MORALITY

A Response to God's Love

JOSEPH STOUTZENBERGER

OurSundayVisitor

Curriculum Division

www.osvcurriculum.com

The Ad Hoc Committee to Oversee the Use of the Catechism, United States Conference of Catholic Bishops, has found this catechetical text, © 2005, to be in conformity with the Catechism of the Catholic Church

Nihil Obstat
Rev. Dr. Steven Olds, S.T.D
Censor Librorum

Imprimatur
✠Most Rev. Norbert M. Dorsey C.P., S.T.D.
Bishop of Orlando
June 4, 2004

Write:
Our Sunday Visitor Curriculum Division
Our Sunday Visitor, Inc.
200 Noll Plaza, Huntington, Indiana 46750

Our Sunday Visitor and the Our Sunday Visitor logo are registered trademarks of Our Sunday Visitor Curriculum Division, Our Sunday Visitor, 200 Noll Plaza, Huntington, Indiana, 46750.

For permission to reprint copyrighted material, grateful acknowledgment is made to the following sources:

The Division of Christian Education of the National Council of the Churches of Christ in the U.S.A: Verses from *The Holy Bible: The New Revised Standard Version, Catholic Edition.* Text copyright © 1993, 1989 by the Division of Christian Education of the National Council of the Churches of Christ in the United States of America.

Excerpts from the English translation of *Rite of Penance* © 1974, International Commission on English in the Liturgy Corporation (ICEL); excerpts from the English translation of *The Roman Missal* © 2010, ICEL. All rights reserved.

United States Catholic Conference, Inc., Washington, D. C.: English translation of the *Catechism of the Catholic Church* for the United States of America. Translation copyright © 1994 by United States Catholic Conference, Inc.—Libreria Editrice Vaticana.

Printed in the United States of America

Morality: A Response to God's Love
ISBN: 978-0-15-901486-8
Item Number: CU0604

10 11 12 13 14 15 16 17   015016   16 15 14 13 12
Webcrafters, Inc., Madison, WI, USA; March 2012; Job# 98429

CONTENTS

PART 1: FOUNDATIONS FOR CATHOLIC MORALITY

PART 2: CATHOLIC MORALITY APPLIED

Chapter Overview

- Moral decision making reflects our nature as persons endowed with intellect and free will.
- Christian morality is our response to Jesus.
- Grace as sharing in God's life is both a comfort and a challenge.
- The grace of the Holy Spirit helps us live our vocation to follow Jesus.

Welcome to your morality course. The goal of the moral life is to achieve holiness, particularly eternal happiness with God. During this course you will be discussing many issues and concerns that you already think about. You will have an opportunity to explore your decisions, your behaviors, the wisdom of the Bible, and the teachings of the Church. Your active participation in reading and reflecting on the many topics under discussion can help you become more conscious of the world you live in and more conscientious, caring, and honest in your daily decision making. In particular, the course invites you to look at morality that comes from Sacred Scripture and Catholic tradition. This course presumes that it is important to view yourself and other people as Jesus does. Use the course to become more fully yourself, living a life worthy of the person you are— a child of God.

Before we begin. . .

1. Think about situations that call for moral decision making. Describe three of these situations.

2. What would your life be like if you did not have to consider the moral implications of your actions? Would you prefer life to be like that?

Let us pray. . .

Jesus, Savior and brother, you have told us that you are never far from us. Your loving Father is also our Father. In the choices that we make day by day and moment by moment may we always seek to walk with you as we face the challenges that come our way. Send your Holy Spirit to guide us on our journey. Amen.

What Is Morality?

Morality refers to human acts and to whether the human acts you choose are good or evil. Thus, this course in morality will:

- explore with you the processes, principles, and wisdom involved in making good moral decisions.
- provide you with valuable information about ways to understand good acts and evil acts.
- help guide you when confronted with difficult decisions that make you wonder, *What should I do?*

God is already assisting us in our moral decision making. He has equipped us with moral law, which provides ways to tell the difference between a good act and a bad act. Moral law is, "the fatherly instruction of God, setting forth the ways which lead to happiness and proscribing those which lead to evil" (*Catechism, Glossary*). Throughout this course you will consider other various expressions of the law: natural, divine or revealed, Church, and civil. God has written on the souls of all human beings a moral sense that enables them to discern the difference between good acts and evil acts, between truth and lies. This original moral sense is called **natural law**. In other words, he has placed in our soul a moral compass that points the way to make good moral decisions.

You can also tell the difference between a good act and a bad act by means of our **conscience**, which is, "the interior voice of a human being, within whose heart the inner law of God is inscribed" (*Catechism, Glossary*). A conscience is like having the voice of God speaking to us from the core of our being. At the appropriate time, this voice indicates those acts that are good and warns of those acts that are evil.

Morality and the Challenge of Decision Making

What does your conscience tell you about the following situations?
What would you choose to do in these situations based on God's voice within you?

- You are with a few classmates at a dance when a person you were friends with in grade school comes into the room. Someone in your group says, "Look at that guy. What a loser!" The others laugh. How do you respond?

- You have been going out with someone for a few weeks. You go out with this person only because you want to have someone to talk with on the phone and to do things with on weekends. This person starts to end many of the conversations you have together by saying, "I love you." You're uncomfortable about this, but you don't want to hurt this person's feelings. What do you do?

- Your parents are going away for the weekend, leaving you and your brother in charge of the house. Your brother, a high school senior, invites some of his friends over on Friday night. They bring a case of beer with them. What do you do?

- You pick up some friends on a Friday night. One of them mentions that there's been a party going on in the woods of a nearby public park. When you arrive, about fifteen classmates are there. Within minutes a police cruiser pulls up. A police officer jumps out of the car near you and yells, "Freeze!"

All of your friends run away. What do you do? If the officer arrests you and says that he'll go easy on you if you give him the names of others who were there, what would you do?

- You are walking along a downtown street in a large city. A poorly clad, older woman comes up to you and asks, "Can you spare some change so I can get something to eat?" How do you respond?

- You are about to go to a party when a friend who has been having family problems calls and asks if she can come over to talk with you. She sounds upset. What do you do?

- One day your math teacher leaves the classroom for a moment, and a student takes a copy of an upcoming test from the teacher's desk. When the teacher returns he notices that a copy of the test is missing. At the end of the period he calls you aside and asks you if you know what happened to the missing test. What do you say to him?

- You finish drinking from an aluminum can. You recall the messages you've heard about recycling, but the others who are with you do not keep their cans separate from the rest of the trash. What do you do with the can?

- The school's chaplain invites students to spend part of their Christmas vacation collecting and delivering toys to children in poor families. How do you respond?

Choosing Good or Evil

There are three elements of moral decision:
- the object chosen
- the intention of the action
- the circumstances surrounding the act.

The object chosen refers to the nature or the matter of a proposed act. For example, on the face of it, giving our mother a birthday card is a good act, and totally ignoring our mother's birthday is a bad

act (and generally a bad idea). In other words, our reason and will will make the judgment that honoring our mother on her birthday is a truly good act and failing to do so is a bad act.

The intention of an act indicates our purpose for doing the act. The intention is concerned with what we hope to achieve by doing a particular action. Thus, intentions involve the goals or ends of our actions. Giving our mother a birthday gift for the sole purpose of manipulating her and possibly getting her to agree to some-

thing we want is an example of a good act with a bad intention. Such an action is not a good moral decision, because an evil intention undermines and spoils even a good act.

When talking about the object chosen and the intention, it is important to bear in mind that some acts are inherently evil.

Jesus made this clear when he said, "If you wish to enter into life, keep the commandments. . .You shall not murder; You shall not commit adultery; You shall not steal; You shall not bear false witness" *(Matthew 19:17–18)*. Thus, there are some acts that are always immoral and thus are always the wrong choice. And as Jesus indicated, the Ten Commandments are our best source for discerning which acts are inherently evil.

Circumstances can influence the moral goodness or evil of a proposed act. Circumstances such as "ignorance, duress, fear, and other psychological or social factors" *(Catechism, #1746)* can lessen or increase the moral goodness or evil of an act. Failing to honor our mother on her birthday because we do not know who she is or the date of her birth does not constitute an immoral decision.

In Chapter 7, we will discuss moral decision making in greater detail. **G**

Freedom is the power, rooted in reason and will, to act or not to act, to do this or that, and so to perform deliberate actions on one's own responsibility.

 Catechism, #1731

Group Talk

1. Think of five acts that require a moral decision. Think of some intentions that might affect these five acts. How would you arrive at a good moral decision?

2. Give an example, other than those mentioned above, of an act that you believe is inherently evil.

3. Discuss the sources of morality (the object chosen, intention, and circumstances) in reference to the examples on the preceding page.

Decision Making Day by Day, Moment by Moment

We are constantly making choices—this is the reality of being human. (Remember the saying, that even not to decide is to decide.) Decision making, therefore, is an everyday thing. It involves the way we spend our money, our time, and our talents; the way we treat our parents, our friends, people we don't like, and even the environment. It involves the way we respond to our neighbor in need and the way we attempt to resolve conflicts. Our moral viewpoints guide what we do with the many decisions that come our way over a lifetime.

The brief sketches opening this chapter represent a mere sampling of the types of decisions that all of us must face. Each new day greets us with the challenge of making decisions that have an impact on ourselves or others in positive or negative ways. Each new encounter with another person calls us to respond—pleasantly or angrily, honestly or deceptively, encouragingly or destructively. With each new piece of information that enters our consciousness, with each new experience that we have, with each yes or no that we say to those around us, we are shaping our moral viewpoints and ourselves as moral decision makers.

Even if you have been an adolescent for only a short time, no doubt you are experiencing the blessings and the burdens of decision making. Not too long ago your choices were simpler: *Do I accept the demands of my parents and other adults, or do I ignore them and do what I want to do?* Now you are being met with so many more decisions—decisions that you never had to face before and for which you alone will be held responsible. You are expected to take charge of your life, to use your talents wisely, to act responsibly, and to consider the welfare of others—without always having someone telling you the right thing to do. How you use this new power now will play a large role in determining who you will become.

Consider two of the many examples illustrating the challenges of decision making. Either you are or soon will arrive at an age when you can legally drive a car. Along with a driver's license comes the excitement of increasing freedom. It also represents the accountability that faces you as a maturing young person. More often you will find yourself in circumstances where you are not under adult supervision, with or without the independence afforded by a car. You will be expected to act in ways that demonstrate greater and greater personal authority.

Similarly, in recent years your wonderful gift of sexuality has blossomed. You will want to share yourself, physically, with another. This developing dimension of yourself certainly makes an important statement about the person you are. However, your decisions about right and wrong in regard to your sexuality make an even greater statement about the person you are.

Moral decision making contributes greatly to defining who you are. Your identity takes shape as you relate with family members, peers, teachers, and even strangers. Constantly, you are called upon to make choices that affect yourself and others. When your conscious choices help or harm someone, then you have entered into the realm of moral decision making.

Moral decision making, then, is a very important dimension of your life right now. It brings joys and demands, challenges and opportunities. Through this capacity, you participate in shaping both yourself and, at least to some degree, your world. To exercise this capacity is to be human; to shirk from making decisions is to diminish your humanity. This course on morality is designed to help you develop the skill of decision making in light of Christ and the Catholic Church. **A R**

Every human person, created in the image of God, has the natural right to be recognized as a free and responsible being.

Catechism, #1738

Activity

Morality cannot be reduced to our individual perception about right and wrong. However, it is important to realize that each person has his or her own sense of what is moral and what is not. It's helpful to know what our own sense of morality is and then to check out our sense of morality against that of Catholic teachings. With that in mind, consider the following twelve actions.

1. Rank these actions from 1 to 10 in terms of the degree to which you consider them to be moral. (1 = "It's not particularly wrong; it wouldn't bother me at all." 10 = "This is a serious wrong; it would bother me a great deal.")

2. When finished, ask, "What might others conclude about me based on my rankings?" Compare your rankings with those of others and discuss your reasoning.

For Review...

1. What is morality? What role does natural law play in decision making? How can you access this natural law that God has etched in your soul?

2. Give an example to illustrate that moral decision making is both a blessing and a burden.

3. Why does being moral require a sense of responsibility?

4. What does it mean to say that morality is an everyday occurrence?

_____ a. I started a fight with a smaller, younger student whom I simply didn't like.

_____ b. My former boyfriend (girlfriend) rejected me. I spread unkind stories about him (her).

_____ c. I helped a friend pay for an abortion.

_____ d. A student who just doesn't fit in was being mocked, and I joined in.

_____ e. I lied to my parents about where I was on Friday night. I was out drinking with friends.

_____ f. In the cafeteria I saw ten dollars drop out of a student's pocket. I kept it.

_____ g. I sold a car stereo system when I knew the system didn't work properly. I lied about it and made money on the deal.

_____ h. I am a boy who fathered a child and then denied that the child was mine.

_____ i. I found an envelope containing $200. It was marked "tuition." I kept it.

_____ j. I looked at another student's answers during a test.

_____ k. I saw a traffic accident occur. I knew some people were hurt. I ignored it because I was late for baseball practice and I might have been cut from the team.

_____ l. I was baby-sitting my younger brother and sister. Against my parents' wishes, I let my siblings watch a violent and sexually explicit movie on cable because I wanted to see it.

Reflection

1. Write down three examples of moral decisions that were important to you four years ago.

2. Write about three areas of moral decision making that you are now being called upon to address that you didn't have to face before.

3. Name the three elements involved in a moral decision.

Catholic Morality

As the previous section pointed out, morality can operate on a strictly human level. Our natural attraction for the good pushes us to use our decision-making capacity in positive ways. However, the teachings of the Catholic faith are central to moral discussion. For one thing, through the gift of faith we recognize the one, true good that fulfills our longing—and that one, true good is God. To be drawn to the good ultimately means to be drawn to him. And rather than staying aloof from us, God the Father loves us, reveals himself to us as love and truth, and gives himself to us. Through his Son Jesus Christ, who is both human and divine, the Father gives us a participation in divine life. We need only to tap into it, which we do when we allow the Holy Spirit to work through us as we live our lives and make the choices that constantly confront us.

Catholic morality, then, refers to the way that we lead our lives in response to God's law of love in our souls. Because of Jesus and the Holy Spirit at work through the Church, we are not alone when faced with the awesome responsibility of moral decision making. Looking to Jesus helps us to make honest, caring, and thoughtful choices. Nonetheless, we find in Jesus and the Church norms for addressing the question, *What should I do?* Much of our decision making takes on new meaning in light of Jesus Christ. Looking to Jesus, we discover three interconnected concepts underlying Catholic morality: human dignity, grace, and vocation. These concepts are keys to answering the question, *Why try to lead good lives?* They also are starting points in our search for answers to the question, *How can I lead my life in a way that reflects my God-given dignity, the grace of the Holy Spirit working within me, and Jesus' call to follow him?* **R A**

> **Catholic morality**—the way that we live our lives as children of God in response to Jesus under the guidance of the Holy Spirit at work in the Catholic Church

... by the sacraments of rebirth, Christians have become "children of God," [Jn 1:12; 1 Jn 3:1] "partakers of the divine nature" [2 Pet 1:4]. Coming to see in the faith their new dignity, Christians are called to lead henceforth a life "worthy of the gospel of Christ" [Phil 1:27]. They are made capable of doing so by the grace of Christ and the gifts of his Spirit, which they receive through the sacraments and through prayer.

 Catechism, #1692

Reflection

Reread the stories on page 3 of this chapter. Now put Jesus into each situation. Would your response change? If yes, how?

Activity

1. Draw a picture, create a collage, or write a song or poem with the theme "Morality—responding to God."

2. Explain why you chose the words or images that you used.

Christian, Recognize Your Dignity. . .

dignity—
the respect owed to all human beings because they are made in God's image

Of all visible creatures only man is "able to know and love his creator." [GS 12 § 3.] He is "the only creature on earth that God has willed for its own sake," [GS 24 § 3.] and he alone is called to share, by knowledge and love, in God's own life. It was for this end that he was created, and this is the fundamental reason for his dignity.

Catechism, #356

The *Catechism of the Catholic Church* begins its discussion of the moral life with the words "Christian, recognize your dignity and, now that you share in God's own nature, do not return to your former base condition by sinning" [St. Leo the Great, *Sermo 21 in Nat. Dom.*, 3:PL54,192C.] *(#1691)*. In other words, the starting point of Christian morality is not *What should we do?* nor even *What do we do?* but rather *Who are we?* We are people with inherent **dignity**, that is, each one of us is beloved of God, made in his image. We are naturally religious beings, whose vocation is to know, love, and serve God. We are children of God, who loves us. Therefore, we are called to live in communion with him and find our happiness through him.

Without losing his own nature as God, Jesus took on our human nature so he could reveal the full extent of his Father's love for his children. Jesus, who is both true God and true man, is our principal model of holiness, our mediator with God the Father, and our Savior. Jesus is our Lord and by our calling him "Lord," we profess our belief in his divinity. In his message and, more importantly, in his very life, Jesus reveals the scope and the depth of his Father's love for us. Only when we see ourselves in the eyes of Jesus do we truly see ourselves. The gaze of Jesus, always a loving gaze, is the gaze of one who shares our humanity as well as the gaze of one who knows our deepest core. In Jesus we discover the beauty, the glory, and the power of who we are. **G**

For Review...

1. Define Catholic morality.

2. With what statement does the Catechism begin its discussion of the moral life?

3. What realization is the starting point for Christian moral decision making?

Group Talk

Answer *agree*, *disagree*, or *uncertain* to the following statements. Explain your choices. If possible, use an example to support your response.

1. Having a strong sense of personal dignity helps people act morally.

2. Experiencing love helps people love others.

3. I can honestly say that I have experienced God's love in my life.

4. "Living my life in response to Jesus" is a good definition of morality for me.

5. When faced with important moral decisions, I have asked myself, *What would Jesus do?*

God's Love

The divine initiative in the work of grace precedes, prepares, and elicits the free response of man. Grace responds to the deepest yearnings of human freedom, calls freedom to cooperate with it, and perfects freedom.

✝ Catechism, #2022

We are the work of God's hand and he loves us. In the Old Testament we see God breaking into human history, gradually revealing his loving nature through words and deeds, and offering men and women a share in his life. He revealed himself to our first parents, and, after they sinned against him, gave them the promise of salvation by offering them a covenant. In time, through such key historical figures as Abraham and Sarah, Moses, and David, God established his covenant with his people. A **covenant** is a solemn agreement between God and human beings involving mutual obligations and promises. In exchange for loving and serving him, he pledged to be our one true God, our caring and protective Father, who would send his people a messiah and savior. In time, God sent his only Son. Jesus, "wanting to make us sharers in his divinity, assumed our nature, so that he, made man, might make men gods" [St. Thomas Aquinas, *Opusc.* 57:1–4.] (*Catechism,* #460).

The term for our participation in the life of God is **grace**. Through grace we partake in the **Holy Trinity**, the very life and nature of God. The grace of the Holy Spirit gives us the gift of the Father's holiness or righteousness. Grace unites us by faith and Baptism to Jesus' life, death, and Resurrection. Grace moves us toward God and away from sin. It helps us accept his forgiveness and justification, which is pardon from sin, growth in grace, and interior renewal.

Grace is a pure gift. God "justifies us," that is, he freely and graciously gives us the grace of the Holy Spirit that cleanses us from sin in Baptism. This justification was won for us by the Passion of Jesus, who offered himself as the spotless victim for man's sins. Nothing we do could possibly earn this gift of grace, otherwise it wouldn't be a gift.

Grace gives us the capacity to engage in the moral life. We are God's children, not robots or slaves. Whenever we do good, it is because of the grace of the Holy Spirit within us. Through grace our moral life grows and matures. The fulfillment of our moral life will be in the glory of heaven.

There are two main forms of grace: sanctifying grace and actual grace. **Sanctifying grace** (or habitual grace) refers to God's freely given gift of his love and constant presence in the soul. Sanctifying grace identifies God's friendship that heals us and enables us to respond to his love. **Actual grace** is the help God gives us for a particular need, such as an important decision, a period of painful loss and grief, or a time of crisis. Actual grace gives us the strength and power to conform our lives to God's will during these times of need.

All of us need the transformation that the gift of grace brings. All of us could use greater freedom, wisdom, courage, and compassion—qualities that come only with God's help. Here are the stories of two young people in need of grace in their lives.

covenant— a solemn agreement between God and human beings involving mutual obligations and agreements

grace— the gift of the Holy Spirit; participation in God's Trinitarian life; the help God gives us to live out our vocation

Holy Trinity— one God in three Persons: the Father, the Son, and the Holy Spirit.

sanctifying grace— a share in God's life; a gift from God that enables the soul to live with him and respond to his friendship

actual grace— the help God gives us for a particular need to help us conform our lives to his will

Amy's Dream World

- Amy is a sophomore in high school. Whenever she goes to a party or any other social gathering, Amy clings desperately to her friends, Lauren and Ashley. If Lauren talks to someone else, there is Amy, always right beside her. If Ashley goes to the bathroom, Amy goes to the bathroom. If Lauren and Ashley are talking to boys, Amy nervously joins in.

- Recently, Amy has begun to make up stories about the things she has done, the places she has been, and the people whom she calls friends. In fact, she spends more time talking about imaginary exploits than actually living life. Her few friends continue to include her in their activities, although with less enthusiasm as time goes by.

Jackie and Her Dad

- Jackie is a freshman in high school. She has always been close with her father, but now that she's in high school their relationship has become difficult. Jackie argues about everything, especially about staying up late and going to late-night parties. Jackie and her dad don't talk as much as they used to and when they do, her father asks questions about what she's doing and where she's going. Jackie ends up yelling because she resents the questioning from her father.

- The family table at mealtime has become a battleground. Jackie's dad inquires, "Who are you going out with tonight?" "Why do you always have to know?" Jackie replies as usual. Whenever her dad asks for more details, Jackie rolls her eyes and starts the next battle between them. **R**

Reflection

1. If you were Amy or Jackie, what would you need to hear about yourself and your actions?

2. If Amy and Jackie were your friends and sought you out for help, what message would you want to convey to them?

3. If Jesus were physically present today, what do you imagine he would say to Amy and Jackie? Would Jesus' message to Amy and Jackie parallel your own message to them?

Grace

Like all of us, Amy is not all that she would like to be. She is not as comfortable with herself in social situations as she desperately wants to be. Like all of us, Dave is stretching to be himself; but with his mother, Dave asserts his independence too aggressively. One message of Jesus' that they both need to hear is the following: "Are not two sparrows sold for a penny? Yet not one of them will fall to the ground unperceived by your Father. And even the hairs of your head are all counted. So do not be afraid; you are of more value than many sparrows." (*Matthew 10:29–31*)

Like all of us, Amy and Dave need to hear that they are so loved by God that the very hairs on their heads have been counted and that they are indeed worth more than many sparrows. God's gift of his loving presence and activity in our lives is what we mean by grace.

The prophet Isaiah uses the image of a mother caring for her children to describe how much greater than any human experience is God's love for us. Such is the intimacy with God that the concept of grace conveys. **G**

"Can a woman forget her nursing child, or show no compassion for the child of her womb? Even these may forget, yet I will not forget you. See, I have inscribed you on the palms of my hands . . . **"**

Isaiah 49:15–16

Grace Brings Challenge

World War II had a profound impact on the modern discussion of morality. Those who have tried to make sense of moral and immoral behavior during that era have come to a disturbing realization. Many people in Germany and other countries contributed to the deaths of millions of people either by simply doing what they were told to do or by not taking steps to confront evil.

In contrast to such people, Dietrich Bonhoeffer, a German Lutheran pastor, actively protested the Nazi regime's policies in his country before and during the war. In the 1930s Bonhoeffer spent some time in the United States. However, at the risk of his life he returned to Germany. He felt that during this troubled time he could influence his country's policies more by living in Germany. As a result of his anti-Nazi activities, he was imprisoned and then executed by hanging just before the war ended.

Bonhoeffer was concerned that many of his fellow Christians found the message of Jesus to be comforting but not personally challenging. He believed that faith in Jesus should lead Christians to resist actively the inhumanity that they saw around them.

Group Talk

Without naming names, tell the story of someone, real or fictional, who could benefit from hearing Jesus' message that God loves her or him.

" Then (Jesus) said to them all, 'If any want to become my followers, let them deny themselves and take up their cross daily and follow me. For those who want to save their life will lose it, and those who lose their life for my sake will save it. What does it profit them if they gain the whole world, but lose or forfeit themselves?' **"**

Luke 9:23–25

Bonhoeffer warned his fellow Christians that a relationship with God involves a response on our part. For that reason, grace brings challenge. When we experience God's love deeply, we are moved to love others in return. Bonhoeffer realized that he needed to resist the evil of his day. In the end he paid a heavy price—death by hanging. Another German whose faith led him to risk his life to fight Nazism was the Jesuit priest, Alfred Delp. Father Delp suffered greatly at the hands of the Nazis before he was eventually hanged. His prison meditations are an inspiring testament to faith. Like Bonhoeffer, he saw that being a Christian called him to oppose evil, to take up his cross even if it meant forfeiting his life.

Pastor Bonhoeffer and Father Delp have something to say about grace. God's love, like all true love, empowers us. Choosing to do the right thing requires personal courage. God the Father's grace, the source of courage, is there for us every step of the way. Remember that Jesus himself remained true to the Father even to his death on the cross. Christians who seek to follow Jesus will certainly find their dedication to him to be a challenge. They will also find support, inspiration, and empowerment through the Holy Spirit. **R**

God's free initiative demands *man's free response*, for God has created man in his image by conferring on him, along with freedom, the power to know him and love him. . . . He has placed in man a longing for truth and goodness that only he can satisfy. The promises of "eternal life" respond, beyond all hope, to this desire.

Catechism, #2002

Reflection

Has being a Christian ever been a challenge for you? If so, describe the situation. Do you think that for most people today being a Christian is viewed as a challenge? Explain your answer.

Challenge and Comfort

How can grace empower Amy and Dave—and us? Both of these young people are faced with their own personal problems. We have difficulty imagining Amy and Dave dedicating themselves to others as many saintly people have done in the past. But actually, the Church is made up of people exactly like Amy and Dave. That is, people don't become heroes and then act heroically. Rather, people struggle to act rightly, respond to God's grace, and grow into heroic people.

Jesus' words of comfort and his words of challenge are not contradictory messages. Actually, they represent two sides of the same message. Amy and Dave need a breakthrough in their lives, a sense of being loved, a burst of courage, and an experience of grace. In other words, Amy and Dave need to hear Jesus' words of comfort, which say that he lives in them and that he loves them. Such an experience of the presence of God and of being loved can free them to explore new patterns of behavior. This is always challenging and often painful. Amy's struggle is to love herself more; Dave's struggle is to practice greater sensitivity toward his mother.

Grace—God's life within us and God's love for us—is a gift to be shared. We do not earn or merit grace; God chooses to share his grace out of love for us. We honor Mary, the Mother of God, as being "full of grace" because God the Holy Spirit acted to preserve her from all sin from the moment of her conception. Free of sin and full of grace, Mary still freely chose to say yes to God and to cooperate with his grace. When we notice that someone is being left out and we take the initiative to include that person in our group, then we are responding to God's grace and acting. When we volunteer to participate in a community-service activity at the cost of sacrificing our time, then we are living out grace. When we risk going against the crowd because we realize that if we don't someone might get hurt, then we are living out grace.

At the end of time Christ will make known to us the secret disposition of our hearts, revealing our works and our response to grace. As Lord of the living and the dead, Christ will judge us according to our acceptance or rejection of grace. At the very moment of our death, at what

is known as the *particular judgment*, we will in our immortal souls be given either entrance into the blessedness of heaven—immediately or through a purification—or immediate and everlasting damnation. For those who die in God's grace but are in need of purification, they will enter a purifying state in order to obtain the holiness necessary to enter heaven. And yet we know that "God did not send the Son into the world to condemn the world, but in order that the world might be saved through him" *(John 3:17)*. Even people who have not heard the Gospel or know the Church, but who still search for God with a sincere heart and try to do his will as it is written in their conscience, they, too, may have eternal salvation.

As we will see later on, Jesus sums up his moral teaching in one word—love *(Matthew 22:37–40)*. However, in our culture love often means no more than a message on a greeting card—cozy, comforting, and not very demanding. In this climate, just as during the World War II era, we need to remember the message of Jesus not only is consoling and comforting but also is very challenging.

Living Grace

Case Study

1. Your religion teacher, whom you like, announces that a service club is having its first meeting today after school. You enjoyed doing a service project over the summer, so you think you'll attend the meeting to find out what's involved.

   When you arrive you discover that none of your friends have come and that all the others in the room are students who are looked down upon by most of your classmates. What do you do?

2. You invite a friend over to your house for the evening. The two of you go to a local video store. You warn your friend that your parents strictly forbid you from watching excessively violent films or ones that contain strong sexual content. There's only one copy remaining of a newly released DVD you know your parents would not approve of. Your friend grabs the DVD and says, "This movie is supposed to be great. Don't listen to your parents. Let's get this one. They'll never know the difference." What do you do?

3. As a soccer player, you spend most of your time with team members. Nonetheless, you also have a friend who has a leading role in the school play. You know that she would appreciate it a great deal if you came to the show. On the night of the play most of the soccer players are going to be hanging out together and they expect you to join them. You think that they'll make fun of you if you go to the play. What do you do?

4. Administrators at your school recently approved use of the auditorium for a "battle of the bands" program. A friend confides to you that one of the bands plans to use the event to showcase a performance that would clearly embarrass the school. Your friend says, "If school officials find out, the band members will know that I told, so make sure you don't tell anyone." What do you do? **G**

Group Talk

Describe possible responses to the above situations. How is the challenge of living a Christian life present in each one?

Grace and the Holy Spirit

For Review...

1. Define grace.

2. Who were Dietrich Bonhoeffer and Alfred Delp?

3. What was their message regarding living the Christian life?

4. Give an example of living a grace-filled life.

5. What does Scripture tell us is Christ's role at the end of time?

6. What is the relationship among the Holy Spirit, grace, and Catholic morality?

About two thousand years ago, a group of people huddled together in a room in the bustling city of Jerusalem. They were frightened, disillusioned, and ill at ease. The link that held them together was Jesus of Nazareth who had spent a few short years astounding them with his words and actions and giving them hope. He died a horrible death, but afterward many of them actually saw Jesus in their midst—changed but very much alive. Before they could comprehend fully what his post-crucifixion appearances meant, Jesus again left them. Now they didn't know what to do. On this day, known as Pentecost, a total transformation took place. Everyone in the room was changed. The Bible says that a strong wind and "tongues of fire" brought about the change. These two images represent the Holy Spirit, the real force behind the wind and fire.

In this incident the Holy Spirit, third person of the Trinity, co-equal with the Father and the Son, took center stage in the Christian story. Those who were touched by the Holy Spirit at Pentecost came to the realization that Christ was not absent from them. Instead, he remains present *through* them.

At Pentecost, Jesus poured out the Holy Spirit on his disciples and gave them the power to spread the gospel. Today, Jesus pours out the Holy Spirit on us through his Church, which he "builds, animates, and sanctifies" (*Catechism, #747*). Thus, the Pentecost story is not just about the earliest Christians receiving the gift of grace. The Pentecost is also our story. The Holy Spirit is the fountain of grace by which persons of faith are enabled to participate in the Trinity's work. Grace brings strength and courage. Just as at the first Pentecost the Holy Spirit was manifest as fire and wind, so today "[t]he human person participates in the light and power of the divine Spirit" (*Catechism, #1704*). Catholic morality means acting as persons filled with the Holy Spirit.

Vocation: Being Co-workers with God

vocation—

calling to love and serve God both now and forever.

Vocation means calling. The way we live out our vocation differs from person to per-son, but everyone's vocation is to serve God and to honor Him with their love. Jesus spent the last years of his life calling people to turn their lives around. His call echoes down through the ages to us today. We are called upon to use our abilities to enhance our own life and the lives of those around us, just like the servants who are given talents in the following story told by Jesus.

"For it is as if a man, going on a journey, summoned his slaves and entrusted his property to them; to one he gave five talents, to another two, to another one, to each according to his ability. Then he went away. The one who had received the five talents went off at once and traded with them, and made five more talents. In the same way, the one who had the two talents made two more talents. But the one who had received the one talent went off and dug a hole in the ground and hid his master's money. After a long time the master of those slaves came and settled accounts with them. Then the one who had received the five talents came forward, bringing five more talents, saying, 'Master, you handed over to me five talents; see, I have made five more talents.' His master said to him, 'Well done, good and trustworthy slave; you have been trustworthy in a few things, I will put you in charge of many things; enter into the joy of your master.' And the one with the two talents also came forward, saying, 'Master, you handed over to me two talents; see, I have made two more talents.' His master said to him, 'Well done, good and trustworthy slave; you have been trustworthy in a few things, I will put you in charge of many things; enter into the joy of your master.' Then the one who had received the one talent also came forward, saying, 'Master. . . I was afraid, and I went and hid your talent in the ground. Here you have what is yours.' But his master replied, 'You wicked and lazy slave! You knew, did you, that I reap where I did not sow, and gather where I did not scatter? Then you ought to have invested my money with the bankers, and on my return I would have received what was my own with interest. . . .'"

Matthew 25:14–27

The English word talent comes from the word used in the Gospel story about the servants who are given talents by their master. In the story the **talent** actually refers to a unit of money in use at the time; but it later came to designate all the natural endowments with which we are born.

All of us have been given many talents. Our vocation is to make something beau-tiful out of the talents that God has given us. God has created us to show forth his truth, goodness, and beauty. Whenever we live his truth, share his goodness, and help to fashion the world to be the way he intends it to be, we are using our talents well. The Catechism calls for the creative use of our talents in these simple words: "God put us in the world to know, to love, and to serve him, and so to come to paradise" *(#1721).* **A**

Activity

Violence, drug abuse, homelessness, eating disorders—the list of societal problems is endless. As a group, describe three problems that currently exist at your school, or in your community. For each problem, describe a creative way that it could be addressed. If possible, determine a role that you might play in solving the problem.

Vocation Means Living a Christian Life

We are created in God's image. Therefore, we have a vocation to be co-workers with God in the continuing story of creation. Humans are co-workers when they help transform the world and the human community into what God intends them to be. We should not make too much of our power to shape ourselves and our world, but we should not minimize our potential as co-workers either. Our aim should be to "fully become 'God's fellow workers' and co-workers for his kingdom *[1 Cor 3:9; 1 Thess 3:2; Col 4:11]" (Catechism, #307)*. That is, the talents that we have been given are to be used to carry on God the Creator's work. **R**

. . . Conclusion

We practice Catholic moral decision-making in all our attempts to love God and others and to promote human welfare. We do not make decisions in isolation, but within a community. Catholics are members of the worldwide Church founded by Christ to be a source of salvation for the world. Catholics are called to respond to God's grace and be faithful to him. We are invited to live out our vocation so that our moral decisions embody the Holy Spirit at work in us and in the world.

For Review...

1. In what sense is *vocation* another term for *Catholic morality*?

2. What did the word *talent* mean in biblical times? What does the word mean now?

3. What does God ask us to do with our talents?

4. What does it mean to be a co-worker with God?

Reflection

Instead of asking *What is God doing for me?* we should ask *What might God do with me?* Think about your life—past, present, and future. What do you envision that God has done with you, is doing with you, or will do with you? Write a response to this question in your notebook.

Model of Morality

Katie and Mark, two young people from Denver, met and hit it off immediately. In time, they fell in love and decided to marry. When they discussed plans for the wedding, they both agreed they didn't want an extravagant wedding. That still left the question of gifts. "I think people tend to overdo it with wedding gifts," Katie said. Mark chimed in, "We think there are a lot better causes that it could be going to."

While searching Internet sites related to weddings, Katie came upon a site of a foundation based in Pennsylvania. The foundation provides services aimed at helping couples add a charitable dimension to their wedding. For instance, it funnels cash gifts in the couple's name to reputable charities. Also, if the couple enters a bridal registry at certain stores through the foundation, the stores donate a percentage of money spent to charitable and service organizations. Finally, the foundation even has available honeymoon packages that also include a percentage of the rate going to charity.

When her mother heard about Katie and Mark's decision to add a spirit of charity to their wedding, she wasn't surprised. After all, she remembered Katie faithfully going off to volunteer at a local hospital when she was just twelve years old. She knew that Katie could use a lot of things that brides often receive on their wedding day, but inside she beamed with pride at the choice Katie and Mark made. This simple, creative step they were taking to think of others in need on their wedding day would help shape their entire marriage together.

Leader: Give glory to God—Father, Son, and Holy Spirit.

All: Now and for ever. Amen.

Reader #1:

"To be alive, to be human, it is not enough to know the real; I must love it: God's people, God's things, God himself. . . . The point is, I am most human when I go out of my small self, when I share not what I have but who I am, when I am "for others". . . . To be human as a Christian should be human, my existence should be Godward and humanward: turned totally to God, totally to God's image on earth." Walter J. Burghardt SJ, *Tell the Next Generation* (New York: Paulist Press 1980).

All: I have come that you may have life and have it to the full.

Reader #2:

" This is my commandment, that you love one another as I have loved you. No one has greater love than this, to lay down one's life for one's friends. You are my friends if you do what I command you. I do not call you servants any longer, because the servant does not know what the master is doing; but I have called you friends, because I have made known to you everything that I have heard from my Father. You did not choose me but I chose you. And I appointed you to go and bear fruit, fruit that will last, so that the Father will give you whatever you ask him in my name. I am giving you these commands so that you may love one another. *"*

John 15:12–17

All: I give you a new commandment: love one another; you must love one another just as I have loved you.

Leader: Let us silently consider . . . our dignity as children of God . . . our participation in God's very life . . . our personal calling.

All: Lord Jesus Christ, may we live our lives seeking always to follow you. May your Holy Spirit come upon us: to inspire us, to guide us, to set us free to live a life filled with grace. We pray that we may praise you with every word we say and every action we take. With wonder and awe, we rejoice that you are with us always. Amen.

Chapter Overview

- Jesus is the starting point of Catholic morality.
- Love is the guiding principle of Catholic morality.
- The kingdom of God is a central theme in the mission of Jesus.
- Jesus models service and calls upon his followers to serve.

Jesus is the foundation stone of Christianity. If we want to know the focus of Catholic moral teaching, then we need to learn about Jesus' mission and ministry. As the Son of God, Jesus was a forgiver of sins, an advocate for the poor, a voice of warning against the destructive power of sin, and a witness of God's love. In this chapter we will examine key Gospel passages related to morality. In particular we will explore the dual messages of consolation and challenge found in Jesus' teachings: God loves us, and we find true happiness only by loving God and others.

Let us pray. . .

Jesus, our brother and our Savior, your carpenter's hands healed the sick, comforted the sorrowing, and reached out to those who were overlooked. May our hands become your hands—healing, comforting, and embracing those who are in need. You were crucified for our sins, may we not add to the burden of your cross by choosing to commit sin. May we find your message to us ever fresh, ever new, and always the guiding light of our lives. Amen.

Come, Lord Jesus

If Christ were to appear today in our own country, where might we search for him? Upon his birth, the wise men from the East looked for him in a palace. He wasn't there. According to the two accounts we have of his birth, it was a lowly affair. In our modern nativity scenes, shepherds and cattle seem cozy and comforting, even glamorous in their own way. The Gospel writers had another intention in mind with this portrayal. They wanted to proclaim that this child, so easily overlooked, was the long await-ed Messiah, the light of the world, the only Son of God the Father, God himself.

Thus the Gospels hint at an answer to the question *Where might we find Christ today?* Perhaps in an inner-city slum, where people of little means live among boarded-up houses and empty factories, while lights from center-city skyscrapers proclaim a world of affluence so close and yet so far away. Perhaps we would find him along a desolate country road, a member of a large family living off an assortment of odd jobs to make ends meet, hoping that the vegetable garden by the house will keep food expenses down. Perhaps he would live with the nurse and the teacher, newly graduated and newly married, trying to build a life while being true to their professions. Perhaps he would be out in a field bent over a long row of fruits or vegetables, putting in long hours before moving on hoping to find work elsewhere.

When they heard the wisdom that the grown-up Jesus spoke, his townspeople were amazed. "Is not this the carpenter?" they marveled *(Mark 6:3)*. This is not where we expect to hear the voice of God!

His person was often surprising, his message occasionally baffling. Unless we, too, can look in unexpected places, we are equally in danger of not seeing Christ among us.

The Person of Jesus

The whole of Christ's life was a continual teaching: his silences, his miracles, his gestures, his prayers, his love for people, his special affection for the little and the poor, his acceptance of the total sacrifice on the Cross for the redemption of the world, and his Resurrection are the actualization of his word and the fulfillment of Revelation [Pope John Paul II, Catechesi Tradendae 9].

 Catechism, #561

The moral questions Jesus asks are very basic and very person-oriented. He asks of us, *How can we avoid sin? How do we prepare for the kingdom of God? How are people hurting?* and *What can we do about it?* He also asks us to consider, *How is God at work in the world today?* and *How can we participate in God's work?*

The life of Jesus is anything but dull. At the appropriate time in human history, the only Son of the Father became incarnate. In the **Incarnation**, without losing his divine nature, Jesus took on our human nature.

Jesus is endearing but challenging, confronting but compassionate. Jesus' point of view on moral questions is not that of a philosopher, one who stands back and makes pronouncements on right and wrong from an ivory tower. He was the Son of God; but he labored with human hands, made human choices, and wept with human eyes. Jesus was a man of the people, a preacher, and a prophet, who spent the last three years of his life traveling around Israel, proclaiming his message and healing people in need.

Jesus does not offer a single systematic presentation of moral principles. Rather, he shows us his morality as he encounters people who are being hurt and people who are hurting others. We discover Jesus' new law of love through stories about him and by him as well as through the specific moral pronouncements that he makes. Nonetheless, we can identify certain Gospel passages, such as the **Sermon on the Mount**, that contain key moral teachings of Jesus' new law of love. **R G**

> **Incarnation—**
> "the mystery of the wonderful union of the divine and human natures" *(Catechism, #483)* in Jesus, the Son of God
>
> **Sermon on the Mount—**
> a part of the Gospel according to Matthew in which Jesus preaches important moral teachings, including the Beatitudes

Reflection

Describe an experience when you had to do "morality on the run"—making a decision in the midst of an immediate problem. What would you recommend as guidelines for people who find themselves in such situations?

Group Talk

The Sermon on the Mount *(Matthew 5–7)* contains many pronouncements about morality beginning with the Beatitudes. However, a parable such as the Good Samaritan story in Luke, chapter 10, also contains moral implications. Choose several of the Gospel verses below. After reading through them, state the moral messages that they contain. Apply the messages to situations that exist today.

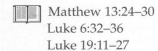 Matthew 13:24–30
Luke 6:32–36
Luke 19:11–27

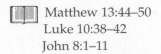 Matthew 13:44–50
Luke 10:38–42
John 8:1–11

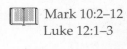 Mark 10:2–12
Luke 12:1–3

The Moral Character of Jesus

Clearly, the Gospels leave us wanting to know so much more about the person of Jesus. The only story we have of him before age thirty can be considered as a foreshadowing of wondrous things to come. Read Luke 2:41–51 about the incident of twelve-year-old Jesus discussing spiritual matters with the priests in the Temple while his parents anxiously search for him.

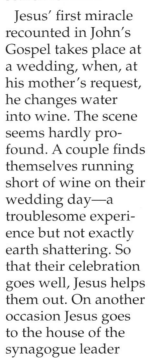

Jesus' first miracle recounted in John's Gospel takes place at a wedding, when, at his mother's request, he changes water into wine. The scene seems hardly profound. A couple finds themselves running short of wine on their wedding day—a troublesome experience but not exactly earth shattering. So that their celebration goes well, Jesus helps them out. On another occasion Jesus goes to the house of the synagogue leader whose daughter is dead *(Mark 5:21–43)*. Jesus pushes through the weeping crowd and, upon entering the house, takes the young girl by the hand and tells her to get up. Again he saves the day in simple, direct fashion.

Even though we have too few accounts of them, the moral character of Jesus comes through in incidents such as these. He regularly demonstrates courage, compassion, and a desire for people to believe in his Father. He shares meals with both the leaders and the outcasts of society. He gets upset when anyone is left out. Jesus serves as our model for morality because of who he is. In other words, we find the answer to our moral quest both in what Jesus says and in the moral character that he keeps demonstrating in his many encounters with others. As we read these accounts we discover, in the words of Pope John Paul II, that: "The light of God's face shines in all its beauty on the countenance of Jesus Christ, 'the image of the invisible God'" *(The Splendor of Truth, #2).*

I once took a count of what sort of things Jesus thought important enough to confront people about in the Gospel of Luke. Nine times Jesus confronted people for not showing love in their actions. Nine times he confronted folks for their greed and hoarding, which get in the way of single-minded service toward God and loving action toward the needy. Nine times Jesus confronted people for having divided loyalties, rather than serving God alone.

Eight times he confronted people for showing by their actions that they did not recognize his authority. Eight times he confronted people who were seeking places of honor and reputation, and urged instead the way of servant-like humility. Seven times he emphasized that the crucial question is whether we actually do what he teaches, versus the hypocrisy of claiming to be on the side of righteousness while not doing God's will.

Seven times he called people explicitly to repent, to take the log out of our own eye, to stop being self-righteously critical of others and insisting on our own way, and instead to be more humble and loving toward him and toward others.

Glen Stassen, "Incarnating Ethics," Sojourners, March/April 1999.

Jesus, the Son of God

It is impossible to summarize the complete identity of Jesus and so here is an incomplete list of some of the many facets of Jesus Christ.

- He is the only Son of the Father. To get a clearer picture of God the Father, we can look to Jesus who is the image of the Father. In fact, everything that Jesus says and does makes a statement about God.

- Jesus is God. He assumed our human nature while retaining his divine nature. "Jesus Christ is true God and true man, in the unity of his divine person; for this reason he is the one and only mediator between God and men" (*Catechism, #480*).

- Jesus is the Savior of humanity. The name Jesus means "God saves." And the name Christ should not be understood as Jesus' last name but rather as a title designating Jesus as the anointed

one. Taken together, the names Jesus and Christ tell us that he is the one sent from God to save us from our sins. "There is salvation in no one else, for there is no other name under heaven given among mortals by which we must be saved" (*Acts 4:12*).

- Jesus is "the way, and the truth, and the life" (*John 14:6*). God sent his Son so that we could dwell in light, both now and forever. Before Jesus came, humanity dwelled in darkness, and God wanted man to have a way out. Jesus is the way of life through which humanity can escape from darkness and sin. He is truth for a people who wonder if there is anything worth believing in. And he is life—abundant and joyful life today and for all eternity—for all people who believe in him and who turn away from sin and death.

Jesus is the model of holiness. He didn't just teach us about loving God and others, he lived what he taught. He told his disciples, "love one another as I have loved you" (*John 15:12*).

By following his example and loving one another, we participate in Jesus' life. It makes all the difference in the world that we recognize our actions as an extension of the work of Christ. Every attempt to follow Jesus' example is not an isolated, individual act. Instead, it is a window through which the light of Christ shines. **R A**

For Review...

1. Which moral questions does Jesus view as more basic than *What should I do?*

2. What does it mean to say that Jesus does "morality on the run"?

3. What does it mean to say that the moral character of Jesus serves as the basis for Christian morality?

4. Who is Jesus? List five ways to describe him.

Reflection

Have you ever had an experience with someone that led you to think, "If there were more people like this, the world would be a much better place?" Describe the experience.

Activity

Read one of the Gospels. Based on your reading, write your own one-page portrait of Jesus.

Even non-Christians associate Jesus with love. Jesus embodied love—through his presence, his healing touch, his words of comfort to the sorrowing, and his words of challenge to the comfortable. Indeed, we can imagine no greater expression of love than Jesus freely offering himself on the cross for our salvation.

Throughout his public life Jesus went to great pains to show us how much God loves us. Here is how the first epistle of John puts it: "In this is love, not that we loved God but that he loved us and sent his Son to be the atoning sacrifice for our sins. Beloved, since God loved us so much, we also ought to love one another." *(1 John 4:10–11).*

Clearly, love is the guiding principle of Christian morality. Jesus revealed the centrality of love when he was tested by a group of religious leaders of his day. He responded to their questioning about commandments by proposing his own commandment—love. **A**

"When the Pharisees heard that he had silenced the Sadducees, they gathered together, and one of them, a lawyer, asked him a question to test him. 'Teacher, which commandment in the law is the greatest?' [Jesus] said to him, 'You shall love the Lord your God with all your heart, and with all your soul, and with all your mind.' This is the greatest and first commandment. And a second is like it: 'You shall love your neighbor as yourself.' On these two commandments hang all the law and the prophets.**"**

 *Matthew 22:34–40*

Guiding Principles for a Christian Moral Life:

- All love comes from God.
- Love on our part is a response to and a participation in God's love.
- Love others as we love ourselves, that is, with our whole being.
- Love of others and love of God are inseparable.

Activity

Saint Paul provides in 1 Corinthians 13 a hymn dedicated to love. Read the passage in your Bible. Choose one of the characteristics and illustrate it with a collage, a photograph, a drawing, or a poem.

Finding Christ in People

Imagine that you are brought into a police station to identify someone in a lineup who claims to be Christ. Standing before you is a hardened prisoner, a strange-looking older woman, a young boy in tattered clothes, and a mother carrying an undernourished baby who is crying. Where is Christ in this motley lineup?

The message that Jesus speaks in the following passage from the Gospel according to Matthew startles us into concluding that Christ is represented in each of them.

"When the Son of Man comes in his glory, and all the angels with him, then he will sit on the throne of his glory. All the nations will be gathered before him, and he will separate people one from another as a shepherd separates the sheep from the goats, and he will put the sheep at his right hand and the goats at the left. Then the king will say to those at his right hand, 'Come, you that are blessed by my Father, inherit the kingdom prepared for you from the foundation of the world; for I was hungry and you gave me food, I was thirsty and you gave me something to drink, I was a stranger and you welcomed me, I was naked and you gave me clothing, I was sick and you took care of me, I was in prison and you visited me.' Then the righteous will answer him, 'Lord, when was it that we saw you hungry and gave you food, or thirsty and gave you something to drink? And when was it that we saw you a stranger and welcomed you, or naked and gave you clothing? And when was it that we saw you sick or in prison and visited you?' And the king will answer them, 'Truly I tell you, just as you did it to one of the least of these who are members of my family, you did it to me.'"

Matthew 25:31–40

When we apply the message of this vivid scene to our own lives, we discover that Jesus is calling us to seek him in the people who are part of our lives. For example, the story reminds us that we are to welcome strangers. Our attitude toward the "strange" student in our school whom nobody likes actually reflects our attitude toward Christ. Likewise, how we respond to people around us who are hungry—for food or for attention or for friendship—indicates how we are responding to Christ. Similarly, actions to alleviate suffering are actions on behalf of Christ.

But Jesus also calls us to reach out to those who are not necessarily in the mainstream of their lives. We will find Christ in our prisons, in our hospitals, and in our shelters for homeless people. Just like Jesus, we must treat each person as our brother or sister no matter what the circumstances of his or her life.

The passage from Matthew invites us to search our souls and question the way that we normally view things. For instance, in contrast to the Gospel story, we probably imagine Christ as being like us and not as being some stranger.

Similarly, we are probably accustomed to looking for Christ in a church—not in a prison. This vivid scene offers a forceful presentation of the Christian challenge. It invites us to care for those who make up the fabric of our lives as well as for those whom we frequently overlook and avoid.

A

For Review...

1. Which word describes the guiding principle of Christian morality?

2. According to the story in Matthew's Gospel, where is Christ to be found?

3. In what context does Jesus put his message to place God first in our lives?

Activity

Write a short story with a modern setting about finding Christ in another person.

The Christian Measure of True Happiness

The Beatitudes are at the heart of Jesus' preaching. . . .they shed light on the actions and attitudes characteristic of the Christian life. . . .The Beatitudes respond to the natural desire for happiness. This desire is of divine origin: God has placed it in the human heart in order to draw man to the One who alone can fulfill it.

✝ **Catechism, #1716–1718**

Sometimes the eight **Beatitudes** are viewed as the Christian equivalent of the Ten Commandments. The Beatitudes are similar to the commandments in the sense that both lists describe what it means to be a member of God's people. However, while the Commandments represent a specific set of laws, the Beatitudes teach us about our goals in life as Christians: building up God's kingdom, participating in the life of the Trinity, attaining happiness on earth and in heaven, and living as daughters and sons of God. The Beatitudes offer hope in time of trouble as they describe the types of blessings and rewards waiting for those who choose to live them. The Beatitudes challenge us to think conscientiously about our attitude toward others so that our attitude reflects love of God above everything else.

As you can clearly tell, the Beatitudes are not a simple list of rules. Neither do they provide us with a series of things to do. Rather, they describe a way of life that results from trying to live the values of Jesus. **Beatitude saints** are people who attempt to live the Beatitudes and who take their message to heart. On the surface, Beatitude saints endure difficult times. Below the surface, they experience joy that comes only from an attitude of trust in God and from acting on that trust. **G**

The Eight Beatitudes

❝When Jesus saw the crowds, he went up the mountain; and after he sat down, his disciples came to him. Then he began to speak, and taught them, saying:

'Blessed are the poor in spirit, for theirs is the kingdom of heaven.'

'Blessed are those who mourn, for they will be comforted.'

'Blessed are the meek, for they will inherit the earth.'

'Blessed are those who hunger and thirst for righteousness, for they will be filled.'

'Blessed are the merciful, for they will receive mercy.'

'Blessed are the pure in heart, for they will see God.'

'Blessed are the peacemakers, for they will be called children of God.'

'Blessed are those who are persecuted for righteousness' sake, for theirs is the kingdom of heaven.'❞

📖 *Matthew 5:1–10*

Group Talk

Divide into small groups and choose one or more of the Beatitudes. For each Beatitude make a list of Beatitude saints—that is, people living or dead, whose lives and actions exemplify that Beatitude's values.

A Beatitude Examination of Conscience

Each of the Beatitudes presents us with life goals, as well as actions that flow from those goals. Use the following questions to determine how close you are to being a Beatitude saint. After reading the entire list, choose one set of questions, and reflect on how you might make these characteristics your own. How might you better follow in the footsteps of the early Beatitude saints of the Christian community?

The Poor in Spirit. Do I trust in God? Does my life become so cluttered that I have little time for God? Do I recognize that the world is not a weight upon my shoulders alone? Can I accept help rather than always trying to go it alone? Do I identify with poor people and, together with them, seek reasons for hope? Do I work to change attitudes and structures that oppress poor people?

Those Who Mourn. Life always involves suffering. Do I appreciate that the suffering that comes from giving myself for others can also bring joy? Can I feel the pain of others, and do I contribute to relieving their anguish?

The Gentle. Do I view other people with profound respect? Do I treat the people whom I meet with care, sensitivity, and even tenderness?

Those Who Hunger and Thirst for Righteousness. Do I relate to others with a sense of fair play? Do I push myself to speak out against injustice and to work for just causes?

The Merciful. Do I wish for others what I would want for myself? When others are down, do I try to help them up rather than take advantage of their misfortune? Would people who know me say that I am truly a kind person?

The Pure in Heart. Am I a person of integrity, someone who cultivates wholesome values and stands up for those values? Am I sincerely honest when making decisions about right and wrong? Are my motives pure, that is, not dominated by self-interest to the exclusion of the interest of others?

Peacemakers. Do I search for peaceful means to resolve conflicts? Am I known as a peacemaker in my family, among my friends, and with the strangers whom I meet? Do I try to understand the points of view of those with whom I have disagreements?

Those Who Are Persecuted in the Cause of Righteousness. Are there beliefs and principles that I hold dear? Am I willing to stand up for my beliefs, even when they are unpopular or lead to personal hardships?

The Kingdom of God

kingdom of God— God's reign or rule—proclaimed by and present in Jesus—in which people serve one another, share their goods with one another, and refuse to retaliate with violence against others

For Review...

1. How are the Beatitudes similar to and different from the Ten Commandments?

2. What do the Beatitudes challenge us to do?

3. Define a "Beatitude saint."

4. What are the two dimensions to God's reign?

5. What is the kingdom of God? How do we participate in this kingdom today?

6. Name two images Jesus uses to help us appreciate the kingdom of God.

The **kingdom of God** is a central theme in the preaching of Jesus. In many of his parables, Jesus taught about a world where God reigns. He provided wondrous images to help us appreciate this kingdom:

- a heavenly banquet to which everyone, especially sinners and outcasts, is invited

- a precious pearl found discarded in a field

- yeast that appears insignificant but, when added to bread, makes the entire loaf rise.

Jesus also pointed out that, even though we may not readily see it, the kingdom of God is already among us and within us. He taught that "no one can enter the kingdom of God without being born of water and Spirit" *(John 3:5)*. And through his death on the cross and his Resurrection, Jesus accomplished the coming of the kingdom.

God's reign has both this worldly and otherworldly dimensions to it. In other words, the kingdom of God is occurring now, as we live our lives in relationship to God. And his reign reaches its fulfillment in heaven. This intertwining of the temporal (time-bound) and eternal dimensions of his reign represents a key element of the Christian message.

Jesus wants us to share in his work of building up God's kingdom here on earth. And we do so as we seek forgiveness of our sins in the Sacrament of Reconciliation, partake in the Eucharist, serve one another, share our goods with one another, and refuse to retaliate with violence against others. We share in the kingdom of God by participating in the Church, which is the "seed and beginning of this kingdom" *(Catechism, # 567)*. By sending the twelve Apostles to preach the kingdom *(Luke 9:1–2)* and by giving Peter the keys of the kingdom, Jesus established the Church as a means to continue the work of building up the kingdom.

Taking the teachings of Jesus seriously certainly will cause us unrest. We see around us a human community that constantly falls short of his ideals, and we know how frequently we ourselves do not measure up. Consequently, we might dismiss Jesus and his message as unrealistic and unworkable. Yet, are there any better directives for creating and cultivating God's reign? As lofty and challenging as his teachings are, the words of Jesus provide our best guide-book for transforming the world and for seeking eternal life. **R**

The kingdom belongs to the poor and lowly, which means those who have accepted it with humble hearts. Jesus is sent to "preach good news to the poor" [Lk 4:18; cf. 7:22]; he declares them blessed, for "theirs is the kingdom of heaven" [Mt 5:3]. To them—the "little ones"—the Father is pleased to reveal what remains hidden from the wise and the learned [cf. Mt. 11:25]. Jesus shares the life of the poor, from the cradle to the cross; he experiences hunger, thirst, and privation [cf. Mt 21:18; Mk 2:23–26; Jn 4:6–7; 19:28; Lk 9:58]. Jesus identifies himself with the poor of every kind and makes active love toward them the condition for entering his kingdom [cf. Mt 25:31–46].

✝ **Catechism, #544**

"Come and Follow Me"

According to John's Gospel, on the night before he was crucified, Jesus shared his last supper with his closest friends. At that first Eucharist, Jesus tied a towel around his waist, got on his knees, and washed his disciples' feet.

Although we can't be certain about first-century customs, one belief is that at the time it was common practice for servants to wash the face and hands of dinner guests; but even servants did not have to wash other people's feet.

(Remember that in first-century Israel there were no paved streets or modern sewage and garbage disposal systems.

People wore open sandals while walking over dusty and dirty roads.)

Jesus' washing of the Apostles' feet was both shocking and purposeful. By doing so he sent a clear message about the type of behavior he expected of his disciples. As he completed the **foot washing** of the

Twelve, Jesus said, "For I have set you an example, that you also should do as I have done to you" *(John 13:15)*.

At one point Jesus gathers together his Apostles and tells them, "Whoever wants to be first must be last of all and servant

of all" *(Mark 9:35)*. Interestingly, when Jesus cures a sick woman and a leper, their immediate response—the sign of their new life—is that they begin to serve. (See Luke 8:43–48 and Mark 1:40–45.) The message of the Gospels is clear: Christians are commissioned by Jesus to serve one another and those who are hurting in their midst. **G**

> **foot washing—** the activity Jesus performed prior to the Last Supper that becomes the model for all Christian service

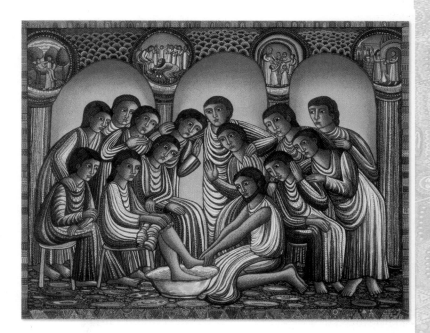

Reflection

The ancient Greeks and Romans had epic poems that rival any current Hollywood blockbuster films in action and adventure. An interesting event is described in book four of the Latin classic, Virgil's Aeneid. A severe storm occurs at sea. After a harrowing time fighting the storm, the sailors who survive experience a shipwreck and then struggle to make their way to shore. Wise old Mentor stands up, gazes along the beach strewn with debris and bodies, and says: "Perhaps someday we will be glad to remember even these things."

Have you ever had a painful, challenging, or difficult experience that later you were able to say you were glad you went through? What was the experience? What did you learn from it? Was there any sense of "joy" that actually accompanied or resulted from the experience? Write about your experience.

Group Talk

1. What message did Jesus want to convey by washing feet and asking his disciples to wash one another's feet?

2. Name three types of activities that today would mirror the spirit of foot washing.

The "Hard Sayings" of Jesus

"hard sayings" of Jesus—

teachings such as the Beatitudes and the Last Judgment that overturn commonly held values and priorities

We cannot avoid the fact that the Gospels contain many **"hard sayings" of Jesus**—teachings such as the Beatitudes and the Last Judgment that overturn commonly held values and priorities. Even his closest friends found many of Jesus' teachings to be hard sayings—teachings that are hard to understand and even harder to follow.

If we paged through the Gospels, we could find many examples of difficult and disturbing teachings. Here are two Gospel passages that exemplify values and priorities that run counter to those typically found in most cultures.

"You know that among the Gentiles those whom they recognize as their rulers lord it over them, and their great ones are tyrants over them. But it is not so among you; but whoever wishes to become great among you must be your servant, and whoever wishes to be first among you must be slave of all."

 *(Mark 10:42–44)*

"But I say to you that listen, Love your enemies, do good to those who hate you, bless those who curse you, pray for those who abuse you. If anyone strikes you on the cheek, offer the other also; and from anyone who takes away your coat do not withhold even your shirt. Give to everyone who begs from you; and if anyone takes away your goods, do not ask for them again. Do to others as you would have them do to you."

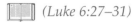 *(Luke 6:27–31)*

Many of us today are accustomed to hearing the words of Jesus about turning the other cheek, serving others, valuing people over property, and becoming like little children. Because of our familiarity with these sayings, we might overlook the challenge found in them. But imagine if we preached these same sentiments in different words and apart from a church setting. No doubt, we would find ourselves ridiculed, labeled troublemakers, or denounced as some sort of crazy religious fanatics. The hard sayings of Jesus create a tension in anyone who attempts to take them seriously. And yet to be his follower means to take seriously that which Jesus took seriously.

Perhaps the hardest part of Jesus' message is that he suffered agonizing torture, rejection, mockery, and finally a slow death on the cross for our sins. The Catholic moral life also leads to suffering at times. However, it is important to remember that for Jesus, Resurrection followed death. His Resurrection makes new life possible for each of us, returning us to grace. We have the hope of rising to new and everlasting life. So, behind his hard sayings, Jesus leaves us a message of hope. **R**

For Review...

1. What action by Jesus modeled his command to serve others? When did Jesus perform this action?

2. What does the text mean by the "hard sayings" of Jesus? Give an example.

Reflection

1. Name three ways that you personally could place God first in your life.

2. If you actually did these things, would your life be more or less burdensome? Explain your answer.

Jesus and the Law

The Old Law is the first stage of revealed Law. Its moral prescriptions are summed up in the Ten Commandments. The precepts of the Decalogue [the Ten Commandments] lay the foundations for the vocation of man fashioned in the image of God; they prohibit what is contrary to the love of God and neighbor and prescribe what is essential to it.

 **Catechism, #1962**

If we look at the incidents when law is mentioned in the Gospels, we discover that often Jesus is presented as being in conflict with the Law. He was confronted for violating Sabbath law—for healing on the Sabbath and for allowing his disciples to pick grain on the Sabbath. He was challenged by advocates of the Law to name the greatest commandments and to pronounce judgment on difficult legal matters. He was baffling to many because he frequently spent time with people who did not keep the Law and who were officially the "outlaws" of his society, such as tax collectors and prostitutes. By examining the references to law in the Gospels, we can name certain perspectives on law held by Jesus.

The Law of the Gospel

Jesus tells his followers, "Do not think that I have come to abolish the law or the prophets; I have come not to abolish but to fulfill" *(Matthew 5:17)*. The Old Law is a good and holy way that shows us what is sinful. But the Old Law is not perfect; it does not give us the strength of the Holy Spirit to fulfill it. Jesus fulfills the Old Law by giving us the grace of the Holy Spirit, which we receive by having faith in Jesus, being people of charity, and receiving the sacraments. Jesus was primarily concerned about communicating God's love for us. On our part, he calls for a change of heart, a conversion in response to our experience of God's love.

Jesus gives us the Law of the gospel that, rather than abolishing the Old Law, builds on it by calling us to change our hearts and give ourselves into God's loving care. Thus Jesus' teachings describe what happens when we change our hearts. For example, we have already studied the famous list of Christian characteristics known as the Beatitudes. In them, Jesus reaches out to those who are open to his New Law of love: the poor in spirit, the gentle, those who are persecuted for their beliefs, those who mourn, justice seekers, the merciful, the pure in heart, and peacemakers. Elsewhere he reminds us to "change and become like children" *(Matthew 18:3)* and to "sell your possessions, and give the money to the poor" *(Matthew 19:21)*. Statements such as these are not laws, but rather are descriptions of people completely changed by the experience of God's love.

The Spirit of the Law

"Do not think that I have come to abolish the law or the prophets; I have come not to abolish but to fulfill. For truly I tell you, until heaven and earth pass away, not one letter, not one stroke of a letter, will pass from the law until all is accomplished."

Matthew 5:17–18

As this passage from Matthew's Gospel makes clear, Jesus brings the Law to fulfillment. Jewish Law names the terms of friendship between God and us; Jesus embodies and makes complete that friendship. Jesus knew and approved of the Law. However, he strongly disapproved of certain attitudes toward and uses of the Law.

For one, Jesus criticized those who used elaborate reasoning to get around the letter of the Law. Secondly, Jesus emphasized the spirit of the Law. Merely following the letter of the Law means doing what the Law commands only because it says so.

Following the spirit of the Law means acting in response to the Holy Spirit who dwells within us. The difference is one of attitude.

- We can approach a school project with the attitude that it is required for a certain grade or with an attitude that of itself it can be a great learning experience.
- We can give a gift because we are expected to or because we truly want to show the person our love.
- We can recycle our paper, aluminum, and glass products because of local laws or because we feel strongly about the benefits of recycling.

As these examples point out, actions based solely on the letter of the Law or based on the underlying spirit of the Law can look the same from the outside and can achieve the same external results. However, whether we follow the letter or the spirit of the Law makes a great difference regarding who we are and regarding our relationship with others. **G**

Group Talk

Give two examples of someone following the letter of a law but not its spirit. Give two examples of someone following the spirit of a law. In light of your examples, explain the difference in terms of possible intentions and results.

Love as the Summation of the Law

As you have no doubt already noticed, love is a recurring theme in any course on Christian morality. Law and love need not be contradictory. More often than not, following the law is the loving thing to do. However, it is possible that when we emphasize strict observance of the law we can lose sight of the true purpose of law, namely, love of God and others. When Jesus' disciples are accused of violating the Sabbath laws by plucking grain, Jesus reminds his accusers that "[t]he sabbath was made for humankind, and not humankind for the sabbath." (Mark 2:27)

Legalism refers to emphasizing strict observance of the law. For that reason, legalism misses the heart of the matter when it comes to the intention of laws. We are legalistic when we begin counting words after writing one sentence of a 500-word essay assignment. We are legalistic when we drive the speed limit even when conditions indicate that lower speeds are called for. We are legalistic when we stick to the rules of a game even when doing so is unnecessarily hurting certain players. We are legalistic when we scheme to figure out how laws and rules can best serve our personal interests. We are legalistic when we decide that people are good guys or bad guys simply on the basis of whether they keep the law.

Clearly, Jesus places concern for people and love of God over observance of law. There must have been many people who held a legalistic attitude toward law during his time, because reminding his listeners of the importance of love over law is a central theme of Jesus' teaching.

> **legalism—**
> attitude of strict observance of laws, regardless of circumstances and possible harm to people involved

Exercise "Moral Muscle"

"You have heard that it was said to those of ancient times, 'You shall not murder'; and 'whoever murders shall be liable to judgment.' But I say to you that if you are angry with a brother or sister, you will be liable to judgment; and if you insult a brother or sister, you will be liable to the council; and if you say 'You fool,' you will be liable to the hell of fire. . . You have heard that it was said, 'You shall love your neighbor and hate your enemy.' But I say to you, Love your enemies and pray for those who persecute you, so that you may be children of your Father in heaven; for he makes his sun rise on the evil and on the good, and sends rain on the righteous and on the unrighteous. For if you love those who love you, what reward do you have? Do not even the tax collectors do the same? And if you greet only your brothers and sisters, what more are you doing than others? Do not even the Gentiles do the same?**"**

Matthew 5:21–22, 43–48

Typically, laws state the least that a person ought to do. Jesus responds to such an attitude toward law with a resounding: Do more! "Do not steal" tells us the minimum of how we should treat property. It does not tell us when we should share our property with others. "Obey traffic laws" does not require us to be exceptionally courteous drivers or to stop and help others who are in trouble by the side of the road. "Do not cheat" specifies what we cannot do during a test. It does not stipulate that we use a test as an educational experience. Performing the two or three weekly chores that we have been assigned says nothing about the many ways that we can also help out at home to make things run smoothly. Voting and paying taxes are merely the minimum requirements of good citizenship.

Minimalism refers to an attitude of doing the bare minimum required of us by law. Minimalism and legalism are deceptive partners in our attempts to lead moral lives. Instead of concentrating on the minimal requirements of the law, Jesus invites us to exercise **moral muscle**—pushing ourselves to take extra steps in making our world a better place. Faithfulness to laws holds a valuable place in Catholic morality. However, of itself such faithfulness is merely a limited part of the Catholic moral teaching. Divorced from personal initiative and thoughtfulness, law keeping is merely moral laziness. Jesus wants more from us. **A**

minimalism—
an attitude of doing only the least that is required by law in our moral life

moral muscle—
pushing ourselves to do more than the minimum in our moral life

For Review...

1. What is most striking about Gospel stories related to Jesus and the Law?

2. Name four perspectives that Jesus held about law.

3. Rather than focusing on what we are supposed to do, what does Jesus focus on in his teachings?

4. According to the text does Jesus renounce the Law?

5. Define legalism and minimalism.

6. What does the text mean by the phrase "exercise moral muscle"?

Activity

Write an essay describing either legalism or minimalism as an attitude toward law. Include in your essay the message of Jesus: Do more!

Making the Jesus Story Our Story

In the midst of his famous Sermon on the Mount, Jesus sums up his challenge to us in these words: "Be perfect, therefore, as your heavenly Father is perfect" *(Matthew 5:48)*. That's quite a proposition he hands us mere mortals. Of course, none of us is perfect. Perfection here means being the person we were intended to be. So Jesus was perfect because he fulfilled completely the purpose for which he was created. It took Jesus his whole human life to complete this task; just as it will each of us. To help us on our journey, Jesus assures us that his story is our story. We celebrate our identification with Christ in our Baptism and Confirmation, in our participation in the Eucharist and the other sacraments, and through all our efforts to live a Christ-like life.

Celebrations of Catholic life should not be separated from our attempts to lead a Catholic moral life. The sacraments offer us a glimpse into our true Catholic identity—that is, how to be those persons and that community we are meant to be. As actions of the Holy Spirit at work in Christ's Body, the Church, the sacraments transform those believers who come to them truly and openly. The sacraments strengthen us to be the people God intended us to be. The task of following Jesus is never-ending, and we need all the help we can get. As the next chapter points out, the Church—its history of truth-tellers and models of sainthood, along with its resources such as prayer and the sacraments—connects us in our imperfection to the perfect one, Jesus. **R**

> **"**Here is a test, to find whether your mission on earth is finished: If you are alive, it isn't.**"**
>
> Richard Bach, *Illusions: The Adventures of a Reluctant Messiah* (New York: Delta, 1997).

...Conclusion

Jesus is our great moral teacher and model. In all of his teachings, Jesus begins with the message of God's love for us. Because of that starting point, Jesus' moral teachings — such as his summary of the Commandments, the Beatitudes, and the reign of God—are expressions of a response to the Father's love. Ultimately, eternal beatitude— heaven—awaits us. This entire course is meant to be an exploration of Jesus' invitation to respond to his love and to love as he loves.

For Review...

1. How can we achieve the perfection to which Jesus challenges us?

2. What is the relationship between the sacraments and Christian identity?

Reflection

1. Have you ever had a moment when you felt particularly close to God? Did the experience suggest anything to you in terms of moral behavior? Explain.

2. If the moral message of Jesus can be summed up in the phrase, "Love one another as I have loved you," what would you say are some characteristics of Jesus' understanding of love as this chapter presents them?

Model of Morality

Pier (Peter) Giorgio Frassati

Pope John Paul II named more saints and blesseds (a stage toward canonization into sainthood) than any pope before him. Many of these new officially recognized holy ones of the Church are not monks and nuns or figures from the distant past. Some, like the Italian Pier Giorgio Frassati, lived lives similar to the way most young people today live their lives. Pier was athletic and outgoing, an avid skier and mountain climber. He was known for being a person of joy and for spreading that joy to others. He also attended Mass daily and performed many acts of charity. Pier saw a natural connection between these two aspects of his spiritual life: "Jesus comes to visit me each morning in Holy Communion. I return his visit to him in the poor."

Alas, during one of his visits to a person sick with polio, he contracted the disease himself. He was only twenty-four years old. Nonetheless, he didn't let the fatal disease dampen his spirit of joy or his concern for others. In fact, the last thing he wrote before his death at the age of twenty-five, was a request for medicine not for himself but for a friend who was ill but unable to afford it. During the beatification ceremony, the pope praised Pier for his embrace of "life's ordinariness," his devotion to the Blessed Sacrament, and the hope he spread through his simple expression of

Pier (Peter) Giorgio Frassati

Christian joy to those around him. Pier lived out his faith and charity where he lived—in his family and school, in the university and society. Pope John Paul called Pier "a living witness and courageous defender of this hope in the name of the Christian youth of the twentieth century which springs from the Gospel and to the grace of salvation which works in human hearts."

Matthew Bunson, et al. *John Paul II's Book of Saints* (Huntingdon, IN: Our Sunday Visitor Publishing, 1999.)

Divide into groups of four to six students. Each group should choose one Gospel passage that inspires the members of the group.

Each group will choose a reader who will proclaim the chosen passage to the class.

After each passage is read, allow time for the students to reflect on the passage.

Conclude the prayer service with the following prayer:

Let us pray... God our Father, we pray that the work we associate with your Son may also become our work: love, service, forgiveness, sharing of goods, relieving burdens, giving ourselves over to you. Sustain us in our attempts to do your will. Carry us by the power of the Holy Spirit throughout our lives. Forgive us always. Bring us home to you as you promised. We ask this through Christ our Lord. Amen.

3

THE CHURCH

Chapter Overview

- The communion of saints refers to holy things, especially the Eucharist. It also refers to holy people from the past, present, and future who are inspired by the Holy Spirit to use their talents for helping others.
- The Church is a God-given gift that assists us in our moral lives.
- The Church's sacraments are the "masterworks of God" that give us grace to follow Christ.
- The Church is a source of moral guidance for Catholics.

The Church provides inspiration, support, fellowship, and guidance as we struggle to be Jesus' disciples. In this chapter we examine the numerous ways that the Church community can assist us in our moral decision making. A key to appreciating the Church and its relationship to the moral life is to remind ourselves that the Church is we, not they or it.

Before we begin ...

1. Draw a symbolic image of the Church and its relationship to the moral life.

2. Discuss the following questions:
   - Why did you select the image that you did?
   - Where are you in this image of Church—inside or outside, active or passive, in communion or in conflict?
   - Based on your drawing, what role are you assigning to the Church in your moral life?

3. Draw an image that would depict your understanding of the ideal relationship between the Church and the moral life. Explain this image.

Let us pray...

Christ our Lord, you are the head of your body, the Church. You are a living presence, across the globe and in the seat next to us. You are within us and among us. As members of your body, we join with all the saints, living and dead, who proclaim your good news: *"We proclaim your Death, O Lord, and profess your Resurrection until you come again."* Amen.

A Teenage Princess Who Cared for the Poor

Imagine that you were born a medieval princess. At the age of four, you were sent off to live in the home of your future husband. At age fourteen you married the man chosen for you, and you took on the dual responsibilities of raising children and assisting your husband in making decisions about affairs of state. (The age is not a misprint. The heroine of our story did indeed begin her life as wife and mother at age fourteen.)

We envision a princess as living a fairy-tale life, surrounded by riches and waited on by countless servants. However, this was not the case for the princess who became known as Saint Elizabeth of Hungary.

Born the daughter of a Hungarian king, Elizabeth was betrothed while still an infant to a German prince. She was sent off to live at her future husband's castle, where she married him at age fourteen. While still a teenager, Princess Elizabeth became a wife and mother. She loved her husband and he loved her. She also felt deep compassion for lepers, famine victims, and suffering peasants—the people most in need during her lifetime. The prince, Elizabeth's husband, admired and respected Elizabeth's untiring efforts on behalf of these people and supported her in her endeavors. Elizabeth saw to it that much of the wealth of the realm went to building hospitals and facilities for poor people. Because of her generosity she gained many enemies, who felt that royal money should be spent on more "important" matters such as grander castles and stronger armies.

One such enemy was her mother-in-law. According to legend, one time Elizabeth

even gave up her own bed to a homeless leper. Elizabeth's mother-in-law felt that this instance of extreme generosity could easily be exposed as misguided. To discredit Elizabeth the mother-in-law dragged her son, the prince, to the bedroom. However, when the two of them entered the room, instead of a leper they found a vision of Jesus Christ.

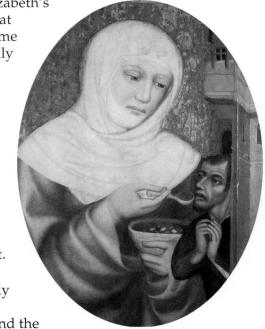

Saint Elizabeth of Hungary (1207–1231)

After bearing four children and selflessly dedicating her life to caring for the poor and the sick, Elizabeth died at the age of twenty-three. Four years later she was proclaimed a saint of the Church. The speed with which she was named a saint indicates that, even though she was young, many people of her time already viewed her as a saint.

As a princess, Elizabeth could have enjoyed all the comforts of courtly life. Instead, she gave herself to the needy people in her realm. For her efforts she suffered rejection, harassment, and physical torment from her enemies. Nonetheless, true to her youthful enthusiasm and deep compassion, she remained undaunted. We can look to Saint Elizabeth of Hungary for inspiration as we search for ways to channel our own enthusiasm and compassion. **A**

Activity

Do research on someone who has recently made a positive contribution to the world. Write the person's story—if possible include a picture. As a class, collect the stories and make a booklet or bulletin board display of these models of saintliness. (Some people to consider are Mother Teresa of Calcutta, Jean Donovan, Maximilian Kolbe, Oscar Romero, Mev Puleo, Alfred Delp, Katharine Drexel, Thea Bowman, Peter Maurin, and Edith Stein.)

The Communion of Saints

"What is the Church if not the assembly of all the saints?"
[Nicetas, Expl. Symb. 10: PL 52:871B.] The communion of saints is the Church.

✝ **Catechism, #946**

communion of saints— this title refers to two realities. First of all, it designates the "holy things" such as charity and the Eucharist, by which the unity of the faithful is brought about. Second, it refers to the unity in Christ of all the redeemed, those on earth and those who have died.

> **"**I believe in the Holy Spirit, the holy catholic Church, the communion of saints . . . **"**
> The Apostles' Creed

> **"**People will always follow a good example; be the one to set a good example, then it won't be long before the others follow. How lovely to think that no one need wait a moment. We can start slowly changing the world! How lovely that everyone, great and small, can make their contribution toward introducing justice straightaway. . . . And you can always, always give something, even if it is only kindness! **"**
> Anne Frank, "Give," March 26, 1944

Eulogies have become increasingly popular recently. In addition to the Mass and formal prayers for someone who has died, often a family member or friend gives a speech commemorating the loved one who has died. ("Dad worked for twenty-seven years at the same factory, where he made his way up to supervisor. He was beloved by all who knew him and was always a calming presence among family and friends." "Mom balanced her work at the supermarket with raising four children. She lived to see great-grandchildren, whom she showered with love.") Good eulogies remind us of the many ways that one person has touched the lives of many others. Most of us won't accomplish feats that grab newspaper headlines. However, each of us has made a significant difference in the lives of any number of people.

A common feature of eulogies is some pronouncement of faith and hope. The speaker may say something like, "We know that Dad is in heaven now where he still watches over us. We look forward to the day when we can all sit around a table with Mom and Dad once again." Whether we are aware of it or not, through these words the eulogist is proclaiming a profound Christian mystery. That is, the cloth we weave that is our lives does not become unraveled at death. The communion we contribute to on earth is part of a larger communion. It is called the **communion of saints**.

One Family of God

Sometimes we are overwhelmed by the darkness, evil, and suffering around us. We overlook the many people who are good and caring in situations where selfishness or complacency seems more rewarding. Elizabeth of Hungary is a member of the communion of saints that is the Church. History provides us with many examples of saintly people, people so filled with the Holy Spirit that they lived heroic lives of goodness.

For instance, even in the inhuman circumstances of Nazi concentration camps during World War II, where every morsel of food was life, we find that saintly people shared their bread with others who were in greater need. The recently canonized saint, Maximilian Kolbe, offered and gave his own life at the hands of the Nazi executioners so that another might live.

The communion of saints is the glory of the Church. The communion of saints refers to all people—past and present—who are united in Christ; it also refers to the holy things such as charity and the sacraments that bring about that unity. The Church is the assembly of all the saints. We are companions with other believers today and with those who have gone before us. Of course, the people who make up the Church are sinners as well as saints. Some more than others stand out as beautiful expressions of saintliness. God continues to raise up saints in every day and age. Where we find a crisis we also find members of our human family who are trying to deal with the crisis.

Where we find people in need we also find saints who are trying to meet those needs. For example, we read about rock musicians who contribute their time, money, and influence to help fight the problems of hunger, homelessness, and racism. We also know that great numbers of young people volunteer their time to help in hospitals, homes for children who have special needs, and hospices for people who are poor. Many school and parish groups dedicate their time and effort to addressing problems in their local communities.

While not everyone who is working to make the world a better place links their involvement directly to their Christian faith, all such people share the Christian spirit spoken of by the bishops of Vatican Council II:

Today there is an inescapable duty to make ourselves the neighbor of every man, no matter who he is, and if we meet him, to come to his aid in a positive way, whether he is an aged person abandoned by all, a foreign worker despised without reason, a refugee, an illegitimate child wrongly suffering for a sin he did not commit, or a starving human who awakens our consciousness by calling to mind the words of Christ: "As you did it to one of the least of these my brethren, you did it to me" (Mt. 25:40).

Pastoral Constitution on the Church in the Modern World, #27 **R**

Reflection

If you were to die at a young age, what tribute would friends, family, and acquaintances make about you? (Don't hold back. Think positively.)

The Gift of the Church

"(God) desires everyone to be saved and to come to the knowledge of the truth" *(1 Timothy 2:4)*. Jesus, the Son of God, is the truth. He is God the Father's fullest revelation of himself. Jesus, the Son of God, entrusted "the knowledge of the truth" to his Apostles, who in turn passed

it on to all generations by means of their preaching, their lives, and their writings. The Holy Spirit, who is inseparable from Jesus, was with the Apostles as they continued Jesus' work and grew the Church.

The Church, then, is Christ's Body on earth. Jesus is her head; he lives in her and with her, and she lives for Jesus and draws life from him.

We can see that the Trinity is fully at work in the Church.

- The Church is the means and the end of God the Father's plan of salvation.
- The Church is born by the Son's total self-giving, Jesus' death and Resurrection.
- The Church is built up, animated, and made holy by the Holy Spirit.

Thus the Church is "the sacrament of the Holy Trinity's communion with men" *(Catechism, #747)*. This means that the Church is the sign and instrument of God's plan of salvation. All salvation comes through the Church from Jesus who is her head.

The Church today plays a vital role in our moral decision making. In obedience to Jesus, the Church strives to preach Christ's gospel to us and to all people. In a world where it is hard to know what is true and worthy of belief, we can rely upon the Church to provide us with "the knowledge of the truth." She is guided by the Holy Spirit and governed by Christ, leading the Church through Peter and the Apostles, "who are present in their successors, the Pope and the college of bishops" *(Catechism, #869)*.

Jesus handed on his mission to his Apostles and entrusted the keys of the Church to Peter. Today, the pope is Peter's successor. As Christ's vicar on earth, the pope is commissioned by Christ with the full and immediate power to care for the souls of the faithful. Under the authority of the pope, the bishops, assisted by priests and deacons, faithfully teach us the gospel, lead us in worship, and guide the Church as true shepherds of Jesus' flock.

Later in this chapter, we will explore some of the ways that the Church acts as our moral guide. **G**

Group Talk

Describe five ways that the Church has been a gift for your life.

Describe five ways that the Church has been a gift to the world.

The Church as the Body of Christ

The word "Church'" means "convocation." It designates the assembly of those whom God's Word "convokes," i.e., gathers together to form the People of God, and who themselves, nourished with the Body of Christ, become the Body of Christ.

(Catechism, #777)

Within the Church we find people who believe in Jesus Christ and who seek to carry on his work, such as the various saintly people described earlier. We also discover people who are hurting and who at times hurt others. We will find them all living together in a community called Church.

The Church can be described in many ways. She is the Bride of Christ in that he loved her, died for her, and called her to be the mother of God's children. The Church is the Temple of the Holy Spirit in that he is her soul and the source of her unity and life.

The Church is also referred to as the people of God, a family of believers formed in Christ. Nevertheless, we often think of the Church as only the select group of people who hold leadership positions within the Church. For instance, we might say: *Why doesn't the Church do more for homeless people in this country? Why doesn't the Church do more for young people? Why doesn't the Church do more to intervene in the many trouble spots of the world? Why doesn't the Church share its wealth?* Quite likely, we actually mean, *Why don't bishops, priests, nuns and other religious, and perhaps the people who are most visible in our parishes do more?* However, we need to remind ourselves constantly that the Church is not *they* or *it*, but *we*.

The Analogy of the Body

In a famous analogy found in his letter to the Corinthians, Saint Paul describes the Church in terms of a body made up of different parts.

"For just as the body is one and has many members . . . so it is with Christ. For in the one Spirit we were all baptized into one body—Jews or Greeks, slaves or free—and we were all made to drink of one Spirit.

Indeed, the body does not consist of one member but of many. If the foot would say, 'Because I am not a hand, I do not belong to the body,' that would not make it any less a part of the body. And if the ear would say, 'Because I am not an eye, I do not belong to the body,' that would not make it any less a part of the body. If the whole body were an eye, where would the hearing be? If the whole body were hearing, where would the sense of smell be? But as it is, God arranged the members in the body, each one of them, as he chose. If all were a single member, where would the body be? As it is, there are many members, yet one body. The eye cannot say to the hand, 'I have no need of you,' nor again the head to the feet, 'I have no need of you.'**"**

1 Corinthians 12:12–21

In Saint Paul's analogy Christ is the head, and all other community members serve different functions that together make one body. The Church is one body in which all the members play vital roles. When we ourselves are suffering from a stomachache or headache, then our entire body feels discomfort—not just the isolated parts. Similarly, if suffering occurs in one part of the world, the effects will eventually touch every part of our increasingly interconnected global community. For instance, if suffering occurs in Africa, China, or Central America, then all parts of the globe eventually will experience the pain. We would be out of touch with our bodies if we commented, "My liver is deteriorating, but that's okay because the rest of my body is fine." Similarly, we would have a poor sense of our interdependent earth if we said, "People are starving in Africa, but that's okay because North Americans have lots to eat."

We might have a better understanding of the body analogy if we would imagine our school community, our family, and our city or town as a human body made up of different parts. In our family and our communities, the health and well-being of each part are vital for the well-being of every other part. For instance, if one family member disrupts the dinner table, everyone's meal is disturbed. If one family member has a drug problem, then the entire family suffers. While on the opposite end of this same comparison, one small group of students working hard to plan dances and other activities benefits the entire school community. **A**

Activity

Write about one of the following as if it were a body made up of interrelated parts:

- Your school community
- Your country
- Your family
- The world community

Body of Christ Means Community of Support

In one high school, a group of students designs a program of skits to demonstrate to other young people some of the dangers related to teenage sex and drinking. In another school students initiate a suicide prevention program. Elsewhere,

a group of young people receives training in peer counseling. Some juniors and seniors prepare to serve as big brothers and big sisters to incoming freshmen in order to ease their transition into high school. Members of the National Honor Society volunteer their time as tutors for other students. Another group of students gathers weekly in the school chapel to pray for the needs of the school community. Youth group members from surrounding parishes organize and participate in sports programs for local youth.

We could easily expand the list of ways that the Church functions as a community of support. One of our words for Church is **ecclesia**, which is also the Greek word for a duly summoned assembly. This reminds us that Christians are not meant to travel solo on their life journeys. Within the Church, everyone is both giver and receiver. Saint Paul makes it clear that, for the Body of Christ, the weakest members are just as important as the strongest: "On the contrary, the members of the body that seem to be weaker are indispensable" (*1 Corinthians 12:22*). Weak and strong, good and bad, in the Body of Christ everyone needs one another.

As Body of Christ the Church is both a here-and-now community as well as a society that is eternal, spiritual, and hierarchical (a society organized into orders or ranks, each subject to the one above it). She is both the means to and the goal of God's plan. Through the bishops, aided by priests and deacons, the Church authentically teaches us the faith handed down by the Apostles. The Church guides us with truth in our moral decision making, celebrates with us divine worship—especially the Eucharist, and shepherds us as the Body of Christ. **G**

For Review...

1. Briefly describe how Elizabeth of Hungary and Maximilian Kolbe modeled saintliness.

2. What is the communion of saints?

3. Describe the ways that the Church is a gift to God's people.

4. How can Saint Paul's analogy of the body be applied to the Church?

5. What does the Greek word for Church imply?

Group Talk

1. Saint Paul says that the weakest members of a body are just as important as the strongest. Does this principle hold true in any of the community bodies to which you belong? Explain.

2. Name groups or organizations with which you are familiar that function as communities of support.

Sacraments and the Moral Life

Sacraments are "powers that come forth" from the Body of Christ, [Cf. Lk 5:17; 6:19; 8:46.] which is ever-living and ever-giving. They are actions of the Holy Spirit at work in his Body, the Church. They are "the masterworks of God" in the new and everlasting covenant.

† **Catechism, #1116**

The moral life can be viewed as a form of spiritual worship. The Church's sacraments nourish and strengthen our moral lives.

Baptism—forgiveness of original and personal sin, a share in the divine life, birth into new life as God's adopted children; entry into the Church

Confirmation—strengthens our bond with Christ and the Church; helps us bear witness by our words and deeds

Eucharist—hearing and pondering God's word; sharing consecrated Bread and Wine in community; receiving and becoming the Body of Christ

Reconciliation—celebrates the receiving of forgiveness for sins confessed with a contrite heart; reconciliation with God and the Church strengthens recipients to live by the law

Anointing of the Sick—celebration of healing and care for the sick; a statement about our call to pray for and assist those who are suffering

Holy Orders—men promise to devote their lives in service of the Church as deacons, priests, and bishops

Matrimony—strengthens the love and unity of the couple, whose love imitates Christ's love for his Church and the Church's love for Christ; celebration of the family as the foundation for involvement in the moral life of the community

Sacraments of Initiation—Joining the Body of Christ

Catholics are familiar with Baptism as the gateway into the Church, and thus a necessary step for salvation. However, we are coming to see the ancient structure of Baptism, Confirmation, and Eucharist as one process of initiation, whether celebrated all at once as an adult or in stages beginning in infancy. The commitment called for in each sacrament doesn't end when the ceremony ends. It's just the beginning.

For instance, newly baptized Christians receive a brand new garment which symbolizes putting on Christ. This simple but powerful ritual says a great deal about how baptized persons are to act for the rest of their lives. Henceforth, regardless of what they are wearing on the outside, inside they represent Christ.

Confirmation strengthens the grace of Baptism and calls its recipients to share the gospel through words and actions. Often young people preparing for Confirmation perform a service to their community as a sign of their Christian commitment.

Finally, full initiation occurs through participation in the Eucharist, "the heart and the summit of the Church's life" *(Catechism, #1407)*. We join with Catholics worldwide to worship Jesus and give thanks to God the Father. We offer perfect worship to the Father because we are united with his Son, Jesus, in offering worship. We "dishonor [the] table" of the Eucharist if we do not move from participating in this meal to sharing with people in need *(Catechism, #1397)*.

Sacraments of Forgiveness

> **"**Then Peter came and said to him, 'Lord, if another member of the church sins against me, how often should I forgive? As many as seven times?' Jesus said to him, 'Not seven times, but, I tell you, seventy-seven times.'**"**

Matthew 18:21–22

alienation—
an experience of isolation and separateness from God and others

reconciliation—
an experience of reuniting and reconnecting with God and others

In biblical symbolism, the number seven signifies completeness. Jesus' response to Peter about how often we should forgive one another suggests that Jesus knows how frequently we humans need forgiveness. We are constantly in need of forgiveness, and Jesus tells us here that we should forgive one another completely and endlessly, as God forgives us always.

Forgiveness is an important step in eliminating the roadblocks that exist in our relationships, including our relationship with God. Thus, Jesus instituted the Sacrament of Penance—also called Confession or Reconciliation—so that all the faithful could receive forgiveness and participate in the process of conversion. Christ gives bishops and priests the authority to absolve, or forgive, sins. If we truly have experienced forgiveness, then we know how refreshing and revitalizing an experience it is. **R**

Baptism is the first sacrament that provides forgiveness of sins, original and personal. All personal sins committed after Baptism are forgiven by the Sacrament of Penance. Our participation in this sacrament presumes our willingness to repent of our sins, genuine sorrow for the sins we have committed, and a resolve to sin no more in the future. The way we partake of the Sacrament of Penance is by confessing our sins to a duly authorized priest, having the intention to make reparation for our sins, and receiving the priest's absolution.

As part of the sacrament, the priest proposes a penance in the form of certain prayers or actions. These acts of penance help us to repair the damage caused by our sins and to lead a life worthy of our call to follow Christ. The benefits of this sacrament are many: reconciliation with God and the Church, pardon from the eternal punishment resulting from mortal sins, a peaceful conscience, and an increase of grace to continue our Christian journey.

Without forgiveness we are out of touch with God and with one another. **Alienation**, a sense of distance and separateness from others and of uneasiness around others, is unsettling and saps our energy. To be renewed and revitalized, we need to experience forgiveness. With forgiveness we find **reconciliation**—a word that means reuniting and getting back in touch with others. Therefore, reconciliation is the means of overcoming alienation and of achieving a return to a sense of belonging.

It's easy to see how alienation fosters immorality while a spirit of reconciliation supports moral behavior.

A primary function of the Church is to be a community in which forgiveness and reconciliation take place. Thus Jesus has given the Church the power to forgive the sins of those who are baptized. Within the Church there are ceremonies to celebrate reconciliation. In a sense, all sacraments celebrate reconciliation since all

sacraments celebrate different ways of keeping in touch with God and with other people. The sacrament that we associate most with forgiveness and straightening out our lives is Reconciliation. **A**

For Review...

1. Describe the relationship between the sacraments and morality.

2. What are the Sacraments of Initiation? Describe one way that each of these three sacraments sets a direction for living a moral life.

3. What does the number seven mean in biblical symbolism? What does it say about Jesus' message of forgiveness?

4. Define the terms alienation and reconciliation.

5. What does the sacrament of Reconciliation celebrate?

Reflection

• Recall a moment in your childhood when your mother or father reprimanded you for doing something wrong. Imagine yourself crying, then your parent hugging you and saying, "It's okay now."

• Imagine that you and your best friend are fighting. You exchange angry words, cutting deeply since each of you knows the other's weaknesses so well. A few lonely and anxious hours later your friend arrives at your door and says, "You know I can't stay angry with you. I'm sorry for those nasty things I said. Please forgive me."

• Imagine that you are baby-sitting a young child. While you are chatting to a friend on the phone, the child scribbles with crayon on new living room furniture. Imagine how troubled and burdened you feel unless you experience forgiveness, both as giver (to the child) and receiver (from the parents).

• Write about a time when you experienced forgiveness.

Activity

1. Write a poem, a story, or an imaginative essay, the theme of which is either alienation or reconciliation.

2. Using specific examples, describe the relationship between alienation, reconciliation, and the moral life.

The Church as Moral Guide

magisterium—
the teaching office of the Church

"The task of giving an authentic interpretation of the Word of God, whether in its written form or in the form of Tradition, has been entrusted to the living, teaching office of the Church alone. Its authority in this matter is exercised in the name of Jesus Christ" [DV 10 § 2]. This means that the task of interpretation has been entrusted to the bishops in communion with the successor of Peter, the Bishop of Rome.

 Catechism, #85

Jesus Christ is obviously the teacher of Christian morality. However, just as we find Christ embodied in his Church, so also we receive continuing guidance in morality through the Church. Jesus appointed the Apostles to be teachers in his name. Likewise, the pope and bishops carry on their role as teachers, ensuring that Church teaching remains faithful to Jesus and the Apostles. As teachers, the pope and the bishops teach us the faith which we apply to our moral lives. They carefully study moral questions involving natural law and reason that arise in this swiftly changing world and provide us guidance for our moral decision making.

The living, ongoing teaching office of the Church is known as the **magisterium**. Guided by the Holy Spirit, the Church's magisterium interprets the word of God found in Scripture and Tradition. That is, the magisterium looks to these two sources of the single deposit of truth—the word of God—to formulate teaching in matters of faith and morals. The Church's magisterium is such a reliable reflection of Jesus' message that her teachings on faith and morals are ensured by the charism of infallibility.

Scripture and Morality

The Church constantly is nourished and strengthened by God's word in Scripture. To truly appreciate the moral wisdom found in the Bible, we must keep in mind the following biblical facts:

- By inspiring its human authors, God is the true author of Scripture.

- To interpret the words of Scripture, "be attentive above all to what God wants to reveal through the sacred authors" (Catechism, #137). In other words, even the devil can quote the Bible for his own purposes.

- The Church defines the Bible as the 46 books of the Old Testament and the 26 books of the New Testament.

- Because Jesus is the focus of the four Gospels, they occupy a place of great importance and centrality in the life of the Church.

The Church and Natural Law

In making statements about morality, Church leaders follow time-honored principles of early Church teachings, constantly looking to the life and message of Jesus for guidance. Then, they seek to provide teachings that address the very real problems facing people in current historical situations and in diverse cultures. To help in applying Scripture and Tradition to current moral issues, the Church teaches us about natural law, an approach to moral reasoning that has guided Christian thinkers since the early centuries of the Church.

Natural law is an important element of the Church's teaching on morality. God has placed within us a way to participate in his wisdom and truth. It is unchangeable, permanent throughout history. He has hard-wired us with a natural law or essential principles, which we can then access using the good sense God gave us. An expression of these principles of natural law are the Ten Commandments. And since everyone, across the globe and throughout history, has the natural law engraved on his or her heart by the Creator, natural law has served as "a necessary foundation for the erection of moral rules and civil law" (*Catechism, #1979*). **G**

With its emphasis on human reason as an instrument capable of arriving at truth, natural law presents a very positive image of us humans. It suggests that reasonable people can speak among themselves about rights and duties and that they can attempt to convince one another of truth through the force of reasonable arguments. In other words, natural law believes that, despite cultural and other obvious differences, Americans can seek universal truth about right and wrong in dialogue with Africans, Asians, and others. Similarly, since morality is not a matter simply of religious beliefs but of rationally presented truths, Christians can discuss moral issues with Hindus, Buddhists, Muslims, and Jews. The United Nations Declaration of Human Rights, developed by representatives of all the world's nations, is an example of common universal truths.

By examining human nature, the natural moral law discovers basic principles that should govern human conduct. Examples of two such moral principles are "Speak truth" and "Respect life." How would advocates of natural law defend such principles? In condensed form, natural-law morality uses the following reasoning process to arrive at these principles.

Humans are endowed with a wonderful, God-given capacity to communicate by using speech. Granted, other creatures also communicate, but human speech is something special. Traditional natural-law morality determines that, by its nature human speech is meant to communicate truth. While it can be used for talking gibberish or for deceiving others, the very design of our ability to speak suggests that we use it for telling the truth. The crowning glory of human speech is its capacity to express deep emotions and to convey lofty ideas, to break down barriers between people, and to communicate with others in fashioning a more human community.

Group Talk

Natural law refers to principles that are so natural to our human condition that they are "engraved on our hearts." Imagine that you are a member of a United Nations commission established to formulate a declaration of universal moral principles—that is, a list of principles that would apply to everyone everywhere simply because they are human. Create this list of principles as universal pronouncements about how people should or should not act.

The Precepts of the Church

As Catholics, our moral lives are intertwined with the life of the Church, especially its liturgical life. Our moral lives are nourished by our participation in the Church's liturgy. The precepts of the Church are laws that name specific actions that all Catholics are obligated to carry out. According to the *National Catechetical Directory*, the following precepts apply to Catholics in the United States.

1. To keep holy the day of the Lord's Resurrection: to worship God by participating in Mass every Sunday and holy day of obligation; to avoid those activities that would hinder renewal of soul and body on the Sabbath (e.g., needless work and business activities, unnecessary shopping, etc.).

2. To lead a sacramental life; to receive Holy Communion frequently and the Sacrament of Reconciliation regularly—minimally, to receive the Sacrament of Reconciliation at least once a year (annual confession is obligatory only if serious sin is involved); minimally also, to receive Holy Communion at least once a year, between the First Sunday of Lent and Trinity Sunday.

3. To study Catholic teaching in preparation for the Sacrament of Confirmation, to be confirmed, and then to continue to study and advance the cause of Christ.

4. To observe the marriage laws of the Church; to give religious training, by example and word, to one's children; to use parish schools and catechetical programs.

5. To strengthen and support the Church—one's own parish community and parish priests, the worldwide Church and the pope.

6. To do penance, including abstaining from meat and fasting from food on the appointed days.

7. To join in the missionary spirit and apostolate of the Church. **A**

Activity

The precepts of the Church spell out the very minimum necessary for our moral and liturgical life. What other practices would you include to energize and strengthen you moral/liturgical life.

Written Sources of Catholic Moral Teaching

In the Gospels, Jesus is more often called teacher (in Hebrew, **rabbi**) than anything else. The Church then, dedicated to following Jesus, takes the teaching vocation very seriously. The primary teachers of children are parents, who have the first responsibility for the education of their children in the faith, in prayer, and in the virtues. However, learning is a lifelong process. Thus, we need guidance throughout our lives.

From the beginning of Christianity, there have been leaders of the community dedicated to preserving and carrying on the teachings of Jesus. Today, the pope and bishops continue that role. Together, and in various ways, they provide teachings, norms, and guidance. Certainly, teaching entails much more than the written word. We know of only one incident when Jesus himself wrote—a few words written on the ground that caused quite a stir. See John, Chapter 8. However, we do use the written word. The following types of writings describe some of the means by which leaders of the Church teach and guide the Catholic community.

Documents of Vatican II—As a result of the international bishops meeting together from 1962 to 1965 at Vatican Council II, numerous documents were published.

This council marked only the second such council in over four hundred years, so obviously it was a significant event for the Church. The documents do address some specific moral issues, especially in the document called *The Pastoral Constitution on the Church in the Modern World*. In addition to specific teachings, however, the documents provide a sense of direction for the Catholic community as it journeys through our fast-paced world.

Catechism of the Catholic Church—No summary of Catholic teaching was produced by the Second Vatican Council. The Second Vatican Council was described as a pastoral council, one concerned about the life and the spirit of the Church today, rather than a council whose primary focus was on defining teaching more exactly. However, twenty years later a number of bishops petitioned the pope that he begin a process of compiling a catechism that would serve as the primary teaching document for the universal church. In 1994 the **Catechism of the Catholic Church** appeared in English and quickly became a bestseller. It is meant to guide Church leaders and teachers as they try to instruct the members of their community on official Catholic teaching.

rabbi—
Hebrew for teacher, a term frequently applied to Jesus

Catechism of the Catholic Church—
a "synthesis of the essential and fundamental contents of Catholic doctrine, as regards both faith and morals, in the light of the Second Vatican Council and the whole of the Church's Tradition" *(Catechism, #11)*

Papal Encyclicals—An **encyclical** is an official letter from the pope to the Catholic community. In the recent past, popes have written encyclicals on such topics as peace, justice, family life, human dignity, treatment of workers, and morality in general. When we look at specific moral topics later in the course, we will refer to various encyclicals to find relevant teachings.

Statements of Vatican Commissions— The pope oversees a large collection of offices dedicated to various areas of Church life, such as education, justice and peace, and relations with other religions. For the most part, members of these commissions work behind the scenes to help make the Church an instrument of peace, justice, and moral betterment in the world. However, on occasion commission members study a specific area of morality or Church life and issue a pronouncement to provide guidance on that question. For instance, as we will examine later, there have been tremendous advances related to artificial reproduction. Such advances are matters not only of technology, but also of morality. A Vatican commission gathered together experts to examine the issue and prepared a document about it.

Pastoral Letters—Traditionally, the bishops of the Church are known as pastors, a word meaning shepherd. In their local area, known as a diocese, they serve as successors to the Apostles. Bishops, either individually or as a regional group, write official letters to their communities. These letters are called pastoral letters. For instance, in pastoral letters the Canadian bishops have addressed concerns of Indian populations in their country. The U.S. bishops have written about immigrant workers and nuclear weapons.

The Catholic Church is both local and universal. Catholic communities celebrating Christ's presence in their lives and seeking to do his will can be found in Hong Kong, Kiev, Nairobi, Detroit—and all over the world. The pope and bishops are visible reminders of the combined local and universal nature of the Church. **A R**

For Review...

1. In the Gospels what title is applied most frequently to Jesus?

2. What instrument for seeking moral truth does natural law emphasize.

3. Distinguish among the five types of written Church documents described in the text.

Activity

Read through an official Church document (choose from one of the types mentioned above) that addresses moral concerns. Write about key teachings found in the document.

Reflection

Think back on your understanding of Church that you had before reading this chapter. How has the information in this chapter supported or changed your understanding of Church? Explain.

...Conclusion

Moral decision making and living an authentic life are important challenges facing all of us. Catholic teaching about the Church reminds us that we are not alone in making decisions and in shaping our lives. We are better decision makers when we look for support, guidance, and direction in the teachings of Jesus, in the great heroes and heroines of Church history, from current Church members and from the many official teachings found in the Church today.

In a world filled with suffering, Church members are called to proclaim that there is a place where suffering can be shared. In a world of confusion, Church members are called to proclaim that Christ offers a focus for the search for wisdom. In a world of war, Church members are called to proclaim that peace can be sought together in Christ. In a world of intense loneliness and alienation, Church members are called to proclaim that we can live together and love one another in Christ. Indeed, this course is a study of what will be required of each of us in order to become such a Church today.

Pope John XXIII

The Catholic Church has been established by Jesus Christ as MOTHER AND TEACHER of nations, so that all who in the course of centuries come to her loving embrace, may find salvation as well as the fullness of a more excellent life.

Mater et Magistra, #1

Blessed Pope John XXIII began his first of the two encyclicals that he wrote with the above words. In so doing, he was proclaiming to the world that the Church established by Jesus offers a loving embrace to all people. Pope John communicated this message not only in words but physically in the way he embraced the people he met. During the short time he was pope (1958–1963) John XXIII met an astounding number of heads of state compared to his predecessors. However, he also made a point of visiting men in the prisons of Rome, even mentioning without guile that he had a family member who had spent time in prison.

Pope John XXIII convened the Second Vatican Council, which did so much to make the Church an even more active and compassionate presence in the world. At the beginning of the council he was carried down the center aisle of St. Peter's Basilica on an elevated throne. The world's bishops were gathered there, and Pope John soon dismounted his throne so that he could greet his friends personally. Pope John knew that a gathering of bishops from all parts of the world would result in heated discussions. He welcomed open and honest exchanges among them. In his opening address he told the assembly that the Church wanted to address disagreements with "the medicine of mercy rather than that of severity." He fostered dialogue not only within the Church but also between the Church and the rest of the world.

Pope John XXIII was truly a pastor who modeled in his very being the two images he applied to the Church—mother and teacher. Because of him, the Church is more than ever an advocate for people who are poor or oppressed, a voice for peace, and a partner working with all people of good will to develop the human family.

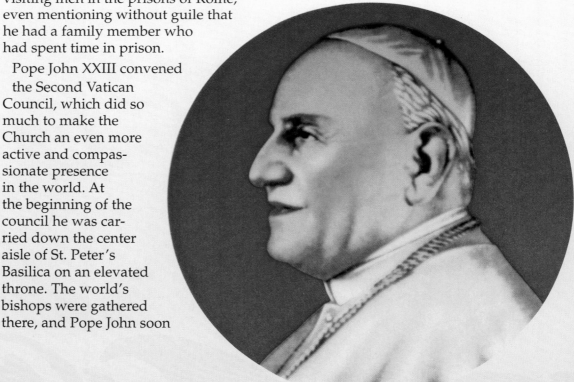

Pope John XXIII

Let us pray ... Lord Jesus Christ, you called us from all the ends of the earth to be one Church, sisters and brothers in you. Help us to be ever mindful that we are members, one of another in you, and that we are to live accordingly.

A reading from St. Paul ...

We will lovingly follow the truth at all times—speaking truly, dealing truly, living truly—and so become more and more in every way like Christ who is head of his body, the Church. Under his direction the whole body is fitted together perfectly, and each part in its own special way helps the other parts, so that the whole body is healthy and growing and full of love (Ephesians 4:15–16).

Litany of the Church

For those who are patient with me and willing to listen to me in good times and in bad . . .

Response: I thank you, God.

For those who are home to me wherever I am, even during the many anxious and unsettling moments I face each week . . .

Response: I thank you, God.

For those who brighten my day, comfort my sorrow, challenge me, and share my joys . . .

Response: I thank you, God.

For those who teach me right understanding and guide me in the way of wisdom . . .

Response: I thank you, God.

For those who manifest the love of Jesus to me . . .

Response: I thank you, God.

For those with whom I can be myself and who remind me that life is good. Together with them, may I come to know your love for us . . .

Response: I thank you, God. Amen.

4

CONSCIENCE Being True to Ourselves

Chapter Overview

- Our dignity as persons created by God requires us to follow our conscience.
- Popular uses of the word conscience are frequently inadequate to describe all that the term involves.
- A fuller understanding of conscience includes three dimensions: awareness, development, and judgment.
- Scripture and Tradition emphasize the importance of using our conscience to make informed moral decisions.

We live our Catholic morality in the day-to-day decisions we make. Conscience has come to be identified both with our capacity for right judgment in making decisions and with our faithfulness to that judgment. In this chapter we will look at popular uses of the term conscience and then define it in a way that reflects its original meaning. We will then summarize recent Church teaching, particularly the groundbreaking perspectives on conscience of the Second Vatican Council.

Before we begin . . .

1. Take a few minutes to draw a symbolic representation of conscience.

2. What does your drawing say about conscience?

Let us pray . . .

Gracious God, you have blessed us with the awesome power of conscience. Gazing inward, we search our hearts and ask: *How are my decisions shaping who I will become? How are my actions affecting others? What is your will for me?* You entrusted us with freedom and the power of choice. In our moral decision making, make us worthy by the power of the Holy Spirit of the trust you have placed in us. Amen.

The Nature of Conscience

hero—
someone who follows
her or his conscience in
the face of difficulties

Both in fictional and in real-life dramas, we often encounter the theme of being true to conscience. The theme deserves frequent treatment. Being true to conscience is an important sign of living an authentic human existence. Conscience represents our dignity and integrity as persons. We recognize a hero as someone who follows conscience in the face of difficulties, sometimes even at the risk of losing one's life.

For instance, during World War II, a young Austrian Catholic named Franz Jägerstätter believed in his conscience that his country—at the time part of Nazi Germany—was fighting a war that was wrong. Therefore, he refused to be drafted into his country's army. He found no support for his conscientious stand—not even from his parish priest. For being true to his conscience, Jägerstätter was executed by the Nazi leaders of his country. At the time Jägerstätter was found guilty of noncompliance with the law. Today we recognize him as a hero of conscience.

The Heroism of Being True to Conscience

During the late 1960s and the 1970s, Cesar Chavez, founder of the United Farm Workers union, led a variety of protest actions to draw attention to the suffering of migrant farm workers in California and elsewhere. Largely through his efforts, poorly paid migrant farm workers gained a union. Even after achieving unionization for the farm workers, Chavez continued his heroic struggle. He fought against the use of cancer-causing pesticides in the growing of fruit and against other dangers faced by farm workers. In 2003 the U.S. Postal Service issued a stamp honoring Chavez for his heroism.

The challenge to be true to our conscience flows naturally from the Christian vision of morality. Throughout history and in our present day, we find many real-life reminders that a call to be a person of conscience is a call to be heroic. **A**

Activity

Many critics of our contemporary culture lament that we have few heroes to imitate and inspire us. However, heroes need not be celebrities. Rank the following people from 1 for most heroic to 8 for least heroic. Then defend your top choices and explain what you believe it means to be a hero.

____ A young girl volunteers one evening a week at a nursing home.

____ A boy whose family is poor attends high school and also works to help support his family.

____ A tenth-grade girl attends a basketball camp where all other participants are boys.

____ A junior in high school works at two jobs during the summer to raise money for a trip to Europe with her school band.

____ Even though cheating would be easy and other students around him are cheating, a boy with poor grades does his own work during a science test.

____ A girl whose eyesight is very poor enrolls in a special program for blind skiers.

____ A boy who believes strongly that abortion should be illegal is arrested while participating in an anti-abortion protest.

____ A Mexican American girl who speaks little English attends a school where everyone else is English-speaking, because she believes that she can get a better education there.

The Voice of God Echoing in Our Hearts

We are required to follow our **conscience** because our dignity as persons created by God requires it. Ignoring conscience diminishes our dignity. Conscience is the voice of God the Father echoing in our hearts. Conscience is a gift from God to lead us to happiness, that is, to himself. Through our conscience, God the Holy Spirit continually works within, reminding us to follow the way of Jesus the Son of God. Conscience is not separate from who we are. Rather, it is at the core of who we are. Nonetheless, we don't decide what conscience dictates; we discover it. In other words, conscience has nothing to do with what we want to do. Many factors, such as our instincts and desires, can muddy our conscience. At the same time, we possess the freedom to accept or reject what conscience—the voice of God within us—directs us to do. Here again, living in accord with conscience often demands heroism.

science—
a moral decision-making ability (or action) centering on what a person has already done or ought to do in the future. It involves an awareness that there is right and wrong, a process of discernment, and finally judgment.

Defining Conscience

Even though conscience is such an important concept in Catholic moral teaching, in popular usage the word is used without much precision. In order to have a fruitful discussion about conscience, it is necessary to define the term much more precisely than the way it is commonly used. How we define the term makes all the difference when we address the questions: Do I follow my conscience? and What does it mean to follow my conscience? Before determining a fuller, more precise definition of conscience, let's look at some of the ways that the term is often used.

- Jen saw the makeup on the drugstore display rack. It was a brand that she had wanted to try, but she had no money. The only person nearby was a young clerk reading a magazine behind a counter. Jen picked up the makeup and examined it. It was small enough to slip into her pocket. She wanted desperately to walk out of the store with it, but a little voice inside her—her conscience—gnawed at her to put the makeup back.

- Mick knew Andrea planned to invite him to her prom. He didn't want to go with her, but his mother had drummed it into him: *Never hurt a girl's feelings.* That saying, like many others that his parents repeated over and over again (*Always clean your plate. Be polite to your elders.*) made it difficult for Mick to go against the upbringing that had molded his conscience.

- With less than a minute remaining in the football game, emotions were at a fever pitch. Defensive captains exhorted their teammates, "If we stop them here, we win the game! Let's hit 'em and hit 'em hard!" Darrell dug in at his defensive-end position. When the ball was snapped, he rushed uncontested toward the quarterback and tackled him fiercely to the ground. For what seemed like an eternity to Darrell, the quarterback lay unconscious in the middle of the football field. Darrell began to feel bad that he had attacked him so savagely. In the weeks that followed, Darrell was racked with feelings of guilt. He had a guilty conscience, bad dreams, and anxious moments. Constantly, he replayed the scene in his mind, and each time he felt terrible about what he had done. **G**

Group Talk

Describe a television show, movie, or novel that depicts a person facing a crisis of conscience. In response to the crisis, what choices does the person make? Is conscience applied in a way similar to or different from the ways the term is described in the above text?

Descriptions of Conscience

The stories of Jen, Mick, and Darrell point out some of the confusion surrounding the term *conscience*. Each example describes elements involved in conscience formation. However, if misinterpreted, each usage can actually distort the true meaning and function of conscience. Let's look at these incidents to see what conscience means in each case.

An Inner Voice

Is conscience merely an *inner voice* such as Jen experienced in the drugstore? In the children's story of *Pinocchio*, Jiminy Cricket is assigned to be Pinocchio's "conscience." Have we been assigned our own Jiminy Cricket who tells us precisely what to do when we face troubling moral decisions? If the two questions above suggest that we have a conscience in the same way that we have a watch or a car, then the answer to these questions is no. Conscience implies that we are valuing creatures drawn toward goodness and truth.

Certainly Jen would do well to listen to the voice of her conscience as it reminds her that what she wants to do is not necessarily what is good to do. However, conscience should not be viewed as an inner voice that we leave untouched, unexamined, and undeveloped.

Our Upbringing

Isn't our conscience actually determined by our upbringing? Like Mick in the above story, all of us were told many things as we were growing up about what is right or proper and about what is wrong or inappropriate. As a result, we walk around as if we have built-in tapes, ready to play a message from our parents or others in authority who have given us advice. Consciously or unconsciously, we carry within us the messages from our early years. Violation of those messages can cause internal conflict.

Certainly, conscience has a cultural and a community dimension. It is formed and molded—cultivated—by our culture and our community. Significant people in our lives, especially in our early lives, shape our sense of right and wrong. **R**

In the above story, Mick should take his parent's advice about not hurting someone's feelings. However, he also might examine critically all the taped messages that he carries around within himself. Likewise, we need to take what has been given to us by those who have gone before us and build on that. In terms of conscience we have received valuable lessons from the authority figures of our past, but there are more lessons to learn. We would not be very conscientious if we did not try to learn them.

Reflection

Significant persons from our childhood can include characters in books, television shows, or movies. Name three such characters who have helped shape your conscience. What positive messages did you receive from each?

A Feeling

If we were asked to write a sentence with the word conscience in it, many of us would include the phrase *guilty conscience*—feeling bad about something we did. On the other hand, a *good conscience* refers to a judgment that we make, after due deliberation, about the rightness of an action. Some people use the expression clear conscience to refer to the fact that a person was not responsible for any wrongdoing in a particular situation. ("Yes, I was at the party, but I wasn't drinking. My conscience is clear.")

In the third example presented above, Darrell feels guilty about hurting an opposing player during a football game. Is such a feeling the work of conscience? Actually, people can feel guilty about their actions even though they are not clearly responsible for the consequences of those actions. For that reason, Darrell's guilt feelings do not offer an adequate explanation for what we mean by conscience.

Our feelings of guilt and of lack of guilt can be connected with conscience. However, just as with an inner voice and with upbringing, feelings are not primarily what conscience involves.

When we look back at our lives, we might discover times when we felt guilty, even though closer examination indicates that we did nothing wrong. For instance, perhaps as a child you accidentally broke something of value that belonged to someone else, and you felt guilty even though you were actually trying to help. Another example might be that you feel guilty about making an unkind remark, one that you did not say with the intention of causing harm. If conscience is the ability to judge the moral right or wrong of a particular action, then it does not depend upon feelings. Feelings are significant and need to be respected and taken seriously. However, of themselves, good or bad feelings are not what is meant by conscience. **R**

Root Meaning of Conscience

Sometimes knowing the origin of a word helps us clarify its meaning. The Latin root of our English word conscience is the active verb to know. From this root meaning we discover two things: Conscience has to do with knowing, and conscience refers to an action rather than a thing. Conscience, therefore, means the act of judging based on one's knowledge of right and wrong. If conscience is central to moral decision making, then we need to retrieve this sense of the term. The Catechism's definition of conscience does just that when it states, "Conscience is a judgment of reason by which the human person recognizes the moral quality of a concrete act" *(#1796)*.

Reflection

1. Have you ever felt guilty for an action that harmed another even though you did not intend to cause harm? If so, explain the situation.

2. Have you ever not felt guilty when doing something that turned out to be wrong or hurtful? If so, explain the situation.

3. Have you ever felt guilty when you knowingly did something wrong or hurtful? If so, explain the situation. What did you do about the feelings? (For instance, did you use the guilt feelings as the motivation to make amends?)

The root meaning of conscience helps us appreciate how this important capacity serves us in our moral decision making. None of the popular applications of the term comprises all that conscience is, for it is more than just an inner voice, more than just a feeling, and more than all the messages about right and wrong that we have accumulated over the years. These popular notions present us with opportunities to reflect more deeply on the meaning of conscience. However, they are incomplete descriptions of conscience. **G**

A fuller definition of conscience includes three interrelated dimensions:

1. Conscience involves our basic awareness of right and wrong and our inclination toward the good.
2. Forming a correct conscience includes everything we do to develop our awareness of truth and goodness.
3. Finally, conscience refers to making a moral judgment about the right and wrong of a particular act. This is done after seeking wisdom and knowledge from Church teachings, the word of God, prayer, significant adults, and other reliable sources.

The Three Dimensions of Conscience

In the following story, Jerry faces a painful dilemma filled with many possible moral decisions. He is faced with making decisions at home that affect his parents. He also recognizes that the tension in his home could influence him to act out in negative ways outside of his home, perhaps even to imitate his father's destructive behavior. In the face of this moral—not to mention psychological—powder keg, Jerry acts in a very conscientious way. He decides to seek help from a counselor.

If we take a look at how Jerry arrived at his decision, we will uncover the three interrelated dimensions of conscience at work. First, Jerry has a basic awareness that he is faced with decisions that could lead to good or bad results. Jerry is drawn to the good and is motivated by an underlying orientation toward goodness and away from evil. This represents the basic groundwork of conscience.

Second, Jerry develops his awareness through self-examination. He is being conscientious insofar as he thinks about the options that are available to him.

Third, Jerry makes a judgment: *Get help.*

So he decides to see a counselor who will help him decide on a course of action.

Looking closely at Jerry's decision making in this instance, we can distinguish the three interrelated dimensions of conscience that are named above.

For Review...

1. Who were Franz Jägerstätter and Cesar Chavez?

2. Name three ways that conscience is sometimes understood in popular usage. Why is each usage insufficient to express all that conscience involves?

3. What does the Latin root of the word conscience mean? What does this root meaning tell us about conscience?

Group Talk

- Name some areas in which your awareness concerning right and wrong has been raised or deepened in recent years.

- Name some areas in which the general awareness of our society has been raised over time.

- Name some areas of moral inquiry about which you would like to gain greater knowledge so that you may make more thoughtful decisions.

- Is it possible for someone to lack conscience? If so, what would some reasons be for such a condition?

Jerry's Problem

Even as a young child, Jerry knew there was an abnormal amount of tension in his family. As he grew older, Jerry realized that the tension arose because of his father's drinking problem. Recently, his mother has been confiding in him her feelings and concerns about Jerry and his father. She has even started asking him questions: "Have you seen Dad drinking lately?" "Has Dad ever talked to you about his drinking?" "You don't drink, do you? You don't want to end up like your father!"

His father, too, has been confiding in Jerry. On a number of Saturday afternoons his father has told him, "I'm going down to the bar to watch some of the ball game, Jerry. Don't tell your mother where I went; she'll just get upset."

Jerry doesn't know what to say or do. He finds that he has been lying to his parents quite a bit lately and spending more time with a crowd that is known for getting into trouble. Jerry wants to do what is right, and he especially doesn't want to hurt either his mother or his father. After some thought, Jerry decides this problem is too big to handle by himself, and so he seeks help. He decides to approach a school counselor. He hopes that with her help, he can unravel some of his own thoughts and feelings and devise some plan to deal with both of his parents as best he can. **A**

Activity

If you were a member of a peer-counseling team at Jerry's school and he came to you for help, what advice would you give him?

Our Inclination to the Good

Not to Decide Is to Decide

Deep within his conscience man discovers a law which he has not laid upon himself but which he must obey. [GS 16.]

✝ **Catechism, #1776**

lax conscience—
when a person does not employ a process of conscientious decision making, thereby not facing or thinking about the morality of actions that he or she performs

In moral decision making, conscience comes into play when people recognize that there are right and wrong acts and that they can choose between the two. We might question the existence of a basic awareness of good and evil in humans. Surely, some people seemingly exhibit no such sense of right and wrong. While this may be true, it does not deny the existence of such a capacity as an essential human trait. We sometimes label a person who takes no responsibility for his or her actions as morally immature or deficient. In other words, to be human means to have a sense of right and wrong; not to have such awareness involves a distortion of one's humanity. In extreme cases, we find people who lack any sense of right or wrong. Sometimes they are referred to as psychopaths.

If we possess an awareness of right and wrong, does it mean that we always act on that awareness in our choices? Not necessarily. We are free to act against conscience. We might also develop the habit of ignoring what our conscience says. We possess many untapped capabilities, and conscience may be one that a person leaves untapped. Nonuse does not equal nonexistence. Just as we have a capacity for learning that might go untapped, so we possess a basic capacity to recognize goodness which might shrivel up from lack of use. The term for conscience when it is either ignored or underemployed is **lax conscience**. A person with a lax conscience does not face or think about the morality of the actions that he or she performs.

Besides awareness of right and wrong, conscience on the most basic level also implies that we are *drawn to the good*. A natural orientation or inclination toward the good marks us as human beings. Despite the reality that this orientation can be distorted by many factors, to be human means to be a seeker of the good. **A**

Activity

1. In a psychology book or other reference source, look up the word psychopath. What does it mean?

2. What factors influence a person's perception of what is right and good?

3. Do you agree that "to be human means to be a seeker of the good"?

Development: Enhancing Our Capacity to Know and to Choose the Good

"Beloved, do not believe every spirit, but test the spirits to see whether they are from God.**"**

📖 *1 John 4:1*

Our basic awareness of and orientation toward goodness is not all that there is to conscience. We must build on and develop this orientation. Therefore, when we speak about following our conscience, we are referring to an **informed conscience**: a conscience that is educated and developed through constant use and examination. **G**

For instance, look at the brief anecdote about Jim in the activity below. We might find Jim's remark to be comical. Certainly, his logic goes counter to what it means to be conscientious. The second dimension of conscience operates against any such ignorance-is-bliss stance. At its very root, conscience seeks more knowledge, greater refinement, and deeper sensitivity. Therefore, the second aspect of conscience refers to all those steps that we take to form and develop our moral capacity.

The Catechism expresses concisely what this dimension of conscience requires: "In the formation of conscience the Word of God is the light for our path; [Cf. Ps 119:105.]

we must assimilate it in faith and prayer and put it into practice. We must also examine our conscience before the Lord's Cross. We are assisted by the gifts of the Holy Spirit, aided by the witness or advice of others and guided by the authoritative teaching of the Church" (#1785).

In other words, as we read about Jesus and about his words and deeds, develop the habit of prayer, study Church teaching on morality, and seek advice from others, we are using the guidance of the Holy Spirit to develop our conscience and to move ourselves along to becoming more informed moral decision makers.

If we make this course a process for deepening our consciousness of ourselves and others and a study of how our actions impact ourselves and others, then the course itself will be the work of developing an informed conscience. As the first level of conscience exemplifies our dignity as human persons, so the second level nurtures and furthers that dignity.

---

informed conscience—

a conscience that is educated and developed through constant use and examination

---

Group Talk

1. Read over the following scenario. Evaluate Jim's response in terms of this second dimension of conscience. What would a conscientious response from him entail?

One day a group of ninth-grade boys was gathered for a talk on moral issues related to sexuality. Jim remarked to his friend, "I don't want to hear about what I shouldn't do. I'm just a freshman. If I don't know something is wrong, then it's okay for me to do it. I can't be held responsible."

2. When college seniors have a morality course, they often say, "This course should be taken in freshman year. By senior year my morality and values are already set." When college freshmen have a morality course, they often say, "This course should be taken in high school. By college my morality and values are already set." High-school juniors and seniors sometimes remark that a morality course should be taken in ninth grade.

State your opinion on the following questions. Give reasons to support your opinions.

- Are a person's values ever completely set? Is moral development ever finished?
- Is junior or senior year of high school too late for a morality course to have an impact on the values and moral decision making of students?
- During which year or years of schooling would you recommend a morality course be given?

Judgment: Making Choices Based on Our Awareness of the Good

"Little children, let us love, not in word or speech, but in truth and action."

 *1 John 3:18*

erroneous conscience— when a person follows a process of conscientious decision making but unwittingly makes a wrong decision

When it comes right down to it, morality involves decisions and acting upon those decisions. Likewise, conscience is not a drama played out endlessly in our mind. It is a judgment of our reason about the morality of our actions. Seeking to be sensitive to our evaluation of goodness and truth, and using as a guide all the information and awareness that our informed conscience can provide, we then choose the best course of action known to us. This involves moral judgment.

An important question related to conscience is *Even though we seek to be as conscientious as possible, can we judge wrongly?* The answer to that question is *yes*. We are imperfect creatures subject to mistakes and misguided judgments. A conscience that judges wrongly, even after a period of conscientious decision making, is an **erroneous conscience**— a conscience in error. Of course, when we follow the directives of our conscience we cannot know that we are wrong. Other people may know better than we do that we are wrong. Likewise, hindsight—looking back after we have acted—might convince us that we were wrong. However, being conscientious means that we make judgments based on our present awareness of the goodness and evil of an action.

We are responsible for seeking truth— especially as Catholics the truths found in Church teaching—and for acting accordingly.

Conscience can remain in ignorance or make erroneous judgments. Such ignorance and errors are not always free of guilt.

Catechism, #1801

A second important question regarding conscience as judgment is *Do people always act according to their best judgment?* The answer to this question is clearly *no*. When people do not follow their conscience on moral matters, then they may be committing a **sin**. In other words, we are obliged to follow the certain judgment of our rightly formed and correct conscience.

Admittedly, since development of conscience differs somewhat with each individual, one person might conscientiously decide upon a course of action that another would find evil. For instance in pre-Civil War United States, conscientious people stood on both sides of the slavery question. Of course, many people advocated slavery for selfish rather than for conscientious reasons. Moreover, many slave owners hardened their hearts and closed their minds to developing their consciences on this particular issue. Nonetheless, at the time, some people apparently adopted slavery in good conscience. That is, they made what we today would consider mistaken judgments with their consciences, and then followed their erroneous consciences.

Whether or not we follow our conscience, we remain subject to the limitations of our human condition. While we must keep this caution in mind, a person striving for the good, seeking truth, and acting conscientiously represents the glory and the grandeur of being created in God's image. **R**

sin—
when people act contrary to their conscience and purposely choose to do wrong; "a deliberate thought, word, deed, or omission contrary to the eternal law of God" *(Catechism, Glossary)*

For Review...

1. An accurate definition of conscience includes three interrelated dimensions. What are they?

2. What is a lax conscience?

3. What does developing an informed conscience involve?

4. Define erroneous conscience.

5. What term is used in Church teaching for not following conscience?

Reflection

Describe a moral dilemma that you or someone you know has faced. Evaluate the process used to arrive at a decision in terms of the three dimensions of conscience described above.

Conscience in Catholic Tradition

To fully understand the term conscience, it must be looked at from the vantage point of Scripture and Church teachings.

Conscience in Scripture: Knowing of the Heart

Except in the Letters of St. Paul, the Bible seldom uses the word conscience. Instead, the Bible's use of the word for heart is the closest equivalent to the concept of conscience. According to Scripture, we can possess a clean heart or speak from an insincere heart. We can ponder God's word in our hearts and take it to heart, or we can be stubborn and harden our hearts. We pray for an upright heart and an understanding heart. The times we go astray we need a change of heart.

Of course the heart that Scripture talks about does not mean the physical organ that pumps blood throughout our body. Rather, it means our entire being. To be conscientious persons we need to develop habits of the heart so that acting with sensitivity and concern for others flows naturally from our awareness of the goodness of God, of our own dignity, and of our oneness with others. When the prophets of old tell us to "change our hearts," they are reminding us that we need to turn away from evil and toward the goodness of God. When Jesus calls for a change of heart—sometimes translated as repentance, or conversion—he is calling us to seek the Father's kingdom before all else (*See Matthew 6:25–33*). **A**

Activity

Use a concordance to research where and how the words conscience and heart are used in the Bible.

The Bible reflects the perspective of a people who were sensual, body-centered, and experiential. Its frequent use of the word heart to denote a concept akin to conscience reminds us that conscience cannot be an intellectual activity that is isolated from our feelings, our experiences, our gut reactions. Conscience must be an activity of our whole person—a knowing of the heart as well as of the mind.

Psalm 119 provides us with a good scriptural description of the knowing of the heart. We find in this psalm many of those traits of conscience that we value so dearly as essential to human dignity. In the psalm, we pray for honesty and authenticity and not the way of deceit in our decision making. We pray to be molded to God's judgment so that we can see ourselves and others through his eyes. We acknowledge our freedom of heart and ask for guidance and understanding as we strive to make decisions in accordance with God's will. We would do well to ponder the psalm's message in our own hearts, for it serves as a fine prayer of conscience. **A**

A Prayer of Conscience

*"Put false ways far from me; and
graciously teach me your law.
I have chosen the way of faithfulness;
I set your ordinances before me.
I cling to your decrees, O LORD;
let me not be put to shame.
I run the way of your commandments,
for you enlarge my understanding.
Teach me, O LORD, the way of your
statutes, and I will observe it to the end.
Give me understanding,
that I may keep your law
and observe it with my whole heart.
Lead me in the path of your commandments,
for I delight in it.
Turn my heart to your decrees,
and not to selfish gain.
Turn my eyes from looking at vanities;
give me life in your ways."*

 Psalm 119:29–37

Activity

1. Read Psalm 119:41–45. Name five things that God gives to those who love him and who attempt to follow their conscience.

2. Using your own words, write a prayer of conscience that you could use when trying to decide the right thing to do when faced with a moral dilemma.

Second Vatican Council on Conscience

When the world's Catholic bishops convened in Rome from 1962 to 1965 for the Second Vatican Council, one issue that concerned them was that of human dignity. Many of them knew firsthand the dehumanizing nature of fascism, Nazism, and communism. They were also concerned about more subtle attacks on human dignity evident in capitalism, individualism, and consumerism.

The bishops published a document known as the *Pastoral Constitution on the Church in the Modern World*. It teaches that conscience represents an essential element of human dignity that should be cultivated and followed in moral decision making. Passages from this document on page 75 illustrate the lofty view of conscience held by the bishops.

The bishops' words summarize the Catholic Church's understanding of moral conscience as an exercise of free will. It is a human action grounded in our human dignity that is itself the action of a judicious and loving God.

Conscience in Church Teaching: Does the Church Say "Follow Your Conscience"?

Thanks to some definitive statements by recent Church leaders, we now have a clearer understanding of conscience. Beginning in particular with Vatican Council II, the Church forcefully has affirmed the importance of conscience. Here are what recent Church documents have stated in response to three fundamental questions about conscience.

Question number one: *Are we called upon to act and live conscientiously, that is, in accord with goodness and truth?* The *Catechism of the Catholic Church* states, "In all he says and does, man is obliged to follow faithfully what he knows to be just and right" (#1778). Clearly, the answer to question number one is *yes*.

Question number two: *Should we think through our decisions and not act solely out of blind obedience or on whim and feelings?* The Vatican II document *Pastoral Constitution on the Church in the Modern World* asserts, "Hence, the more a correct conscience prevails, the more do persons and groups turn aside from blind choice and endeavor to conform to the objective standards of moral conduct" (#16). Thus, the answer to question number two also is *yes*.

Question number three: *Should we act according to the dictates of an informed and developed conscience in our moral decision making?* Turning to the Catechism once again, we read, "Man has the right to act in conscience and in freedom so as personally to make moral decisions. 'He must not be forced to act contrary to his conscience. Nor must he be prevented from acting according to his conscience, especially in religious matters' [DH 3 § 2.]" (#1782). Again, we find *yes* to be the answer given by Church leaders to this pivotal question. **R**

Reflection

List five practical actions you can perform to better follow your conscience.

Quotes on Conscience

Conscience Represents Our Dignity as Human Persons.

Deep within his conscience man discovers a law which he has not laid upon himself but which he must obey. Its voice, ever calling him to love and to do what is good and to avoid evil, tells him inwardly at the right moment: do this, shun that. For man has in his heart a law inscribed by God. His dignity lies in observing this law, and by it he will be judged [Cf. Rom. 2:15–16]. *His conscience is man's most secret core, and his sanctuary. There he is alone with God whose voice echoes in his depths* [Cf. Pius XII, radio message on rightly forming the Christian conscience in youth. 23 March 1952: AAS 44 (1952), p. 271]. *By conscience, in a wonderful way, that law is made known which is fulfilled in the love of God and of one's neighbor* [Cf. Mt. 22:37–40; Gal. 5:14] (Gaudium et Spes, #16).

Conscience Is Present in All People, Urging Them to Seek Truth and Solutions to Problems.

Through loyalty to conscience, Christians are joined to other men in the search for truth and for the right solution to so many moral problems which arise both in the life of individuals and from social relationships. . . .Yet it often happens that conscience goes astray through ignorance which it is unable to avoid, without thereby losing its dignity (Gaudium et Spes, #16).

Freedom is required for People to Choose Good.

It is, however, only in freedom that man can turn himself towards what is good. . . . Man's dignity therefore requires him to act out of conscious and free choice, as moved and drawn in a personal way from within, and not by blind impulses in himself or by external constraint (Gaudium et Spes, #17).

The bishops approved one document specifically titled, *Of Human Dignity*. It is also known as the *Declaration on Religious Liberty*. In this document the bishops speak strongly about the need for freedom and free choice if human dignity is to be served: *God calls people to serve him in spirit and in truth. Consequently, they are bound to him in conscience, but not coerced. God has regard for the dignity of the human person which he himself created; human persons are to be guided by their own judgment and to enjoy freedom* (#11). **A**

Activity

Create a logo that conveys an important principle from the Bishops' teachings.

Pope John Paul II on Conscience

"The Splendor of Truth"—

an encyclopedia on morality by Pope John Paul II

In 1993 Pope John Paul II wrote an encyclical, an official letter from the pope, called **"The Splendor of Truth."** In it he offers his thoughts on morality and moral decision making. He reaffirmed what the bishops of Vatican II said about conscience. However, he expressed great misgivings about the way many modern people interpret their responsibility to follow their conscience. In our strongly individualistic climate, many people view "follow your conscience" as an invitation to do "whatever I want to do." John Paul II pointed out that for Christians, following conscience means doing what Jesus would want them to do.

According to John Paul II, conscience involves intense, honest searching for the truth and then living in line with the dictates of that truth. (Recall the title of his encyclical.) Strangely enough, some people hear "follow your conscience" and believe it lets them off the hook. To them it resembles a parent taking a child to a candy store and saying, "You can get whatever you want." In fact, conscience more often requires self-denial than self-indulgence and looking out for the good of others more than for oneself. In short, conscientious living requires great heroism—a word used frequently in the pope's encyclical.

John Paul II offered the following points for a more accurate and challenging understanding of conscience:

- Conscience can never be divorced from Jesus, who is truth.

- Our seeking to be true to conscience is not the same as an individualistic con-science. An individualistic conscience disregards the will of Jesus, Church teaching, and the wisdom and concerns of the broader community. Therefore, an individualistic conscience is not really conscience at all.

- The teaching of the magisterium holds a privileged place as source of moral guidance. That is, Jesus appointed the Apostles to teach in his name. The pope and the bishops, the successors of the Apostles, continue to teach in his name.

Being true to conscience requires heroism. Thus, the pope ends his discussion of conscience where this chapter began—with the call to be heroic. **R**

For Review...

1. What biblical term is the closest equivalent of the concept of conscience?

2. What attacks on human dignity was the world facing that influenced Church leaders to convene Vatican Council II?

3. Name two documents of Vatican Council II that address the question of conscience.

4. In "The Splendor of Truth," what are the four points about conscience that Pope John Paul II offered?

Reflection

Recall an incident when you tried to follow your conscience. Look over the checklist of steps in the box on the next page involved in following conscience. Note which of the steps you took, deliberately or unconsciously, when making your decision. If possible, add to the list any other steps that helped you make a conscientious decision.

When we follow our conscience we...

- always strive for the truth.
- look to Jesus Christ, the source of truth.
- recognize that what is right and good may not be what we seem to want.
- pursue information and guidance as best we can.
- take seriously Church teaching.
- listen to past wisdom.
- look toward possible future consequences.
- learn from others, especially from parents, family, friends, and fellow Christians.
- are sensitive to others.
- investigate personal motives, pressures, and past patterns of behavior.
- take positive steps rather than settle for indifference and inaction.
- look critically at the messages that surround us in our culture.
- make moral judgments to the best of our ability.
- remain open to the possibility that we may be mistaken in our moral judgments.
- evaluate the quality of our decisions during and after making moral judgments.

...Conclusion

God has given us many gifts—of speech, of sight, of thinking, of our own unique personality. Yet his gift of conscience is one of the most wonderful of them all, for it directs us to use all our gifts for the good of the community, the common good. At times such faithfulness to conscience calls for real heroism on our part.

Catholic teaching on conscience affirms that we possess a basic capacity to search for and to choose goodness. Through prayer and reflection leading to a change of heart, we can befriend and become more familiar with this God-given gift at the core of our being. Through our sincere efforts, conscience can become vital and active in our day-to-day decisions.

We also possess the ability to cultivate and develop conscience. We can do this through the study of Scripture, through seeking advice, through faithful investigation of Church teaching, and through engaging in discussions on important issues with others. (Chapter 7 outlines a process of moral decision making that suggests an entire program of conscience development.)

Finally, conscience is a God-given gift. Used correctly it can lead us to ultimate happiness with God. We show our gratitude to him by its constant and deliberate use.

Model of Morality

St. Thomas More

St. Thomas More (1478–1535) is an example in history of someone known for following his conscience. More was a lawyer who rose to the rank of Chancellor of England during the reign of King Henry VIII. He was married and had three daughters and one son. While More served as chancellor, the pope was petitioned by King Henry to nullify Henry's marriage to his wife Catherine of Aragon so that he could marry someone else. (Henry wanted a son as heir to the throne, and none was forthcoming with Catherine.) The pope refused Henry's request. The king then declared himself head of the Church in England and quickly declared his marriage invalid.

Naturally, such an action caused disruption within England. The king wished to rally whatever support he could. Thomas More was a pivotal person who was highly regarded for being upright and scholarly; if he would approve of the king's action, surely most other English subjects would do the same. However, in conscience More could not approve of the king's declaring himself head of the Church in England. When he refused to sign an oath to that effect, More was found guilty of treason and beheaded. Thomas More was a family man who enjoyed life and in no way desired martyrdom. However, he placed being true to his conscience above all other considerations. He felt that he could not face God if he did not do what he knew to be true and right. More followed his correctly formed conscience.

Was More wrong? Many of his contemporaries in England—even important Church people—did sign the oath that More refused to sign. No doubt some acted out of cowardice. But, on the other hand, some signers might have acted in good conscience. Certainly a case can be made for signing the oath as being a good act. By refusing to sign, More knew that he was in danger of death. However, he listened to his conscience and acted upon it, knowing it to be the right thing to do.

Thomas More was certain of his judgment—even though he disliked tremendously the consequences of remaining true to that judgment. Because of his faithfulness to conscience unto death, More has become a model of integrity and a saint and hero of the Church.

St. Thomas More

> **"**Little as I meddle in the conscience of others, I am certain that my conscience belongs to me alone. It is the last thing that a man can do for his salvation: to be at one with himself. **"**
>
> Thomas More in Robert Ellsberg, *All Saints* (New York: Crossroad, 1997).

Celebrating Morality

A reading from Paul's Letter to the Philippians:

"And this is my prayer, that your love may overflow more and more with knowledge and full insight to help you to determine what is best, so that in the day of Christ you may be pure and blameless.**"**

(Philippians 1:9–10)

Petition #1: God of goodness, we pray that your love takes root within us so that in all cases, in all places, we seek to do your will. We recognize that our hearts are restless until they rest in you. Free us from being timid and fearful; fill us with your spirit of courage and compassion.

Response: We pray to seek your will.

Petition #2: God of truth, we pray that we may grow in wisdom and knowledge. Grant us an understanding heart to know right from wrong, the good from the misdirected, truth from ignorance. May we pursue your truth with endless passion.

Response: We pray to know your will.

Petition #3: God of love, when we grapple with difficult questions, may we always ask, *What is God's will for me right here, right now? What would Jesus want me to do?* The road that we travel is filled with detours and dead ends. When we stray from the straight path, may your Holy Spirit renew in us the fire of love, the courage of our convictions, and the freedom to choose wisely.

Response: We pray to choose your will.

Shared Prayer: (At this time, offer your own prayers of conscience.)

Closing Prayer (recite together):

Lord, make me an instrument of your peace.

Where there is hatred, let me sow love;

Where there is injury, pardon;

Where there is doubt, faith;

Where there is despair, hope;

Where there is darkness, light;

And where there is sadness, joy.

O, Divine Master, grant that I may not so much seek to be consoled as to console;

To be understood as to understand;

To be loved as to love;

For it is in giving that we receive;

It is in pardoning that we are pardoned;

And it is in dying that we are born to eternal life.

(Prayer attributed to St. Francis of Assisi)

5 SIN AND MORALITY

Chapter Overview

- Two images of sin that are frequently used in scripture are missing the mark and hardness of heart.
- In Christianity the primary message about sin is one of forgiveness.
- Distinction among types of sin is intended to help people overcome sin.
- Social sin refers to behavior patterns, values, and social structures that encourage or support sin in a society.

In this chapter we examine Catholic teaching regarding sin. Sin is the dark side of our human condition. As Catholics we can never treat lightly or dismiss our dark side, but neither can we dwell on it. Rather, we view sin in light of the broader Christian message. In the Christian vision, Jesus conquers the sin of the world and graciously offers us forgiveness for our own sinfulness so that we may be free to live our lives lovingly and creatively.

Let us pray . . .

Gracious and forgiving Father, we place before you all the misdeeds, unkind thoughts, and hurtful actions that have marked our lives. We thank you for the gift of your Son Jesus, who sacrificed his life for the forgiveness of sin. Through him, and with him, and in him, we possess the wisdom and the strength to live life passionately and creatively. Through him, and with him, and in him, we know your boundless love. Amen.

Before we begin . . .

Use of the word sin is not as popular today as it once was. And yet, wrongdoing certainly continues, almost in epidemic proportions. To begin your examination of this traditional Christian concept, rate the following behaviors in terms of their degree of sinfulness. (Keep in mind that your ratings will be biased. Church teaching recognizes that both circumstances and the persons involved color the sinfulness of actions.) Explain your rankings.

1. A vacationer takes two large bath towels from the luxury hotel where she is staying.
   not a sin 1 2 3 4 5 *serious sin*

2. An employee at a computer firm quits his job and begins his own business using technology developed by his former company.
   not a sin 1 2 3 4 5 *serious sin*

3. A senior high-school boy pretends to be interested in a sophomore girl in order to persuade her to have sexual intercourse with him.
   not a sin 1 2 3 4 5 *serious sin*

4. Two unmarried sixteen-year-olds have sexual intercourse.
   not a sin 1 2 3 4 5 *serious sin*

5. A person throws a plastic container out of a car window.
   not a sin 1 2 3 4 5 *serious sin*

6. In an attempt to fit in, a boy lies to his friends about seeing a strongly violent movie. Actually he hasn't seen the movie, because his parents have forbidden him to see it.
   not a sin 1 2 3 4 5 *serious sin*

7. A student regularly copies homework from other students
   not a sin 1 2 3 4 5 *serious sin*

8. Because of a long-standing agreement with local government officials, a company legally empties harmful chemical waste into a river.
   not a sin 1 2 3 4 5 *serious sin*

The Pervasive Mystery of Sin

The young teacher told his class, "Today, I have invited a friend of mine to speak with us about our topic, sin. I know him to be old and wise, so listen to his words."

An old man sat at the teacher's desk. He began slowly and thoughtfully. "I cannot define sin, but I can tell you only what sin looks like. To me, sin is present when humans hurt one another. When one nation destroys another nation with deadly weapons—that is sin. When we destroy one another with deadly words—that, too, is sin. Sin can be fiery hot like war and fighting, or it can be icy cold like ignoring someone in need. Sin can become very complicated, like the tangled web of lying. Sin can also be as simple as yelling at a younger brother who wants attention, coming home late when we know our parents will worry, or not keeping our part of an agreement. Sin is an unfounded burst of anger aimed at someone who meant well; sin is also being too lazy to help out at home."

The old man paused, then continued. "Unfortunately, we find sin splashed across the headlines of our newspapers: Public officials accept bribes, children gun down other children without reason, corporations place profits over people, and drugs destroy young lives. But sin also lies hidden in the dark corners of our country, resulting in homeless persons seeking shelter in the subways beneath our cities or nameless farmworkers receiving inadequate pay for harvesting the fruits and vegetables we eat.

"When I think about sin, I picture it as water heating on a stove. For a while, sin simmers—much like pornography that is peddled in corner convenience stores and at neighborhood video outlets. Then later as time passes, the same sinfulness bubbles forth onto the streets in the forms of child pornography and prostitution."

"Why does sin exist?" inquired one student.

"If we knew that answer," responded the old man, "then we would truly be wise. We know that sins exists—we see too much of it to deny its existence.

"But we know little of the reasons why it holds such power over us. Ancient wisdom often pointed to selfishness as the root of sin— a misguided placing of our own will and desires above and against the will of God and the needs of others. However, naming the root of sin does not solve its mystery or destroy its power."

"Is there no escape from sin, then?" another student finally asked.

"That is an important question," the old man replied. "I have told you today that sin surrounds us and that it is lodged in our very hearts. And yet, I want to leave you with words of hope. We have this assurance from someone who faced sin with all of its terrible power, the one we call Jesus. I trust in Jesus that whenever we plant seeds of love, sin is diminished. And where love flourishes, sin withers. Because of the wonder of God's love, I assure you that we can face sin and sing an Easter song: 'O sin, your reign has ended; O sin, you are destroyed!'" **R**

Reflection

If you were invited to address a group of young people about sin, what would you say? What examples would you give? What would be the primary message that you would want to communicate about sin?

Sin and God's Love

"Come, O children, listen to me; I will teach you the fear of the LORD. Which of you desires life, and covets many days to enjoy good? Keep your tongue from evil, and your lips from speaking deceit. Depart from evil, and do good; seek peace, and pursue it.**"**

Psalm 34:11–14

As the old man points out, sin surrounds us. That assessment may sound unpleasant and harsh, but even a quick look at our lives and our neighborhoods, our newspapers and our newscasts, our thoughts and our daily interactions with others, leads us to readily agree with his observations. We find evidence of sin and its consequences at every turn. Sin plagues our world, keeping it from being what it can be. Sin also burdens us, keeping us from being what we are called to be.

Sin is an offense against God. It is a failure to respond to his love as Christ has made it known to us. Our sins wound and violate our nature as his children and brothers and sisters to Christ. Sin may begin at a personal level but it never ends there. Sin also injures the entire human community. Therefore, our failures at loving—God, others, and even ourselves—are what Christianity calls sin.

From the beginning of salvation history, sin has played a major role. In the first book of the Bible, the scriptural passage about the first humans, traditionally called Adam and Eve, tells us the story of our first parents' sin, which is called "original sin." You can read their story in Genesis, chapters 2–3. The story indicates that God intends the world to be a place of harmony, solidarity, and love. The story also insists that people are accountable for their actions and that sin violates God's intention for creation. The story of Adam and Eve sets the stage for another story that places evil and sin in a Christian context—the story of Christ's conquering of sin through his death on the cross. The mystery of human sinfulness is frightening; the mystery of God's love is infinitely more wonderful. **A**

Activity

Draw a symbol or image that you think would illustrate sin. After completing your drawing, create a written analysis of what the image suggests about your impression of sin.

Two Images from Scripture

We can gain a better understanding of what Christianity means by sin if we examine the way the term is used in Scripture. The Bible uses many images to refer to sin. Two images used frequently to describe the mystery of sin are missing the mark and hardness of heart. By exploring the meaning of these two biblical images of sin, we can come to a greater appreciation of how sin might operate in our own lives.

Missing the Mark: The Failure to Love

One image for sin in Scripture is "missing the mark."

"And now, my children, listen to me: happy are those who keep my ways. Hear instruction and be wise, and do not neglect it. Happy is the one who listens to me, watching daily at my gates, waiting beside my doors. For whoever finds me finds life and obtains favor from the Lord; but those who miss me injure themselves; all who hate me love death."

Proverbs 8:32–36

The people of the Bible believed that there was a mark or goal to aim for, and that sin meant missing that mark. The term for "sin" actually was the same word as that used in archery for missing the mark, for being "off center." Ultimately, the mark we aim for is God—the joy of life with God and with God's family both now and in the future. We sin, or "miss the mark," when we settle for behavior that does not reflect love for God, ourselves, and others. **R**

Reflection

The biblical image of sin as "missing the mark" invites us to consider some important questions. Write about the following:

• State goals for living a Christian life.

• How are you trying to live out these goals in specific ways right now?

• What actions, attitudes, or values are moving you along toward the goals of living a Christian life? What actions, attitudes, or values are interfering with your attaining those goals?

Here are examples of behaviors that might not appear on many people's list of sins. However, when we consider that our true goal is God-like love, then we can recognize these actions as "missing the mark."

- Sitting at his desk at school, Bill carves obscenities into the desktop. Now the desk looks unsightly, and no one can write smoothly on it. The obscenities will have a negative impact on younger children, other students, or visitors, as well as create added work for school personnel. With little thought, Bill actually has chosen destruction over concern for others.

- Kim's mother asks her to stay home and watch her younger brother on Friday night. Kim says, "You know I always go out with my friends on Friday nights. I'm not giving that up!" In this case, Kim does not see beyond her own wants to another's needs.

- The regular teacher is absent, and a substitute is taking over for the day. When the substitute asks the class where they left off in the lesson, a student purposely directs her to material they covered the previous week. No one else speaks up, and the student who misdirected the substitute snickers with his friends about

his successful prank. When presented with an opportunity to rise to a higher level of consideration, the students instead settle for less.

- Hannah's parents have expressly forbidden her to drink. Hannah assures them that she doesn't. Nevertheless, every Saturday Hannah and her friends gather in a section of a local park where they know beer will be readily available. With this weekly routine, Hannah diminishes the level of trust in her family, and she participates in behavior that is illegal and potentially dangerous.

- Steve's homeroom has an intramural basketball team, and everyone who shows up for the games must play. One boy is a terrible player and, since he has come to every game, he is entered in the championship game. The boy makes a lot of mistakes, and the team loses. Steve joins his classmates in deriding the boy for losing the game. In so doing, Steve is displaying insensitivity to the boy, who at this moment needs just the opposite shown to him. The biblical image of sin as missing the mark helps us recognize that when we make choices that are uncaring, insensitive, and selfish, we hamper our journey toward our ultimate goal of being a loving person. G

Group Talk

If you were to illustrate sin as missing the mark, which two examples would you use? Explain why these two examples illustrate this understanding of sin.

Hardness of Heart: The Failure to Be Human

It's easy to imagine attitudes that would reflect a stony heart in need of transformation.

- Don't bother me. That's your problem!
- I wish this new student would just leave me alone.
- Can't these homeless people stay off our city streets? They bother me while I'm trying to shop.
- I'm not picking it up. I didn't put it there.
- Why did she get so upset about what I said? I was only joking.
- Mrs. Smith is really having a bad day with the experiments in her biology lab sessions today. Let's give her a hard time.

Scripture often uses bodily images such as "hard-hearted" to describe sin, because the "root of sin lies in the heart of man" (*Catechism, #1853*). This image of a hard heart suggests a closing in upon ourselves—the way we might stiffen when we are being touched by someone whom we don't want to touch us. Such images do not portray humanity at its best. A heart of stone is not a human heart.

In the book of Ezekiel, God promises to replace hearts of stone with hearts of flesh:

"*I will sprinkle clean water upon you, and you shall be clean from all your uncleannesses, and from all your idols I will cleanse you. A new heart I will give you, and a new spirit I will put within you; and I will remove from your body the heart of stone and give you a heart of flesh.***"**

 *Ezekiel 36:25–26*

Scripture is reminding us that sin has as much to do with our attitudes as with our actions, with our being as with our behavior. A heart of flesh is one that can be touched and also wounded. But only with a new heart of flesh can we embrace others and allow others to embrace us. **A**

For Review...

1. What does the story of Adam and Eve indicate about a Christian understanding of sin?

2. How does the story of Jesus respond to and complete the Adam and Eve story?

3. Name two biblical images used for sin.

Activity

Write a song or a poem about being "hard-hearted" or about having a "heart of stone."

Sin in Christian Tradition

A number of years ago a noted psychiatrist named Karl Menninger wrote a book titled, Whatever *Became of Sin?* In the book Dr. Menninger decried

our modern tendency to avoid speaking about sin. He pointed out two dangers to this tendency. For one, if we lose our sense of sin, then we run the risk of losing authority over our lives. In other words, if we blame our parents or our culture for all of our actions, then we eliminate accountability for our decisions. Rather than being subjects, we make ourselves out to be objects. Secondly, without a sense of sin any choices that we make are valueless. If nothing is wrong, then it doesn't matter what we do. Into what kind of murky future would this attitude take us? Menninger and others are reminding us that if we don't recognize our dark side for what it is, then we give it power over us.

Throughout history Christian teachers have taught about sin. A basic, common-sense reason why they have done so supports Dr. Menninger's insight: Only when we recognize that a problem exists can we overcome the problem. Imagine if your car became hopelessly stuck in a snowdrift and you told all those who offered to help you, "There's no problem!" Imagine if you forgot that you had an important test one day, and you walked into class totally unprepared and said, "We have a test today? No problem!" Imagine if your drinking became so out of control that even your friends try to tell you to cool it and instead you say, "Don't be silly! I can handle my drinking. It's not a problem." By drawing our attention to the reality of sin, Church teachers remind us that we do have problems hampering us from being what we would like to be. **G**

Group Talk

In our society there is a tendency for people to blame circumstances rather than to take responsibility for their behavior. What kinds of problems are caused by our not taking responsibility for our behavior? Use examples to defend your answer.

Forgiveness of Sin

The Gospel is the revelation in Jesus Christ of God's mercy to sinners. [Cf. Lk 15.]

✝ **Catechism, #1846**

A young boy took a trophy that his father had won when he was in high school down from its shelf. The father had received the most valuable player award in the state baseball tournament. The trophy was one of his prized possessions. The young boy had been told not to touch it, but he couldn't resist. He was placing it on a table when it fell off, hit the floor, and broke in two.

The boy was stunned. What was he to do? He quickly picked up the broken trophy and hid it in a drawer, hoping no one would notice the empty spot on the shelf.

At dinner, the boy was nervous, but no one seemed to have noticed. However, that night while watching television his father asked him if he had seen the trophy. "No, Dad," the boy replied.

Suspicious, the father turned off the TV and asked his son again. This time the boy confessed. "I'm sorry, Dad. It was an accident."

After inspecting the broken trophy, the father said, "You were told not to touch this trophy. I hope you've learned a lesson about disobeying and about not lying to your parents. I know you're sorry. I forgive you. Now don't be down on yourself—you're more important than any trophy." **R**

Reflection

1. Is the father's reaction in this story realistic?

2. Do you agree that the son's feelings are more important than the trophy?

3. Do you think it is still important for the son to experience some consequences for his actions? Why or why not?

4. If Jesus were the father, how do you think he would have reacted? Why?

Christic Conquers Sin

Lamb of God, you take away the sins of the world, grant us peace.

Since God alone can forgive sin, to be cleansed of sin is a true gift from the Father, given to the Church by Jesus, through the grace of the Holy Spirit. When we read about sin in the Gospels, we find the word almost always used in connection with forgiveness. When we read about the amount of time that Jesus spends with sinners, we can't help but note his special affection for them. He wants the power that sin has over them to be eliminated. Throughout the Gospels, we find instances of Jesus forgiving sinners. Even when people are seeking a cure for their physical ailments, he forgives their sins as well! The Gospel message, then, is a message of God's mercy for sinners.

The essential message about sin in the Christian story is that Christ conquers sin. Sin is a transgression against God that is overcome with Christ's death on the cross on Good Friday and his Resurrection on Easter. In other words, sin is clearly neither the central theme nor the final

chapter in the Christian story. Christ, the sacrificial lamb offering his life for the sins of the world, takes on all evil and conquers it.

We need to remain ever watchful about sin. And yet Christian belief is that we can celebrate Christ's victory over sin and know that his victory is ours as well. Therefore, we have faith and hope that our participation in transforming evil into good contributes to God's plan of salvation. We should try not to let the fear of sin and its many manifestations prevent us from doing good, from taking a chance on love, or from joining other "sinners" in doing our part in furthering God's kingdom on earth. **A**

Activity

One of the most significant ways that Jesus stands out as unique is in his treatment of sinners. Read the following Gospel passages and for each one describe the attitude that Jesus exhibits toward sin or sinners in the story. Then, use these passages to describe in concrete terms how Jesus' message of forgiveness could be applied today.

Matthew 9:9–13 (the call of Matthew)

Luke 7:36–50 (the penitent woman)

Luke 15:1–10 (the parable of divine mercy)

Luke 15:11–32 (the prodigal son)

Luke 18:9–14 (the pharisee and the tax collector)

Luke 23:39–43 (the good thief)

John 9:1–14 (the man born blind)

Luke 17:3–4 (the forgiveness of those who sin)

Original Sin and the Story of Salvation

Saint Paul wrote the following reflection about his own tendency toward sinfulness:

"... I am of the flesh, sold into slavery under sin. I do not understand my own actions. For I do not do what I want, but I do the very thing I hate.*"*

Romans 7:14–15

Saint Paul is being brutally honest here.

He could be speaking for all of us when he admits to giving in to what he calls the "sin that dwells within me." (Romans 7:17, 20). He found the pull of sin to be a powerful force within him. This inclination to evil is a result of **original sin**. As a result of original sin, we are wounded at our very core, subject to error, and have a tendency toward evil as we exercise our freedom. Therefore, we find ourselves constantly doing battle with our darker side.

Original sin harkens back to the biblical account of Adam and Eve. As you know from the story, humans—created good and filled with bright promise—didn't take long before they gave in to sin and misused their God-given free will. According to the very beginning of the Book of Genesis, the world is good. Following each stage of creation, Genesis includes the refrain "And God saw that it was good." Human beings are counted among God's good creation. In fact, human beings hold an exalted position in the order of creation; they are made in his very image. Our wounded nature occurs not through God's handiwork but through human beings abusing their freedom and disobeying him. Through their disobedience, sin enters the world. Original sin does not refer to any actions that people from that time on have done, but rather it refers to the human condition resulting from what is known as "the Fall", a primeval event that took place at the very beginning of human history. Like so many human traits, the effects of original sin have been passed down. It requires divine intervention for members of the human family to be restored to God's good graces.

In other words, original sin has wounded humans beings. It cries out for a redeemer to restore the human condition back to its original grandeur. As creation first occurred at God's hands, so new creation occurs through a Redeemer who is one with him—Jesus Christ. Therefore, the Adam and Eve event leads directly to the event of Jesus Christ. As Scripture tells us, "For just as by the one man's disobedience the many were made sinners, so by the one man's obedience the many will be made righteous" *(Romans 5:19)*.

Jesus' Paschal mystery, his Passion, death, Resurrection, Ascension, and Pentecost won redemption for humanity. Jesus saved us to the very end, and by doing so gave his life for the lives of all people.

The Word became flesh for us *in order to save us by reconciling us with God...*

Catechism, #457

Sin and the Mercy of God

Sins can be viewed according to their degree of seriousness—less serious sins are called **venial sins**; the most serious sins are called mortal. While venial sins are like wounds to our relationship with God, **mortal sins**—as the term implies—are "deadly." In addition, we can sin by doing something wrong—a **sin of commission**—or not doing something that we should do—a **sin of omission**. Situations in which we are more likely to sin are known as "occasions of sin"—for example, a recovering alcoholic who frequents a bar is in a place where he would be tempted to sin.

Keep in mind that all this talk of sin is meant to loosen its power over us. We seek to identify and acknowledge sin insofar as it prevents us from cooperating with the Holy Spirit at work in us. **G**

Mortal Sin—A Complete Rejection of God

Our lives find meaning through our relationship with God the Father in his son Jesus. When we talk about our Christian life and the place of sin in our life, we are talking about a relationship. Therefore, we can better understand the traditional Catholic concept of mortal sin by comparing it to our friendships. Treating a best friend cruelly is not treating that person with love and respect. Such mistreatment may or may not involve complete rejection; it may not deliver a mortal blow to the relationship. Even best friends can treat each other very harshly on occasion. It doesn't necessarily mean that they cast off from each other forever. Also, deliberately rejecting someone can occur only in an atmosphere of freedom. At times the pressures of living are great. These pressures, internal and external, affect our freedom to relate to others in healthy and wholesome ways. They also can diminish our **culpability**, or moral responsibility.

We sin mortally when we reject God completely. Like the death of a friendship, then, mortal sin involves serious actions, attitudes, and freedom. A sin is mortal when it meets three criteria: it must involve "grave matter," it must be done with full knowledge, and the one performing the action must do so deliberately *(Catechism, #1857)*. The Catechism points out that "our freedom has the power to make choices for ever, with no turning back" *(#1861)*. In other words, we have the freedom to reject God completely and forever. Freely and forever saying no to God's love results in our exclusion from God's eternal presence in heaven and our living forever without God's presence in **hell**. However, God wants all of us with him forever, and thus repentance and God's forgiveness are always available to those who don't seek such a fate. This is why mortal sins must be confessed in the Sacrament of Reconciliation. Finally, we need to keep in mind the Catechism's last statement about mortal sin: "we must entrust judgment of persons to the justice and mercy of God" *(#1861)*. **G**

---

venial sin—
an action that weakens our relationship with God

mortal sin—
an action so destructive that it mortally wounds our relationship with God; complete rejection of God

sin of omission—
not doing an action that is called for

sin of commission—
purposely doing an action that is harmful to oneself or another

culpability—
the degree to which people are responsible for their actions

hell—
"The state of definitive self-exclusion from communion with God and the blessed, reserved for those who refuse by their own free choice to believe and be converted from sin, even to the end of their lives" *(Catechism, Glossary)*

Venial Sin—Weakening Our Relationship with God

Most of our sinful actions are not so serious as to be considered mortal. We perform small acts, which weakens our relationship with God. Venial sins often result from bad habits or laziness. Repeated venial sins weaken our ability to avoid sinning in the future. Unless we work at overcoming venial sins, we could eventually find ourselves turning completely away from God through mortal sin. Again, comparing this to a human relationship, think of a marriage relationship—separation and divorce often happen in small steps, not all at once.

A final word about Catholic teaching on sin: Sin is a statement about the way we treat our relationship with God; it does not describe his relationship with us. We may work very hard at rejecting God, but he never rejects us! We look to Jesus on the cross who died for us and know that God is ever-faithful to us, ever-forgiving, and ever-loving. **A**

For Review...

1. What modern tendency did Karl Menninger caution against? What are the two negative consequences that can result from this tendency? How does Christian teaching counteract this tendency?

2. In the Gospels, what association is frequently made in discussions about sin?

3. What is the essential message about sin in the Christian story?

4. Define original sin.

5. What is the difference between mortal sin and venial sin?

6. Describe mortal sins and venial sins in terms of relationship.

7. What does it mean to say that "sin is a statement about the way we treat our relationship with God; it does not describe God's relationship with us"?

Group Talk

Answer *true* or *false* to the following statements. Explain your answers.

1. The Church talks too much about sin.

2. Sin is no longer a helpful category for naming the world's problems.

3. The Christian message must include sin.

4. I hear mention of sin regularly in Church circles.

5. More than other Christians, Catholics emphasize sin.

6. When people do wrong, it's important that they understand that they are sinning.

7. Talk of sin leads to feelings of guilt, which are never healthy.

8. Jesus focused quite a bit on sin.

9. My understanding of sin has changed since I was a child.

Activity

Catholic teaching recognizes that bad habits or vices can lead to sinful actions. It lists seven underlying vices called "capital sins." They are:

pride	lust
avarice	gluttony
envy	sloth
wrath	

Define each word and give one concrete example of how it can be manifest as sin.

A Gospel-Based Perspective on Sin

There is vast goodness in our world, yet sin's effects are also visible everywhere: in exploitative relationships, in loveless families, in unjust social structures and policies, in crimes by and against individuals and against God's creation.

Everywhere we encounter the suffering and destruction wrought by egoism and lack of community, by oppression of the weak and manipulation of the vulnerable; we experience explosive tensions among nations, ideological, racial, and religious groups, and social classes; we witness the scandalous gulf between those who waste goods and resources and those who live and die amid deprivation and underdevelopment—and all this in an atmosphere of wars and ceaseless preparations for war. Ours is a sinful world.

To Live in Christ Jesus, #10

In 1976 the U.S. bishops gave the above description of the effects of sin. Unfortunately, their catalog of sinfulness continues to plague our world decades later. What would Jesus have to say about this state of affairs? After Vatican Council II, Catholic teachers and leaders explored what points of emphasis regarding sin can be found in the Gospels. Here are five points of emphasis regarding sin that emerge from a close reading of the Gospels. **R**

Five Characteristics of a Gospel-Based Perspective on Sin:

1. views sin primarily in terms of relationships,
2. stresses doing the positive,
3. focuses on overall life patterns as well as specific acts,
4. emphasizes sin as being an offense against God and neighbor, and
5. recognizes the social dimension of sin.

Reflection

1. Name five specific examples of sin that would mirror the bishops' description of our "sinful world."

2. Do these examples of sin broaden or deepen your own understanding of sin? Explain why or why not.

Relationships and Apathy

apathy—
an attitude of not getting involved, not caring, not acting when action is called for

In the Gospels, sin is portrayed more as a breakdown in our relationships than as the breaking of a law. In fact, Jesus sums up the law in terms of a loving relationship with God and with our neighbor. (See Matthew 22:36–40.) Therefore, in determining sin from a Gospel-based perspective we need to ask: *What effect do my actions have on my relationship with God? How do my actions harm or enhance the people around me and the quality of my relationship with them?*

"No one has a right to sit down and feel hopeless. There's too much work to do."

Dorothy Day, in *Peace Prayers* (Harper San Francisco, 1992)

"When the Nazis came to get the Communists, I was silent because I was not a Communist. When they came to get the Socialists, I was silent. When they came to get the Catholics, I was silent. When they came to get the Jews, I was silent. And when they came to get me, there was no one left to speak."

Martin Niemoeller in Robert Ellsberg, *All Saints* (New York: Crossroad, 1997).

The Gospels speak more about what we need to do than about what we should avoid doing. Certainly, we need to avoid wrongdoing, such as driving while drinking alcohol, drinking to excess, or taking what doesn't belong to us. However, we must not overlook positive contributions that we can make in our moral life. In this light, **apathy**—not getting involved, not caring, and not doing what needs to be done—can be sinful. Visiting a friend in the hospital and helping someone who urgently needs help are expressions of our moral life. Not to do so could fall into the classification of sins of omission. Sin can involve harming others through inaction just as much as through action. To paraphrase the English political writer Edmund Burke, "The only thing necessary for the triumph of evil is for good people to do nothing." **R A**

Reflection

Complete each of the following sentences.

• Three people with whom I relate on a regular basis are . . .

• I enhance their lives when I . . .

• I would describe the quality of my relationships with them as . . .

• I would harm their lives if I . . .

Activity

High school yearbooks frequently include a picture of students sleeping in study hall with the caption, "a meeting of the Apathy Club." In your own words, define apathy. Write a story whose theme and plot are "the sin of apathy." If possible, illustrate the story with a drawing or a picture.

The Effects of Sin

A lthough it is important to be specific about which of our actions are sinful it is also important to relate our actions more closely to who we are and who we want to become.

Our earlier discussion of the biblical image of sin as hardness of heart reminds us that our actions flow from who we are. In the words of the Catechism, "sin tends to reproduce itself and reinforce itself . . ." *(#1865).* Therefore, we need to examine our overall life patterns, ascertain the fundamental direction of our lives, and determine whether or not we are heading in the direction God wants for us. Our actions make a statement about where we are going. It's helpful at times to step back and look at the patterns of behavior that we have established for ourselves. **R**

Combining the Vertical and the Horizontal

A Gospel-based perspective on sin links the vertical and the horizontal. That is, sin is not between us and a God who is distant and absent from us; rather, sin is between us and God who is close at hand and present in the people around us. When we choose not to love others, we affect our relationship with God. The horizontal view of sin is reflected in the Gospel passage: *So when you are offering your gift at the altar, if you remember that your brother or sister has something against you, leave your gift there before the altar and go; first be reconciled to your brother or sister, and then come and offer your gift.*

Matthew 5:23–24

Reflection

In your notebook or journal, write about how you view the overall direction of your life. How does morality fit in?

Social Sin

social sin—
a term comparable to "structures of sin" referring to sinful structures resulting from personal sin and leading to social conditions and institutions that do not embody God's law of love.

sinful social structures—
ways societies are structured resulting in unjust distribution of power, benefits, and privileges

From a Gospel-based perspective the Christian life is often a matter of *we* and not *I*. Thus there is often a social dimension to sin. Emphasis on the social dimension of morality brings us to what the Church calls social sin *(#1869)*. **Social sin** is sin that exists within a society. It refers to the many ways that groups of people suffer even when responsibility for that suffering may not lie solely on the shoulders of specific individuals. Instead, the culprits are both personal actions as well as the way a particular society is structured. What the Catechism calls "structures of sin" are those that help create a harmful state of affairs in a society. These structures lead to entire groups of victims and accomplices.

Are certain people unjustly hurt because of the way our educational, criminal justice, business, and health-care systems are arranged? Insofar as the answer to this question is *yes*, then we can speak of **sinful social structures**. For instance, if members of one race or gender hold an unfair advantage over others in the workplace or in the court system, then sinful social structures exist in these important social institutions. Sinful social structures are ways that a society is organized that can result in certain groups of people being unfairly deprived of the power, benefits, and privileges available to others.

To demonstrate how societal structures can be sinful, ask yourself the question: *Would a poor, black young man accused of a crime typically receive the same treatment at the hands of our criminal justice system as an older, wealthy, white person?* Statistics reveal that if you are young, poor, uneducated, or a member of certain racial groups, you are more likely to go to prison if you commit a crime. This information suggests that inequalities and disadvantages exist within the criminal justice system itself—one of the "structures of society." When we examine sin in our society we need to consider not only the actions of individuals but also social structures. Sin is at least as much a social affair as it is an isolated, individual one.

We will look more closely at the social dimension of morality in the chapter on justice. For now, we will examine social sin in terms of the following three categories: sinful social structures, social behavior patterns that encourage or support sin, and societal values that cause harm.

"We become victors not by holding our adversary down, but rather by not allowing him to fall . . ."

St. Gregory of Nyssa

In our society, we find many accepted behavior patterns that actually support or encourage sin. This does not mean that we should lessen our sense of individual responsibility for our actions. Rather, we should broaden responsibility to include indirect influences on behavior.

For instance, for many older teenagers and young adults "partying" means drinking. To appreciate the extensive social dimension to problem drinking, imagine that a good friend is struck and killed by an under-aged drunk driver. How far does responsibility extend for this tragedy? An individual who drinks to excess is responsible for his or her actions. However, today someone who serves alcohol to another person who is inebriated can also be held responsible for that person's actions. If, while her parents are away, a teenage girl hosts a party where people are drinking and subsequently a fatal accident occurs, the parents and the girl bear some responsibility. Stepping back even further, are producers of films that are aimed at a teenage audience responsible at all for presenting drinking as "cool," innocent fun rather than as behavior that can have tragic consequences? Might we even include community leaders who provide few alternatives to drinking among those who share responsibility for the problem?

Deaths related to alcohol point to the social nature of sin. We cannot blame "society" and dismiss individual responsibility. On the other hand, we should not accuse individuals of sin and close our eyes to the society in which the sin occurs.

Values dominant in a society that directly or indirectly hurt people are another expression of social sin. For instance, excessive individualism can lead to a "me-first" attitude that is destructive, especially for weaker members of a society. **G**

...Conclusion

We have a dark side, a shadow side that marks us as human. It is important for us to recognize sin, to name it for what it is, and to dread its horror. However, every aspect of Christianity seeks to lead us from a recognition of sin to a celebration of Christ's great victory over sin. Through the power of the Holy Spirit, we are freed from sin so that we can live life and love others in imitation of Christ.

For Review...

1. Name the five characteristics of a Gospel-based perspective on sin.

2. Define *apathy*.

3. What is the difference between a vertical and a horizontal view of God?

4. Name three expressions of social sin.

5. Define the concept of *sinful social structures*.

Group Talk

Look over the following incidents and identify possible social behavior patterns or societal values that might have contributed to such behavior. (Again, social and cultural influences do not eliminate personal responsibility but rather pinpoint factors that help shape people.)

1. Two older teens harass a twelve-year-old boy who refuses to become involved in their neighborhood drug trade.

2. A month after receiving her license, a girl who is late for work drives her car through a red light, causing an accident.

3. A boy who has been sexually active for some time contracts a venereal disease.

4. A seventeen-year-old whose friends participate in illegal drug use becomes addicted to cocaine.

Model of Morality

Jacques Fesch

In 1957 a young man was guillotined in France. (Yes, the guillotine was used just fifty years ago!) The young man, Jacques Fesch, shot a police officer to death in a botched robbery attempt. When the police officer arrived on the scene, Jacques callously shot him three times. The officer had a four-year-old daughter. For Jacques, it was not an isolated incident. Earlier he had embezzled money from his employer—who also happened to be his father-in-law! Jacques hadn't entered a life of crime because he was poor. Newspapers of the time called him "the playboy son of a wealthy family." When his mother gave him money to invest in a business, he instead used half of it to buy a sports car.

Jacques Fesch

Jacques had been baptized in the Catholic Church as an infant, not out of religious convictions on the part of his parents but because it was customary in France. He even received his First Holy Communion despite the fact that it meant nothing to him. Although he had received these sacraments, he called himself a non-believer and lived life without concern for anyone else. During interrogations after his crime Jacques showed no remorse, saying only that he wished he had a machine gun rather than just a pistol. After his arrest in 1954, Jacques was sent to prison. When the prison chaplain first visited him he simply told the priest, "Don't bother. I'm not a believer."

However, over time Jacques felt faith in Christ seeping into his being. Then one night it exploded, and Jacques experienced a profound conversion. He described the event in these words:

I was in bed, eyes open, really suffering for the first time in my life. . . . It was then that a cry burst from my breast, an appeal for help—"My God"—and instantly like a violent wind which passes over before anyone knows where it comes from, the Spirit of the Lord seized me by the throat. I had an impression of infinite power and kindness and, from that moment onward, I believed with an unshakeable conviction that never left me.

After his conversion Jacques began to live his life in prison as if he were a monk in a monastery. He knew that the guillotine awaited him, and he wanted to die a holy death. He wrote letters to his mother and his young daughter, speaking of his deep faith in Jesus. On the night of his execution he completed the journal he kept for his daughter with the words, "In five hours I shall see Jesus." Jacques Fesch was executed on October 1, 1957.

Interestingly enough, the story of Jacques Fesch does not end there. Thirty years later the Archbishop of Paris signed a decree seeking his beatification, a step toward sainthood. Not everyone was happy. After all, Jacques had killed a police officer in cold blood! Nonetheless, the archbishop said that, "Nobody is lost in God's eyes, even when society has condemned him." The archbishop believed that beatification of this man who underwent such a dramatic conversion would "give a great hope to those who despise themselves, who see themselves as irredeemably lost."

(Quotes and information from: Leo Knowles, "Sinner to Saint, the Story of Jacques Fesch," in *The Word Among Us*, Lent 2003 edition, pages 72–76.)

Celebrating Morality

Leader: Let us pray. Jesus our savior and brother, you healed the sick and forgave sinners, you welcomed strangers and shared meals with outcasts, and you showed love to those who felt no love. We gather together seeking to experience your love and forgiveness so that we too will know the freedom you offer.

Reader #1:

Luke 5:1–26

All: Be mindful of your mercy, O LORD, and of your steadfast love, for they have been from of old. Do not remember the sins of my youth or my transgressions; according to your steadfast love remember me, for your goodness' sake, O LORD!

(Psalm 25:6–7)

Reader #2:

Luke 7:36–50

All: Wash me, O LORD, from my iniquity and cleanse me from my sin.

(see Psalm 51:2–3)

Leader: Let us examine our conscience.

All: Lord Jesus, you opened the eyes of the blind, healed the sick, forgave the sinful woman, and after Peter's denial confirmed him in your love. Listen to my prayer: Forgive all my sins, renew your love in my heart, help me to live in perfect unity with my fellow Christians that I may proclaim your saving power to all the world. Lord Jesus, you chose to be called the friend of sinners. By your saving death and Resurrection, free me from my sins. May your peace take root in my heart and bring forth a harvest of love, holiness, and truth. Lord Jesus Christ, you are the Lamb of God; you take away the sins of the world. Through the grace of the Holy Spirit, restore me to friendship with your Father, cleanse me from every stain of sin in the blood you shed for me, and raise me to new life for the glory of your name. Amen.

Based on *The Rites of the Catholic Church* (New York: Pueblo Publishing Company, 1976), pages 382–83.

THE VIRTUES Cultivating Character

Chapter Overview

- Virtues are character strengths that we develop over time and through consistent use.
- The theological virtues of faith, hope, and love are gifts from God.
- The cardinal virtues are prudence, justice, fortitude, and temperance.
- An important aspect of the moral life is creating communities of character.

We make many decisions without a great deal of thought. Often, we act according to our upbringing and the norms of the society of which we are a part. This chapter explores more closely the link between our *being* and our *doing*. On the one hand, *who we are* precedes and shapes *what we do*. On the other hand, as the first chapter suggests, our actions shape who we are. In its long tradition, Catholicism has proposed cultivating virtues, which are good qualities of behavior and character strengths that enable us to make good moral decisions.

Before we begin . . .

Review the following scenarios. Select one that you feel most closely relates to an experience that you have had. What does that experience say about your understanding of moral character?

- Walking alone down a school corridor, you spot an open locker. A few dollars and some coins are clearly visible in the locker. Is your immediate reaction, *I should close this locker so that nothing is stolen or I wonder if I could take the money and get away with it?*

- Your parent asks you to help with some work around the house. Are you thinking, *What excuse can I come up with to get out of this or I'm happy to do my part?*

- Because of an accident that just occurred ahead of you on a busy freeway, you are one of many drivers caught in traffic. Do you think, *Unbelievable! Now I'll be delayed for hours or I hope nobody is seriously hurt?*

- When a new student arrives at your school, is your reaction, *I'll try to make her feel welcome or She'd better not try to move in on my friends?*

- Your parents work late. They tell you not to have friends over until they get home. Since they will have no way of checking on you, do you plan on ignoring their request?

Let us pray . . .

God our Father, you give us the grace to form ourselves into persons of good character and to shape our world into communities of faith, hope, and charity. Give us the courage to accept this grace. Help us see others through your eyes. Enable us to treat others as you treat us— with love and forgiveness. We ask this through Christ our Lord. Amen.

Virtues: *Habits of the Heart*

character—
the attributes and features that make up our individuality

virtues—
good qualities, habits, or patterns of behavior that incline us to live justly; character strengths manifested on a consistent basis in decision making

vices—
bad qualities, habits, or patterns of behavior that incline us to actions that are harmful to ourselves and others

A virtue is an habitual and firm disposition to do the good.

 Catechism, #1803

In each of the scenarios on the previous page, you would have little time to think through any decision that you make. What you end up doing would depend greatly on the values and inclinations that you have internalized over the years. **Character** refers to those features and attributes that make up our individuality. Our character, then, is shaped by many different elements, including our family background, habitual patterns of behavior, the influence of friends, genetic makeup, religious upbringing, and much more. And the composition of our character can incline us toward goodness or evil.

Good character results when we cultivate our unique traits and use them in positive ways. **Virtues** are character strengths—good qualities, habits, and patterns of behavior—that incline us to make good moral decisions. Conversely, **vices** are character weaknesses—bad qualities, habits, and patterns of behavior—that incline us to actions that are harmful to ourselves and others. Even though our character is uniquely ours and we in fact shape and sustain it, it's important to keep in mind that our unique power to do good is a gift of God's grace. With his help, virtues help us in building our character, as well as in doing good. Jesus' free gift of salvation offers us the grace necessary to persevere in virtuous living.

The word virtue comes from a Latin root meaning strength or power. Virtues are good habits that strengthen character, and cultivated by those who exhibit them. In a sense, then, virtues are habits of the heart. Sometimes we think of habits as actions that we do unthinkingly, as if we had no control over them. In fact, good habits and good character do not take away our freedom but instead channel our freedom toward positive ends. In the same way that a person becomes a good swimmer or learns to speak a foreign language, we cultivate virtues through hard work and practice.

Virtuous living resembles good eating habits. In the long run, quick weight-loss programs seldom work. Cultivating healthy eating, sleeping, and exercise habits are the best ways to maintain good health. Similarly, in the face of daily decisions, a virtuous person tends to make wholesome choices. Why? The reason is that virtue is not a one-time event; it is an ongoing pattern of behavior.

Virtuous persons—persons of good character—cultivate fundamental values, convictions, a sense of self-discipline, and behavior patterns that become almost second nature to them. These virtues serve as the basis for consistent responses to the many moral decisions that come their way. **R**

Reflection

Of the following behaviors, select one that might be a virtue that you choose to cultivate in yourself. Explain your choice.

- saying no when I really do not want to do something

- demonstrating concern for the environment
- developing enthusiasm for learning
- showing patience with my friends
- speaking more positively about myself
- taking better care of my body

Authentic Freedom

Character development leads to authentic freedom. It's important to speak about authentic freedom since today so many imitations are passed off as the genuine article. "Freedom is the

power to act or not to act, and so to perform deliberate acts of one's own. Freedom attains perfection in its acts when directed toward God" (*Catechism, #1744*). Freedom and responsibility, however, can be diminished by "ignorance, duress, fear, and other psychological and social factors" (*Catechism, #1746*).

- Ignorance is lack of knowledge, education, or comprehension.

- Duress means threats and/or unlawful or forcible restraints.

- Fear can be brought about by real and imagined dangers.

- Psychological factors include mental and physical problems or limitations.

- Social factors include the violation of economic, political, and other conditions needed for the exercise of freedom.

The "right to exercise freedom" is inherent in our dignity as humans (*Catechism, #1747*). Put simply, authentic freedom includes having a sense of who we are called to be and what we are called to do. Freedom includes having the stamina, the skills, and the inner strength to work toward achieving our goals.

If we think that freedom sounds simple or easy, we are mistaken. The above notion of freedom takes guts, bravery, and courage—in short, strength of character. It is an overwhelming task, and we often fail to use our freedom wisely. Authentic freedom is so challenging that many people settle for a distorted version of freedom—license. License is a permission slip, granting us approval to say or do whatever we want. License lets us off the hook; authentic freedom challenges us to strive to be more and better than we ever imagined. **G**

For Review...

1. Define the terms *character* and *virtue*.

2. What is the root meaning of the word *virtue*?

3. What is the relationship between good character and freedom?

4. In what way does virtue affect behavior patterns?

5. What is authentic freedom? How is it different from license?

Group Talk

Write a response to the following questions:

- How would you define authentic freedom?
- Do you believe that many people mean license when they talk about freedom? Give examples.
- On a scale of one to ten, how free do you think you are? Explain.
- Would you like to become freer as defined in the text? What would it take to increase your freedom?
- What do you think the Catechism means by the following statement: "The more one does what is good, the freer one becomes" (*#1733*)?

The Theological Virtues

theological virtues— faith, hope, and charity; good habits, given by God and directed toward him as their object or major focus

Catholicism identifies three pivotal virtues—faith, hope, and love. The term charity is sometimes used for love. These three are known as theological virtues because they are rooted in God and help us to live in a relationship with the Holy Trinity; in Greek, *theos* means god. Like grace, they are gifts from God, but they also call for a response on our part. Virtues are identifying marks—positive character traits—that show themselves in patterns of behavior exhibited over a long period of time. That is, by living faithfully, hopefully, and lovingly, we cooperate with God's gifts of faith, hope, and love. Let's look at these three virtues as they might be demonstrated in decisions we make.

faith— a gift from God and a human act by which we believe in him and all that he has revealed; the theological virtue of seeking to know and to do God's will

Faith—Trusting and Believing in God

Faith is a gift from God. It is the theological virtue by which the grace of the Holy Spirit moves our hearts, opens our minds, and enables us to believe all that he has revealed to us. "Faith in God leads us to turn to him alone as our first origin and ultimate goal, and neither to prefer anything to him nor to substitute anything for him" *(Catechism, #229)*. Faith, then, works on a number of levels: it is a grace given to us by God; it is a human act, a conscious and free act on our part to respond to God's grace; and it is an act of the Church which precedes and makes possible individual faith, supporting and nourishing the faith of all believers.

Only by faith can we come to know and experience God as one as the Holy Trinity—the Father, the Son and the Holy Spirit. Without faith we cannot believe in the Trinity and thus without faith we are not saved. As Jesus said, "The one who believes and is baptized will be saved; but the one who does not believe will be condemned" *(Mark 16:16)*.

Jesus models faithfulness when he prays in the Garden of Gethsemane the night before his death: "Abba, Father, for you all things are possible; remove this cup from me; yet, not what I want, but what you want" *(Mark 14:36)*. Jesus is alone in the garden. His disciples are off sleeping.

He has one last chance to abandon the message to which he had committed himself. Instead, no doubt knowing that dire consequences would result, he prays to his Father: "not what I want, but what you want."

Faith leads to a faith-filled life. The Blessed Virgin Mary models faith in action when she freely says *yes* to God's invitation to be the mother of the savior. *(see Luke 1:26–38.)* By her faith and obedience Mary becomes the Mother of God and the "mother of the living" *(Catechism, #511)*.

A Test of Faith

Case Study

Jana desperately wants to make the soccer team this year. Playing around before regular practice sessions begin, she shows herself to be a strong candidate to make the team and contribute.

She definitely is becoming part of the "in" group among the best players.

However, Jana notices that a number of players, ones who undoubtedly will be the mainstay of the team, constantly make cutting remarks about a girl named Rhea who also shows some talent.

As time goes by the badgering worsens. Jana doesn't join in. She keeps quiet and concentrates on her game. But even by not participating in the jokes, Jana realizes that she is distancing herself from the better players and not helping Rhea from suffering their taunts. Feeling more and more uncomfortable, she wants to yell, "Leave her alone!" Instead, she hopes that Rhea realizes that she isn't wanted and just goes away. **A**

Activity

Rewrite Jana's story so that her action reflects being a person of virtue. Based on your rewrite, make up a slogan that could serve as a brief description of the virtue of faith.

Hope—A Virtue of Trust and Responsibility

"May the God of hope fill you with all joy and peace in believing, so that you may abound in hope by the power of the Holy Spirit.**"**

Romans 15:13

On a class trip, Madison joins a large group of students in a crowded restaurant. After her meal, a friend suggests that they leave the restaurant without paying the bill. "Let's take a chance and hope that we don't get caught," the friend whispers to Madison.

Tim is prodded by his parents to get involved in school activities. A service club looks for help with a variety of projects aimed at assisting poor people. "Why don't you volunteer some time in the service club?" Tim's father asks. "You can help other people, and it also might be interesting." "It wouldn't do any good, so why should I bother?" Tim responds.

"Besides, after school is the only time I get to watch TV and relax."

hope—

trusting in God, in everything that Christ has promised, and in the help of the Holy Spirit. Hope focuses on obtaining eternal happiness in heaven and the help from God (grace) to achieve it.

In these brief stories Madison's friend, who considers walking out of the restaurant without paying the bill, hopes that she won't get caught. Tim has little hope that he can influence the future. In these instances hope obviously does not reflect the virtue that it is meant to be.

In popular usage the word hope often describes a passive quality and not an active virtue. For instance, in the following popular uses, hope implies passivity—standing by, letting things happen, and not taking charge of the situation:

- I hope it doesn't rain today. I didn't bring a raincoat.
- I hope we don't have a test today. I didn't study.
- I hope my parents don't notice the scratch on the car.

In these uses of the word, hope really means wish, since none of the statements imply any sense of taking action or taking responsibility. By contrast, hope as a virtue does not comprise a wish list of things that we would like to see happen apart from our involvement in them. Rather, our hopes are those things to which we are willing to dedicate ourselves; instead of passivity, **hope** implies trusting in God and cooperating with his grace. Hope is intimately tied to responsibility. It is future-oriented and means taking seriously the consequences of our actions.

Hope is the theological virtue by which we "strive first for the kingdom of God" *(Matthew 6:33)* and eternal life and happiness with God. Hope is trusting in Christ, trusting not on our own resources but on the grace of the Holy Spirit. What better vision of the world exists than the Kingdom proclaimed by Jesus—trust in the existence and fulfillment of God's kingdom. Jesus provides hope that, no matter how hopeless our current circumstances appear and despite trials and setbacks, in the end all will be well. This message of hope and trust in God frees us to act with heroic, never-give-up enthusiasm for life and goodness.

If hope became an active force in their lives, both Madison and Tim would choose behaviors that are far-sighted and filled with promise. As with the virtue of faith, it is through their actions that people demonstrate their hope. Also, hope is not an isolating, individualistic virtue. Hope is contagious. As such, an important dimension of hope is living with such deep trust in God that others grow in hope. **A**

Activity

1. The Catechism uses the following terms to help us appreciate how hope can motivate us to act morally: desire, trust, response, inspiration, a cure for discouragement, and expectation. Write your own description of hope using four of these terms.

2. Hope inspires us to trust that God wants us to be happy here on earth and eternally in heaven. Make up a story of someone who is losing hope or who feels that life isn't worth living. In the story, what do you say to this person to help renew his or her hope?

Charity—The Cornerstone of Virtues

Antoinette recently broke up with her boyfriend, Doug. Through friends she discovers that Doug has been telling embarrassing stories and making insulting comments about her. Angry and hurt, Antoinette wonders how best to respond to Doug's accusations.

Since her grandmother had a stroke, Kathleen's family life has been greatly disrupted. Her grandmother now needs constant attention. Kathleen tells her mother that she wants to help out in whatever way she can, so she begins spending quite a bit of her free time by her grandmother's side. Consequently, she ends up missing out on some social activities in which she normally would participate. When her mother asks her if she feels that her social life is being neglected, Kathleen tells her that she is happy to give the gift of her time to her grandmother.

Charity is the cornerstone of all virtues. One of the most beautiful descriptions ever written about charity (love) is found in the thirteenth chapter of Paul's first letter to the Church at Corinth:

❝*Love is patient; love is kind; love is not envious or boastful or arrogant or rude. It does not insist on its own way; it is not irritable or resentful; it does not rejoice in wrongdoing, but rejoices in the truth. It bears all things, believes all things, hopes all things, endures all things. Love never ends. And now faith, hope, and love abide, these three; and the greatest of these is love.***❞**

📖 *1 Corinthians 13:4–8, 13*

Every other virtue that we might practice represents some dimension of Christian love; every time we practice any virtue, we are giving expression to love. In the above stories Kathleen practices love when she spends time with her grandmother at personal sacrifice to herself. Doug violates love when he spreads stories about his former girlfriend, Antoinette.

Love, like hope, can be misunderstood. The theological virtue of love does not mirror the romantic love that is often referred to in the media, novels, movies, and popular songs. As with hope, sometimes we consider love to be only a passive quality. We might emphasize a passive *being lovable* rather than actively *loving*. Also, people sometimes suggest that selfish and possessive behaviors are motivated by love. (For instance, Doug might claim that he is really demeaning Antoinette because he loves her so much and is angry that she broke up with him.) In fact, selfish love is a contradiction in terms. The Catechism defines love in the words of the medieval theologian St. Thomas Aquinas: "To love is to will the good of another" [St. Thomas Aquinas, *STh*, 26, 4, corp. art.] (#1766). **G**

charity— (sometimes called love) the theological virtue representing the core of the Christian life. Charity is the virtue "by which we love God above all things for his own sake, and our neighbor as ourselves for the love of God" *(Catechism, #1822)*. Charity is the virtue that places concern for God, manifest especially through concern for others, above everything else.

Group Talk

1. Give three examples of misusing or misinterpreting the concept love—examples that you might find in popular culture.

2. Describe three specific situations when the Catechism's description of love—to will the good of another—might be a real challenge for those involved.

The Art of Christian Loving

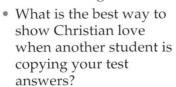

Pope Benedict XVI's first papal encyclical *Deus Caritas Est* (God is Love) states, "Since God has first loved us (cf. 1 Jn 4:10), love is now no longer a mere 'command'; it is the response to the gift of love with which God draws near to us." Like all virtues, love is an art. What does the art of loving look like?

- What is the best way to show Christian love when another student is copying your test answers?

- What specifically does it mean to be charitable to a group of students who act like snobs and exclude you from their activities?

- How can you feel free to love the people you meet on a day when a few extra pimples or some added weight makes you feel anything but lovable?

- How do you show Christian love to the boy or girl who over the weekend pledges loyalty to you and then on Monday tells you that he or she still cares for someone else?

- How do you show Christian love when you discover that some people from your old crowd are now involved in organized shoplifting and invite you to join them on a "shopping spree"?

- What is the best way for you to give at least some expression of love to the multitude of hungry people whom you hear about in the news or in religion class?

Like every art, Christian love—and moral decision making—is not an exact science. As new parents soon discover, sometimes love means hugs and kisses; at other times *tough love* is called for. For instance, in many of the above situations, the art of Christian loving clearly requires saying *no* rather than complacently complying with another's wishes. In other situations the art of Christian loving involves the art of honest confrontation and of being assertive. Despite our possible reluctance to act on our negative feelings toward others, the art of Christian loving suggests that we should respond with care and respect for ourselves and for whoever else is involved.

In his classic work called *The Art of Loving*, psychoanalyst Erich Fromm suggests the following five characteristics common to the practice of loving:

Characteristics of Love

- Giving—sharing oneself with another
- Caring—concern for the life and the growth of another
- Responsibility—the readiness and the ability to respond to another
- Respect—appreciating and admiring another
- Knowledge—knowing the inner core, not merely the outward appearance, of another

Even though Fromm was not referring to Christian love, his list of characteristics has much to offer Christians who seek to follow Jesus' law of love. When applied to Christian life, all dimensions of morality make sense only in relation to the art of Christian loving. That is, moral laws are norms for love; moral principles are the principles of love. Sin indicates a failure to love. In short, moral decision making involves the process of practicing the art of Christian loving. **R**

Prayer and the Theological Virtues

Since they flow from God and direct us toward him, the theological virtues foster all other virtues and give them life. Therefore, a necessary dimension of living the virtues is prayer. In the words of the Catechism, prayer is a "mysterious encounter" with God (#2591). Through prayer we reach out to him and discover that he is already reaching out to us. God takes the initiative; prayer is always a response to his presence within us. Each of the theological virtues is ultimately connected with prayer. *Faith* is prayerful longing to encounter the mystery of God, confident that he makes such an encounter possible. We always pray in *hope*, trusting that he will answer our prayers even if not in the fashion we would like. And finally, *love* is the source and goal of all prayer since ultimately prayer is a loving relationship with God. (*See Catechism, #s 2656–2658.*)

How is the Holy Spirit, encountered through prayer and sacraments, manifest in our lives? There are seven gifts that flow from the Holy Spirit within us. They are known as the "seven gifts of the Holy Spirit." Just like prayer itself, these gifts are two-directional—a back-and-forth between God and us. We need to do our part to gain knowledge and understanding, to find counsel that would reveal his wisdom, and to develop the moral strength needed to face the challenges of the moral life. In the end, however, they are truly gifts. The Holy Spirit offers them to us; through prayer we seek to tap into them. In a sense, prayer is like floating on water. We do what we can to learn how to float, but ultimately we need to let go and simply allow the water to carry us. In our lives, that which keeps us afloat is the Holy Spirit. **A**

The Seven Gifts of the Holy Spirit

Wisdom
Understanding
Counsel
Fortitude
Knowledge
Piety
Fear of the Lord

1. Name and define the theological virtues.

2. Describe faith-in-action as it applies to moral decision making.

3. What is the difference between a hope and a wish?

4. What is the cornerstone of all virtues?

5. How does St. Thomas Aquinas define love?

6. According to Erich Fromm, what are the five characteristics of the art of loving?

7. What is the relationship between prayer and the theological virtues?

8. Name the gifts of the Holy Spirit.

Reflection

1. Tough love means challenging or confronting another person for his or her own benefit. Have you ever attempted tough love or been on the receiving end of tough love? Describe the experience.

2. Explain the difference between "love" and "romance."

Activity

1. Compose a prayer related to one of the gifts of the Holy Spirit.

2. Look up the word "piety." Describe it in a way so that it could be applied to you personally.

3. In the Confirmation ceremony fear of the Lord is also called "wonder and awe in God's presence." How might this gift help us in leading a moral life?

The Cardinal Virtues

cardinal virtues— prudence, justice, fortitude, and temperance; personal character strengths that direct us toward Christ-like behavior and provide discipline for our passions and emotions.

During the Middle Ages theater troupes traveled throughout Europe putting on morality plays in which performers would portray various virtues and vices. Just as in today's television sit-coms, the vices—gluttony, lust, envy, and laziness—often received more attention. The reason for this is obvious—virtuous people get into less trouble than those who live a life of vice. Repeating a line from the beginning of this chapter, virtuous people tend to make wholesome choices. Most of the people portrayed in TV sit-coms are making unwholesome choices. TV plots consist of these characters trying to correct or cover the problems their bad choices have caused.

What are the key Christian virtues? Even though they have ancient-sounding names, they still hold an appeal and serve a purpose in today's television-saturated world. Four pivotal virtues traditionally advocated in Christianity are prudence, justice, fortitude, and temperance. They are called the **cardinal virtues** based on the Latin root of the word—*cardo*, which means hinge. The Christian moral life hinges on these four virtues working together smoothly, just as the hinges of a door keep it centered, stable, and workable. Not as abstract and lofty as faith, hope, and love can appear to be, the cardinal virtues are practical, common sense virtues. Neglected, they weaken our character. Used consistently, they support all our endeavors to live a good life. Like all virtues, they are gifts from God, which grow in us through education, practice, and perseverance. **G**

Group Talk

1. Make a list of vices (negative behavior patterns) and virtues (positive behavior patterns).

2. Name some television characters who exhibit a particular vice. Describe an incident when they exhibited that vice.

3. Name some television characters who exhibit a particular virtue. Describe an incident when they exhibited that virtue.

Prudence—Practical Judgment

prudence—
the virtue that helps us make a correct judgment about what to do and to choose the right way to do it

justice—
the virtue stating that all people have rights and should have their basic needs met; "the firm and constant will to give God and neighbor their due" *(Catechism #1836)*

fortitude—
courage; strength when confronted with difficulties and perseverance in pursuing that which is good

Driving onto train tracks when red lights are flashing at a railroad crossing is not prudent. Talking on a cell phone outdoors during a thunderstorm is not prudent. Organizing your study time during exams is prudent. Staying home the night before a big test or a big game is prudent behavior. **Prudence** is the virtue of making right judgments. It asks the question: What is the right thing to do in this particular situation? Prudence operates a lot like common sense. It is the art of making sensible choices in spur-of-the-moment decisions. The Book of Proverbs describes prudence concisely in these words: "the prudent man looks where he is going [Proverbs 14:15]" *(Catechism, #1806)*. The Catechism goes on to say that "[p]rudence disposes the practical reason to discern, in every circumstance, our true good and to choose the right means for achieving it" *(#1835)*.

Justice—The Virtue of Rights and Responsibilities

Justice is the virtue that reminds us that the people with whom we share our world have rights and that, as much as possible, all people deserve to have basic needs met. Justice is the subject of much discussion throughout Scripture and remains as relevant as today's newspaper headlines. A just person recognizes the dignity of everyone and strives to treat rich and poor, friends and strangers—those like us and those unlike us—with equal dignity. Living up to the virtue of justice is particularly challenging in a world where there is drastically unequal distribution of basic goods, social amenities, opportunities, and justice itself. In justice, all people possess equal rights. Therefore, our own good is never separate from the common good, an important concept in Catholic teaching on justice. Since matters of justice are such an important aspect of morality, we will examine them more closely in a later chapter.

Fortitude—The Courage to Act

Fortitude is simply a fancy term for the virtue that the Cowardly Lion requests from the Wizard of Oz—courage. It "ensures firmness in difficulties and constancy in the pursuit of the good" *(Catechism #1837)*. "Being good" is easy when everyone else is. The challenge is to stand up for what is right in the face of peer pressure or in circumstances when we are being called upon to step out of our usual patterns of behavior. Without the courage to act, all the other virtues are useless. In an atmosphere where even wearing the wrong brand of sneakers takes great courage and opens us up to ridicule, how much more courage is required to follow our beliefs when it really means going against the grain of the society in which we live?

Temperance—The Virtue of Self-Control

temperance—
self-control and a
balanced lifestyle

North Americans know the word **temperance** from the movement to ban alcohol that resulted in Prohibition in the United States. The temperance movement was made up mostly of women. The image they promoted was that of a male factory worker receiving his pay on Friday and heading straight for the nearest bar where he spent a large chunk of his paycheck on whiskey and beer. Meanwhile, his poor wife was home trying to figure out how to feed the children.

As the temperance movement called for control over the consumption of alcohol, so the virtue of temperance disposes us to self-control and helps us to a balanced use of God's created gifts.

Interestingly, self-control has taken on a negative connotation in some circles—as if self-control were an affront to our freedom. In fact, freedom requires self-control. If we are incapable of regulating the amount of food we eat or the amount of alcohol we consume, we're not very free. Being addicted to drugs or to cigarettes is not freedom. Being consumed with possessing the latest clothes styles or the latest gadget is not freedom. As justice is the virtue of social harmony and balance, so temperance is the virtue of personal harmony and balance. As justice advocates wholesome ordering of social resources, so temperance advocates a wholesome personal lifestyle.

The American temperance movement led to making all alcohol consumption illegal. As a virtue, temperance need not eliminate having a good time or other healthy interpersonal relationships. Instead, temperance reminds us that even good things turn sour when they control us.

A life of harmony and wholeness is not a life devoid of pleasure. It is one that aims to keep things in balance. "Temperance moderates the attraction of the pleasures of the senses and provides balance in the use of created goods" *(Catechism, #1838).* **R**

For Review...

1. Name the four cardinal virtues.

2. What is the root meaning of the word cardinal? How does this root meaning explain the role of the cardinal virtues in the Christian moral life?

3. Define prudence.

4. What does justice emphasize about virtuous living?

5. Define fortitude.

6. What social problem did the American temperance movement address?

7. Define temperance.

Reflection

Use the following questions to do a self-assessment of what you typically bring to your decision making.

1. If you were to receive an award today for a virtue that you exhibit, what would the award be for? Describe how you think you came to possess this virtue.

2. If you were to die in five years, what would you hope people would say about you?

3. How are you doing with self-control and balance in your life? Do you think that these are goals worth striving for?

Persons of Integrity

The poem below attests to the way our being influences our actions and the way our actions shape our being. We form our character through what we think, what we say, and what we do. In turn, our character sustains us during the many circumstances in which we find ourselves.

Character does not manifest itself only when we are at home or at school, when we are with our friends or with our family, when we are at work or at play. Character implies that we operate in an overall consistent pattern. A term for this unity of character is **integrity**. (As an integer is a whole number, so persons of integrity manifest wholeness in their behavior.) Integrity is closely associated with being honest and genuine. Its opposite is being dishonest and phony.

Integrity means being true to God and to oneself. What could be more natural, you might ask. In fact, if you are like most of us, when you look back over your actions for the past week or so you quite likely could name numerous times when you weren't true to God or to yourself.

integrity—
honesty, genuineness, and consistency in behavior patterns

> *"Watch your thoughts; they become your words. Watch your words; they become actions. Watch your actions; they become habits. Watch your habits; they become character. Watch your character; it becomes your destiny."*
>
> an anonymous poem quoted by Richard M. Gula, *Moral Discernment* (New York: Paulist Press, 1997).

Genuineness and Consistency

genuine—
not hiding behind a role or image; seeking honest communication with others

lived values—
qualities and concerns that we demonstrate as being important through our actions

stated values—
qualities and concerns that we claim are important to us

Persons of integrity are genuine. They do not hide behind a role or an image—being cute, being the rebel or the misfit, acting like the class clown—but allow multiple dimensions of their personality to come out. A **genuine** person tries to neither play games nor manipulate people but instead seeks to make honest connections with people. **A**

"Selfishness is not identical with self-love but its very opposite."

Erich Fromm

We can say that we care about the environment, but do we show that care in our actions? We can say that we take our education seriously, but do the choices we make back that up? We can say that family is important to us, but if we complain every time our parents ask us to join them on a family outing, then we are not living that value. It is important to distinguish between our stated values and our lived values. Stated values are those values that we claim are important to us. Lived values are the values that we demonstrate in our actions. Persons of integrity investigate their stated values and seek to determine whether there is a gap between what they claim to be a value and the values that they consistently act upon. If they discover that their lived values are not in line with their stated values, then narrowing the gap between the two is an important step toward personal integrity. **R A**

Activity

Place a + next to the following terms that you associate with integrity. Place a 0 next to the terms that you do not associate with integrity. If a particular term sometimes may and sometimes may not reflect integrity, put +0. When finished, use a few of the terms to describe integrity or lack of integrity displayed in a specific way.

—— judgmental

—— spontaneous

—— straightforward

—— selfish

—— aggressive

—— self-accepting

—— expressive of feelings

—— manipulative

—— fair

—— involved

—— critical

—— defensive

—— truthful

—— open-minded

—— conscientious

Reflection

Stated and Lived Values

Based on how important you think each item is to you, rank the following from 1 (of little value) to 10 (of great value). Write the appropriate number in the left-hand column.

Then in the column on the right rank items in terms of the amount of time, thought, and energy you give to each, from 1 *(very little)* to 10 *(a great deal)*.

—— watching television   ——

—— listening to music   ——

—— doing well in school   ——

—— keeping physically fit   ——

—— career goals   ——

—— religion   ——

—— sports   ——

—— friendships   ——

When you are finished, explain what your rankings say about your stated and lived values.

Activity

Write about an incident when you or someone you know was treated in a manipulative way. (We are manipulative when we treat people in a way that can control what they do for us rather than treat people out of a sense of care and mutual respect.) Then write about an incident when you or someone you know was treated with genuineness. Describe the difference between the two experiences.

Taking a Risk

While driving on the expressway, the engine of Joe's car starts to sputter and then it makes a loud *ping*. The engine is still running, but with little power. Joe is approaching an exit off the expressway and decides to take it. He pulls into a mini-mart and calls home to explain the situation. While leaving a message on the answering machine, he realizes that he may be stuck here in the middle of nowhere for a long time. When he gets off the phone, he notices an older couple looking at him from a few feet away. Seeing Joe's dilemma, the man says, "Excuse me. I couldn't help but overhear your conversation. I used to be a truck driver, so I know what it's like to be in your situation. It sounds like one of your cylinders is gone. If the car can run even slowly, you could follow me to a local gas station. The owner is very honest and he'll check it out for you. Then, if you want, my wife and I could drive you into town where you could get a bus."

Joe ponders this offer. Not knowing what else to do, he accepts. At the gas station, the mechanic assures him that he'll take a look at it the following morning and then call him with an estimate. As the couple is driving Joe into town, the wife tells Joe that she has two sons about Joe's age and she would hope that someone would help them if they were ever in trouble. When they arrive at the bus station, Joe thanks the couple and catches a bus home. During the ride, Joe thinks about the fact that so many people are actually amazingly kind and generous. He hopes to remember this incident when he sees someone in trouble. **G**

Group Talk

Joe reflects that, "many people are actually amazingly kind and generous." Regardless of whether you agree with him, give examples to support his claim.

1. What situations tend to bring out virtue and good behavior in people? What situations tend to hinder virtue and good behavior in people?

2. Which virtues do you believe are particularly strong in our society? Which virtues tend to be lacking in our society?

3. In our current social climate, would you have accepted the couple's offer if you were Joe? Why or why not?

4. Would you have offered to help Joe?

Communities of Character

The dignity of the human person requires pursuit of the common good. Everyone should be concerned to create and support institutions that improve the conditions of human life.

✝ Catechism, #1926

community of good character—
a community that promotes rather than obstructs the exercise of virtue; a community that is energized by the practice of values

In addition to acting virtuously on a personal level, we should also think about ways to create an environment where

virtue is the norm. That is, an important goal of the moral life is creating communities of good character.

A **community of good character** promotes the common good and provides the conditions such as peace and respect that allow its people to grow and develop. In such communities, those in authority work for the common good, recognize that they exist in an order established by God, and guarantee laws and conditions that sustain the exercise of freedom.

Catholics often repeat stories such as the parable of the good Samaritan (*Luke 10:25–37*) in order to foster patterns of generosity and to counteract patterns of selfishness and fear. Jesus did not simply call individuals to be persons of virtuous character. All indications are that he wanted to form a community where living in the Holy Spirit would become a way of life. In other words, Catholic morality does not simply ask, *What should I do to be good? It also asks, What should I do to help others be good as well?* To live a consistent moral life we ask ourselves, *How can I develop virtues in myself? We also ask, How can I help create virtuous living as the standard in my community?* Obviously, the first question supports the second; but the second question must not be overlooked.

...Conclusion

Virtue, character, and integrity are formidable-sounding words. An important part of Christian tradition, they still call us to think about how our lives and our communities foster goodness. They lay before us the question: *Do we want to be known simply as a "character" or as a person of good character?* Only by living a life of integrity, a virtuous life, do we become persons of good character. As we struggle to lead Christian lives of faith, hope, and love, we are shaping our identity. The identity we cultivate today in large measure stays with us over a lifetime.

For Review...

1. Define integrity. What would its opposite be?

2. Name and explain the guidelines that help us be persons of integrity.

3. What is the difference between stated values and lived values?

4. What is the relationship between lived values and being a person of integrity?

5. What does it mean to say that a goal of the Catholic moral life is to create communities of character?

Model of Morality

Richie Fernando

In 1996 twenty-six-year-old Richie Fernando was a Filipino Jesuit working in Cambodia at a center for persons with disabilities—most of whom were maimed by land mines remaining from the years of civil war that had ravaged the country. One night an incident occurred that led to his death but also showed him to be a person of deep faith. Here is his story as told by a fellow Jesuit.

On the night of October 16, several students were reprimanded for gambling, an activity that is strictly forbidden because a months' wages can be lost in an evening. The staff met the following day and decided that the ringleader, a former soldier, would be suspended from school but he would be allowed to graduate. In retaliation, the man appeared at school with a hand grenade and threatened to throw it into the midst of the staff and students. While a Thai volunteer restrained the man by holding the man's hands behind his back, Richie helped get the students with disabilities to safety. When all were at a safe distance, the volunteer released the man and dashed out of the building.

But Richie saw the armed man move toward a classroom where the director was teaching another group of students with disabilities. He rushed back into the building and tried to restrain and disarm the man. As the man with the grenade struggled to get free, the grenade got tossed or dropped—no one is quite sure—behind Richie. It exploded, and the impact struck Richie in the head and back. He died on the way to the hospital.

This most uncontroversial and fun-loving of young men, with a sunny, optimistic personality, belied the cynical suspicion that martyrs are gloomy fanatics who somehow "bring it on themselves." He explained his desire to commit himself to the Cambodia mission by simply stating: "Jesus came to be good news to the poorest. I want to be with Cambodian people and work with them to rebuild their country after the years of killing and war." After his death Richie's retreat diary was found.

On January 3, nine months before his death, he had written:

"I wish, when I die, that people remember not how great, powerful, or talented I was, but that I served and spoke for the truth. I gave witness to what is right. I was sincere with all my words and actions. In other words, I loved and I followed Christ."

Reprinted with the permission of Thomas Michel, S.J., and America Press, Inc., 106 West 56th Street, New York, NY. Originally published in *America*, 177:2, July 19–26, 1997.

Celebrating Morality

Let us pray for prudence—common sense and wise judgment. Dear God, may we be attentive to the consequences of our decisions and thoughtful and cautious in our actions. May we act with foresight. May we strive to see the whole picture and not just a limited, narrow view. Let us pray for prudence . . .

(Pause to reflect on wise judgment.)

Let us pray for fortitude—courage and conviction. Dear God, may we have the strength to stand up for what is right, even in the face of challenges and dangers. May we have the determination to follow through on achieving our goals and the moral strength to stand against the crowd when we need to do so. May we find inspiration in David, who stood his ground against mighty Goliath and, with youthful courage, won the day. Let us pray for fortitude . . .

(Pause to reflect on courage.)

Let us pray for temperance—self-control and balance. May we live lives of moderation—a balance of work and play, eating and sleeping, time alone and time with others, studying and just relaxing. In any area of our lives where we have lost control, we pray for the guidance and strength of the Holy Spirit to help us find and hold to the path that will allow us to regain mastery over ourselves. Let us pray for the virtue of temperance . . .

(Pause to reflect on balance and self-control.)

Let us pray for justice—fair play and social harmony. May we seek constantly to see things from the perspective of others. From this wider viewpoint, may we seek the good of all. May we be particularly attentive to those who are hurting or left out, those whose basic needs are not met, those who usually get overlooked. May we find inspiration in the great men and women of history who stood for justice and gave their lives for others. Let us pray for justice . . .

(Pause to reflect on fairness.)

Let us pray . . .

"Those who are kind reward themselves, but the cruel do themselves harm. The wicked earn no real gain, but those who sow righteousness get a true reward. Whoever is steadfast in righteousness will live, but whoever pursues evil will die."

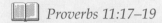 *Proverbs 11:17–19*

Lord Jesus Christ, help us to increase in virtue and come to be recognized as persons of good character. May we join with others to build a community of character filled with virtuous people. Amen.

7 MORAL DECISION MAKING

Chapter Overview

- Three sources of moral decision making are: the object chosen, the intentions, and the circumstances.
- Moral decision making involves asking *what* and *who*.
- Moral decision making involves asking *why, how, when,* and *where.*
- Discernment means calling upon as many resources as possible to evaluate whether an action is right or wrong.

A text on moral decision making cannot be reduced to a how-to book. Moral decision making is more than a skill. Nonetheless, we can identify action steps that can make our moral decision making better. As with all important projects in our lives, moral decision making deserves careful planning and thoughtful execution. Some steps listed in this chapter will appear obvious; others are frequently overlooked. Attention to the process results in moral decisions that are closer to being the best judgments that we can make—that is, judgments in line with the values and teachings of Jesus.

Let us pray . . .

O Lord our God, you have fashioned us in your own image, you have endowed us with the capacity to make decisions. May we use your gifts wisely and lovingly. May your Holy Spirit enlighten us with clear thinking and enliven us with care for others as we seek to do your will. Amen.

Before we begin . . .

1. A friend of yours is away from home at a sports camp. Your friend phones you and mentions that all team members are going into town that night to get matching tattoos. Your friend asks you for advice as to whether you think it would be wrong for him or her to get one, too. How would you recommend that your friend make this decision? What questions should be asked? Who should be consulted? What steps do you recommend that he or she take in order to arrive at the best course of action? Make your list of suggestions as complete as possible.

2. Another friend of yours is working for the summer as a lifeguard at a neighborhood pool. Part of her responsibility is to check the chlorine level of the pool on a regular basis. Now that it is getting near the end of the season, she has stopped checking the chlorine level. Instead, she merely writes down on the chart the same information as the previous lifeguard reported. If you wanted to convince your friend that her actions are wrong, what arguments would you use? What questions should she be asking herself? What steps should she consider to help her see that this is unacceptable conduct?

3. Ask two or three people how they typically go about making an important moral decision. Compare the steps you suggest for the above cases with the steps that they follow. Would you add any of their steps to your process?

Preparing for the Big Game

The school band marched along the driveway in preparation for Friday's big football game. In the parking lot, cheerleaders practiced their cheers until the entire squad could clap and kick and shout in unison. Students and staff in charge of sound equipment and videotaping checked microphones, loudspeakers, and camera equipment. Ticket-takers were assigned. Programs containing the player numbers and positions were printed and folded. Concession-stand workers double-checked their supplies and made sure that extra help would be available on Friday.

On the playing field itself, the football team ran through its drills. Quarterbacks and receivers worked on pass patterns. Place kickers and punters practiced by the goalposts. Running backs coordinated their timing with the offensive line. The defensive team captain yelled out different numbers, and the defense scrambled to set up its predesigned defensive patterns.

On this day filled with preparation, each facet involved in making the championship game a success stood apart as a separate unit. Yet everyone involved knew that attention to these separate details was important for creating a winning combination and a day the entire school would be proud of.

Traditional Sources of Morality

Moral decision making is like preparing for a football game. Attention to the many factors involved in a football game results in a better overall game. Similarly, if we were seriously ill we would seek as much information, advice, and guidance as possible to help us make the best decision about how to treat the illness. If we were faced with other decisions, such as what kind of car to buy or whether to go to college, we would take steps to ensure that our decisions are thoughtful and responsible.

Likewise, the decisions that affect our moral life should not be made quickly or without forethought. Being alert to the many factors involved will improve our moral decision making.

We have the freedom and the wisdom to judge whether an act is good or bad. That wisdom comes from God the Father, who has placed his natural law within us, endowed us with a conscience, and has given us the Ten Commandments, the witness of his Son, and the grace of the Holy Spirit. And if that isn't enough, God has given us the Church to teach us about faith and morals. The Church identifies three traditional sources of morality—the object chosen, the intention, and the circumstances surrounding the act—to help us judge the goodness or evil of an act.

The *object chosen* refers to what we do. Good acts involve something we know is good—feeding the poor, refusing to ridicule a classmate, visiting the sick, telling the truth, and so on. Bad acts involve matters that we know are bad—selling drugs, killing an innocent person, stealing, deliberately harming another person's reputation, and so on.

The *intention* refers to our motive or intention in performing an act. Giving a blanket to a homeless person because we are concerned for her well-being is a good act with a good intention. Cleaning a neighbor's house because we want to steal from that neighbor is an example of a good act done with an evil motive. Murdering a tyrannical dictator because we want to free a nation from oppression is an evil act for what appears to be good reasons. But we cannot justify an evil act performed for good reasons.

The *circumstances* of an act refers to conditions surrounding the act that affect its goodness or evil. Certain factors can "contribute to increasing or diminishing the moral goodness or evil of human acts (for example, the amount of a theft). They can also diminish or increase the agent's responsibility (such as acting out of a fear of death)" *(Catechism, #1754)*. Thus, there are factors that come into play when judging the goodness and evil of an act. Fear, ignorance, and pressure are some examples of these mitigating factors.

It is important to realize that a "morally good act requires the goodness of its object, of its end [intention], and of its circumstances together" *(Catechism, #1760)*. However there are certain acts that are always wrong to choose, such as blasphemy and perjury, murder and adultery. "One may not do evil so that good may result from it" *(Catechism, #1761)*.

Moral decision making is a matter of judgment. Certain skills, such as prayer, can assist this move from discernment to judgment. We might not think of it as a skill, but during decision making, prayer adds an important dimension to the process. In prayer we seek to diminish our self-absorption in order to be more open to God and to his will. Indeed, the goal of every aspect of our moral decision making is to make the best judgments that we can—that is, judgments in line with the values and teachings of Jesus.

Moral Decision Making and Conscience

It's important that you do not separate the process of moral decision making outlined in this chapter from the rest of the course. For instance, the process helps explain what "follow your conscience" involves. It helps us answer the question *What would Jesus want me to do?* Moral decision making serves as a building block for virtuous living. In particular, the process can be applied to specific areas of morality addressed in the second part of the book. **R**

Reflection

Think back to the situations mentioned earlier—the case of the friend contemplating getting a tattoo and the lifeguard who discontinues testing the pool water. Look over the steps involved in moral decision making: the object chosen, the intention, and the circumstances. Then read over the following case study. Based on the information you have just read, what additional steps, if any, would you now take to arrive at a decision? What would your decision be on the following case? Explain why you would take this position.

Friday night and all day Saturday the radio station of the local university featured the music of a group known for its graphic lyrics suggesting violence against women. On Saturday night at a club near the university, three women are attacked by a group of men chanting lyrics from one of these songs.

After the incident some campus student groups argue that such songs should be banned from being played on the radio station. They want a committee to oversee the type of music played. Other students argue that free speech would be compromised if these songs were kept off the air.

Since your high school is near the campus and the radio station is popular with your fellow students, you are invited to present your views on the subject at a special on-the-air forum. You gather together some of your classmates to decide which position you will advocate at the forum and what arguments you will use to support your position.

Fact-Finding: What and Who

If we actually took time to investigate situations calling for moral decision making, what questions could we ask ourselves to help us understand moral dilemmas that come our way?

What?—Opinion or Fact

As in all areas of life, in morality it is important to know what we are talking about. Before we jump to conclusions about moral questions, we need to make a reality check. For instance, imagine that we confront a friend about her drinking. "Marci, I think that you have a drinking problem. I believe you need help." Upon what basis would we make such a statement? If we expect Marci to take our observation seriously, we would need to present her with a number of facts to back up our claim.

To arrive at good moral judgments, we need to know what we are talking about. To illustrate the importance of the *what* question to moral decision making, let us examine two different statements. A necessary first step in evaluating the moral content of each statement is to determine whether it is an unfounded opinion or an observation based on facts.

Statement one: "Don't buy that product. It destroys the earth's ozone layer." This opinion suggests that the purchasing of certain products is immoral because of their effect on the ozone layer. Before we can say that this opinion has merit, we need to know:

- What is ozone? What purpose does the earth's ozone layer serve?
- Is there something in this particular product that harms the ozone layer?
- If yes, how serious is the damage to the ozone layer that is caused by the product?
- How essential is this product? Do alternative products exist?

Based on the information gleaned from asking these questions, we now should be clearer as to whether the statement is an opinion or a fact.

Questions That Help Identify the Facts:

What are the facts and what is merely opinion?

Who performs the action? Who is affected by it?

Why does the person intend to do this action? (motivation)

How will the goals be achieved? (means)

When and Where will the action happen? (time and place)

Another such example would be "Cigarette advertising should be banned. It purposely misleads people, especially children."

Concerning this statement, many cigarette ads portray athletic-looking people engaged in strenuous exercise. Some tobacco companies have sponsored sports events, such as tennis tournaments. Also, some companies have been accused of purposely aiming their ads at a youth market. In other words, cigarette advertising associates smoking with youth and vitality. To seek the truth, we need to ask:

- Do medical facts about the effects of smoking support or deny reports of its dangers?

- Can it be proven that certain cigarette logos and ads are targeted to children?

- Does cigarette advertising encourage smoking among young people?

The *what* question reminds us that moral decision making occurs only when real people make choices in concrete situations. Therefore, first we need to ask, "What are the facts about an issue?" before we jump to the second question, "Who will be affected by my decision?" **A**

Activity

For each of the following topics, write down questions about basic information that a person should have before coming to a moral position on the matter. As a follow-up, research one of the topics and seek answers to the questions you posed.

- buying a fur coat
- nuclear energy plants
- gun control legislation
- laws on the driving age
- violence in sports
- violence on television
- premarital sexual intercourse
- using illegal drugs
- smoking
- unlawfully copying software

What and Who Matter

The person or people involved in an action can make a difference in moral decisions. *Who* figures into morality in two ways: Who does an action and who is affected by an action. The following examples demonstrate ways in which the people who are involved in the decision can be significant.

- Marie is sitting with her friends at a cafeteria table at lunchtime and she jokes about the eating habits of two of them. To one person, Marie's comment is taken all in fun; to the other, it is devastating.

- Even though they come from fairly wealthy families, a group of young people regularly steal just for the fun of it and are finally caught. In a similar situation Anthony, too, is caught stealing. His family has been having a rough time financially and needed food.

- As he enters the restroom at school, John overhears a group of students joking about him. Their comments are cutting and not playful. When he realizes that his good friend Steve is among those making fun of him, John is particularly upset.

Just as morality always refers to specific actions—the *what* of our moral decisions—so, too, morality always involves individual persons. Therefore, who is involved can make a difference in deciding how to act. In the above examples, the emotional state of the person acting or being affected, economic differences, and our relationship to another person all need to be taken into consideration in deciding how to act.

Age differences and cultural backgrounds are other factors that need to be raised when studying the *who* question. For instance, in traditional Vietnamese culture it is considered impolite to say no to someone. This uniqueness suggests a need for sensitivity to cultural differences in our interactions with others.

If a history of racial tension exists in our community, greater sensitivity is required when we make general comments about a person of another race. Actions that are acceptable for children may not be acceptable for adolescents or adults, and vice versa. The various age ratings for television and movies are an example of this. **G**

Group Talk

Give three examples in which *who* is involved can make a difference regarding the morality of actions.

Why, How, When, and Where

motives—
the reasons people do
what they do

The *why* question seeks to determine whether we act out of selfish motives or out of concern for others.

Here are examples of actions that, on the surface, may appear acceptable or even good. However, the motive underlying each action paints a much different picture of the persons involved.

- Mr. and Mrs. Smith invite some of their friends to their house for a party. When the guests arrive, the Smiths use the occasion to attempt to get financial support from everyone for a business opportunity they have recently begun.

- Now that the school year is coming to a close and warm weather is coming, Ted and Angelo have begun to include P.J. in their activities. P.J. has a pool in his backyard; Ted and Angelo do not.

- Amelia knows that she and her brother are supposed to clean the house right after school. On the way home, Amelia decides to spend a few hours at the library to work on a report that's not due for two weeks.

In these examples, even though the acts themselves seem positive, there are negative or self-serving intentions obviously at work. The question of motives adds a very personal touch to our moral decision making. Our **motives** tell us a great deal about who we are. Regardless of whether our decisions are right or wrong, we can have good or bad intentions for those decisions. For that reason, the *why* question moves us from morality as *doing* to morality as *being*. While our intentions are seldom if ever pure, they do make a statement about our integrity as persons and are important for us in evaluating our moral decision making. **R**

Reflection

1. Describe how motives could affect the morality of the following decisions:

   - A student volunteers to help the school chaplain because it will get him out of after-school detention.

   - A politician running for office promises more jobs for the community if she is elected.

   - A male student notices that an attractive female student is having difficulty with course work and offers to help her study.

2. Describe three other situations in which motives can affect the morality of actions.

How?—The Question of Methods

- Katie wants to break up with Ron, a boy she has been going out with for a few months, in order to go out with Joe. At this point, Ron feels madly in love with Katie and presumes that Katie's feelings for him are mutually intense. Katie decides to give Ron the "silent treatment," ignoring him at school and refusing to answer his phone calls and instant messages.

- Dan is concerned that his weightlifting program is not sufficient to help him rehabilitate his knee and get him back into shape for his final year of college football. He feels that if he has a good senior year he will have a chance to make a professional team. He considers taking illegal drugs that he thinks will speed up his rehabilitation.

- The big game between O'Hare High School and Wilson High School is two days away. Late that night, some O'Hare students, wanting to show their spirit, go to their rival school and spray-paint "Beat Wilson" in big letters on the sign by the entrance of the school.

How we do things influences the morality of our actions. In the three examples described above, each person has a goal to achieve: Katie wishes to break up with her current boyfriend, Dan wants to play football at his best, and some students decide to exhibit school spirit. Simply stated, their goals are honorable; however, they can choose any number of different means to achieve their goals. Those means can range between more caring and less caring for the people involved. In these cases,

deception, harmful and illegal drug use, and destruction of property are evil means to achieve a supposedly good end.

An overemphasis on goals can lead to losing sight of the importance of the means used to achieve those goals. For instance, a goal of *Win at any cost* can result in harmful behavior by a student, an athlete, or a friend. Likewise, a business philosophy that advocates *Do whatever it takes to close the deal* opens the door to possible immoral business practices. Even during warfare, some means of attaining goals have traditionally been deemed unacceptable. According to the Catechism, "[t]he end does not justify the means" *(#1753)*. Both the goals and the means to our goals need to be examined in determining a course of action. *How* we do things is one more important factor in determining the morality of our decisions. **A**

Activity

Choose one of the following conflict situations and describe possible positive and negative approaches to resolving the conflict.

- breaking up with a boyfriend or girlfriend
- a disagreement with a parent
- hearing that someone is telling harmful stories about you

When and Where?—Circumstances That Can Color Our Actions

The difference between someone stealing a candy bar from a grocery store and someone stealing the last couple dollars from a poor man who needed the cash for medication can mark the difference between venial and mortal sin. Similarly, lying about why one was unable to turn in one's homework is significantly different than lying under oath. The circumstances, here, change the gravity of the sin.

We could continue this list, naming cases in which *when* or *where* significantly alters the impact of our actions. Of course, questions about *when* and *where* do not always tip the scales from right action to wrong or vice versa. However, since our moral decisions always occur in a time and a place, *when* and *where* are two more questions that can help us ground our moral decisions in concrete reality. **A**

Activity

Explain how using one or more of the questions—What? Who? Why? How? When? and Where?—affects the degree of moral goodness or evil of a person's actions.

1. A teenage boy irritates his younger brother while on a long trip in the family car.

2. In class a tenth grader who is hoping to delay a scheduled test asks a lot of questions to which she already knows the answers.

3. A girl tells her father, "In driver's education class today we saw a film about using seat belts and air bags. From now on I know the first thing I'm going to do when I get in a car."

4. A boy comments to some friends who are trying out for the school play, "All theater people are gay."

5. In order to get money to attend an upcoming rock concert, three boys canvass their neighborhood pretending to be collecting money for a charity.

6. Because he doesn't want them to feel left out, a boy invites to a party some classmates whom his friends dislike.

7. As he boards a plane, a passenger jokes about carrying a bomb in his suitcase.

8. A sports figure known for using illegal drugs is invited to speak at an awards banquet for young athletes.

9. A teenage girl who is seeking to lose weight takes diet pills that are potentially harmful.

10. A farmer uses chemical fertilizers and insecticides on his crops.

11. A coach who wants to embarrass the opposing team's coach tells his players to run up the score even though victory is already assured.

Emotions and Morality

Issues of morality frequently have underlying emotional dimensions. Our principal emotions, or *passions*, are "love and hatred, desire and fear, joy, sadness, and anger" *(Catechism, #1772)*. Taken by themselves, our emotions are neither good nor bad. Their impact comes, however, when they affect our willpower and good sense and thus the way we make our moral decisions. Our emotions, or passions, are morally good when they help us make good decisions; they are morally evil when they lead us in the opposite direction.

There are certain acts that are intrinsically evil—such as murder—and a well-informed conscience will tell us not to choose such an act. Emotions and passions might cloud moral decision making, but they do not determine whether a certain act is right or wrong. **R**

Reflection

Choose one of the following issues and name six to ten different positions that a person might have about it:

- using marijuana and other illegal drugs
- treatment of people convicted of crimes
- Internet pornography
- stealing
- telling the truth versus lying

Considering Possible Effects

Another way to identify facts is to imagine possible effects of different choices that we might make. Our present actions are the seeds out of which future consequences grow.

Remember, though, that consequences do not determine whether an act is good or evil. The consequences of a moral act can, however, increase or decrease the goodness or evil chosen. As mentioned earlier, moral decision making is not an exact science. We cannot know beforehand all that will result from our actions. However, we can envision possible effects. For instance, the excuse "I didn't mean it!" rings hollow from someone who plays baseball dangerously close to backyard windows. We are equally unsatisfied with, "I didn't mean it!" from the boy whose friend is hurt after he pulls a chair out from under her. Similarly, someone who consistently drives recklessly should not be surprised when an accident happens. In each case, the people involved would benefit from considering possible effects of their actions.

The fast pace of much modern development makes attention to

foreseeable effects difficult. A philosophy that states *If it can be done, then do it* has led to scientific and technological developments whose effects have not always benefited humanity.

For example, it is unclear what long-term effects will result from genetic research and continued use of fossil fuels. Nonetheless, we would not be acting conscientiously if we didn't attempt to determine possible repercussions of both.

Issues such as these, as well as many of our everyday decisions, remind us that *our actions have consequences*. We are shortsighted when we fail to consider probable effects of our actions. **G**

For Review...

1. Name and explain the questions that we can ask ourselves to help us understand the actions involved in moral decision making.

2. Explain the three traditional sources of Christian morality: the object chosen, the intention, and the circumstances. How do we use these sources to judge the goodness or evil of an act?

3. Explain how people could distort the means used in achieving their goals.

4. Name two ways that we can stretch our point of view during moral decision making.

Group Talk

Name some possible effects that should be considered before doing any of the following:

- attending an unsupervised party where young people will be drinking
- going for a drive with a friend who does not have a license
- signing a petition stating that one of your teachers is unfair
- teasing someone whom you don't know very well about his family
- having a community grant a permit to a developer to build a shopping mall on the site of a wheat field
- staying out an hour past your curfew

Moral Discernment

What assistance is available to us in our attempts to evaluate our choices? If morality is a prescription for leading a good life, what would a *moral prescription* typically include? Here is a list of helps that we can call upon when we are honestly and thoughtfully trying to make the best moral decisions possible.

Talking to Others

In making our moral decisions, we need all the help we can get. Usually, the most important function served by a friend is to be an active listener while we sort out the jumbled thoughts and feelings that we are carrying around inside us. However, we need not confine our resources to the shared wisdom of friends from our own age group. Often young people rule out seeking help from parents, teachers, priests, or school counselors by saying, "They wouldn't understand." Yet when they finally do talk over their problems with responsible adults, they declare, "Their understanding really helped."

Consider the following questions about how you typically respond to difficult decisions that you face:

- Do I talk over my decisions with anyone?
- Who are the people from whom I normally seek counsel?
- Would it be beneficial for me to consult other people when faced with a difficult decision?

When faced with moral decisions, remember: Deciding *for* yourself does not mean deciding *by* yourself. **R**

Reflection

- Has there ever been a time when talking things over with a friend proved helpful? If so, describe the situation.

- Has there ever been a time when talking things over with a responsible adult proved helpful? If so, describe the situation.

Consulting the Church

As already described in Chapter 3, the Church's teachings are a great repository of resources that can assist us in making moral decisions. The Catholic Church and her magisterium are strong and infallible teachers when it comes to morality and what is right or wrong. The pope and the bishops, as authentic teachers, work diligently to apply the wisdom of faith to moral questions. The Church community of which we are a part is committed to carrying on the message of the great teacher, Jesus. The Church has a role to play when we consider the ways that we, too, can best mirror the message of Jesus in our lives.

When we examine specific areas of morality later in the course, we will refer to insights from official Church teaching on the issues involved. Sometimes Catholics of high school age or older believe that they received the final word on Church teaching during their grade school years. More often than not, actual Church pronouncements on moral matters are much more subtle and insightful than Church members expect. Imagine how silly it would be to believe that we heard the full story about science or history in grade school. The same is true for Catholic moral teaching. This entire course considers consulting the Church's teachings as an essential component of moral discernment.

Check with Your Thoughts and Feelings

During the Vietnam War, which occurred during the late 1960s and early 1970s, one particular photograph received much media attention. It showed a young Vietnamese girl running away from a village that was in flames. She was screaming in pain because she was burning from a plastic explosive known as napalm. Over twenty years later, this young girl—now a woman—again made the newspapers when she paid a visit to the Vietnam Veterans Memorial in Washington, D.C.

The picture of the burning girl touched many people in a way that news reports about the war did not. We might wonder why this particular picture should have had the impact that it did. Young children were being burned with napalm bombs for years during this particular war. The difference was that this picture moved people; it touched their feelings as no news reports of war casualties had previously done.

We know that our feelings can lead us astray. They can be manipulated and misguided and should not be the only word and certainly not the final word in our moral decision making. As the Catechism says, "Strong feelings are not decisive for the morality or the holiness of persons; they are simply the inexhaustible reservoir of images and affections in which the moral life is expressed" *(#1768)*. However, feelings can also lead us to an awareness of truth that we might otherwise miss if we left feelings out of our decisions. To be moral does not mean to be cold, passionless, and inhumanely detached from our feelings. Rather, it means to live life with enthusiasm, afire with Christian love. **A**

Activity

1. Write an essay about an incident when your feelings influenced your behavior in a positive way or in a negative way.

2. How important a role do feelings play in your moral decision making? What role would you like feelings to play in your moral decision making?

Learn from Personal Experience

We are narrow-minded if we never branch out beyond our limited experience of things. However, we are wise to learn from past experiences and to consider their lessons in our current moral decision making. Here are examples of viewing current dilemmas in a fruitful way through the lens of past experience.

- I'm not going to a party with those guys. I know from experience what will happen.

- Maybe you do better at writing a paper the night before it's due, but I need to work on it for days before I come up with something.

- One drink may not affect you, but I know what one drink does to me.

- My parents are divorced. Whenever I come home from visiting my father, I know my mother will be upset. I need to be very careful about what I say.

As we go about living, we experience many things about life, about people, and about who we are. We might discover that certain circumstances bring out the best in us, while in other situations we tend to fall short of what we would like ourselves to be. We might recall that certain past decisions were good ones and others were not.

Such reflection on personal experience is a valuable asset in moral decision making. Each of us is unique. Each of us carries around some information that no one else has; each of us has an exclusive viewpoint that no one else has in exactly the same way. In moral decision making, we should tap into our unique resource known as personal experience. **R**

Relection

Reflect on past events in your life by using the following experiences. Give an example of how each experience—positive or negative—can help you in future decision making.

- an experience with an authority figure
- an experience with someone of the other gender
- an experience with someone very different from my usual acquaintances
- an experience that brought forth positive qualities in me
- an experience in which I responded with concern for another

Recognize and Scrutinize Your Values

scrutinize—
to examine or look over with care various dimensions of a challenging situation so that overlooked aspects can come to light

- To me, being popular is very important. I want people at school to know me and to like me. I take care that I say the right things and wear the right clothes. I pay attention to the people who hang out with me. I want to belong to the group that people look up to.

- I value having a good time. Sure, I want to go to college and do well in life. But for now my philosophy is, "You're only young once."

- When I get older, I want to make lots of money so that I can lead a comfortable life and buy the things that make life enjoyable. I know that many people are deprived of basics, but I think that if you work hard you deserve the fruits of your labor. I intend to be a person who is a success in life.

- I believe that God is always with me and that the best way to listen to him is through prayer and participating at Mass on Sunday.

Values, such as those expressed in the four statements above, influence the choices that people make.

Often the values that are the most influential are so much a part of us that we don't even recognize them. For example, we may become aware of the wastefulness of a typical North American lifestyle only when we travel and encounter people in poor countries who share a bowl of rice for a family meal.

Since our values so often come into play in our decision making, it is important to recognize them as much as possible and to **scrutinize** where they tend to lead us. **G**

For Review...

1. According to the text what is typically the most important function that talking to others serves?

2. What contribution to decision making do feelings make?

3. What does it mean to scrutinize our values?

Group Talk

How could the elements of moral discernment—seeking God's help in prayer, talking to others, consulting the Church, checking our feelings, learning from personal experiences, and examining our values—be applied to the following cases?

1. At a friend's party, seventeen-year-old Mitchell became intoxicated and while driving home, he struck a twelve-year-old boy who was crossing a street on his bike. Mitchell is found guilty of drunk driving and death by homicide. Since you have known Mitchell for many years, you are brought to court as a character witness before sentencing. While you are on the stand, a lawyer asks you, "What do you think should happen to Mitchell?"

2. You have just completed a lifesaving course and would like to work as a lifeguard at your local pool. A friend of yours who worked at the pool last year informs you that a sure way to get the job is to help in the re-election campaign of a local politician whose views on major issues are ones you disagree with.

Judgment Guided by Prayer

Making a judgment about what is right or wrong can feel like a solitary, isolated experience. Since God resides in the very depth of our being, we are never alone in our moral judgments. Turning inward to discover God's will is an important part of moral decision-making. As the Catechism points out, "How can the Holy Spirit be our life if our heart is far from him?" *(#2744)*

Before Jesus made the decision about beginning his active life of ministry, after years of unassuming work as a carpenter, he went aside to a desert place to be alone with God his Father. Before facing the trials of his upcoming torture and death, he went to a garden to pray. In similar fashion, it is a vital necessity of our Christian life to pray constantly. As part of our own judgment process, we would do well to go to a desert place—our room, a walk around the neighborhood, a church—to be alone with God. When faced with a difficult decision, praying about it echoes Jesus' prayer in the garden: "not what I want but what you want . . . your will be done" *(Matthew 26:39,42).* **A**

"The people of God believes that it is led by the Spirit of the Lord who fills the whole world. Moved by that faith, it tries to discern in the events, the needs, and the longings which it shares with other men of our time, what may be genuine signs of the presence of the purpose of God."

Pastoral Constitution on the Church in the Modern World, #11.

...Conclusion

Conscientious decision making involves many steps. We begin by asking for God's help. We then try to uncover the facts. From there we engage in discernment, seeking to determine the morality of all the possible choices we could make. Finally, we arrive at a judgment—as best we can, seeking to do God's will. Decision making, especially in the big decisions we face, deserves this careful attention. Remember, through the many decisions we make, we are creating who we are and we are helping to build God's kingdom in our world.

For Review...

1. Why is moral decision making not meant to be a solitary experience for Christians?

2. What is the role of prayer in moral decision making?

3. What prayer did Jesus say in the garden the night before his death?

Activity

Read through recent newspapers or news magazines. Find a situation that called for moral decision-making. Look back over the many elements of moral decision-making described in this chapter. Apply each one to the problem you selected. Explain whether each step could help a person—and if so, how—in making a responsible decision about the problem.

Model of Morality

Saint Teresa Benedicta of the Cross

In 1998, Pope John Paul II proclaimed a saint of the Catholic Church a Carmelite nun who died at the hands of the Nazis. Although born of a devout Jewish family, early in her teen years Edith Stein questioned those beliefs and declared herself an atheist. She became enamored of modern intellectual life, especially the psychology and philosophy dominant in German universities of the early twentieth century.

Saint Teresa Benedicta of the Cross

When she entered university herself, people soon came to recognize her intellectual brilliance. She shared happy moments at the home of a philosopher, Adolph Reinach and his wife Anna, who were Jewish but becoming Christian. Unfortunately, Adolph died during World War I. His wife asked Edith to come to the house to sort through her husband's papers. Edith dreaded the thought of returning to this home that had been so happy and lively. She presumed that Anna would be somber and tearful because of her husband's death. Edith found instead that Anna's faith in God, especially of Christ on the cross, sustained her, filled her with abiding joy, and gave her hope despite her tragic loss.

This experience began Edith on a process of discernment. She was an avowed atheist and a highly regarded philosopher, but she also would not deny her experience. Although drawn to the Christian faith that was sustaining her friend Anna, Edith did not ask for Baptism immediately. She sought guidance for this monumental decision that she was contemplating. She received the insight she needed by reading the autobiography of the great Spanish mystic, Saint Teresa of Ávila. After being baptized she felt drawn to join the order of nuns to which Saint Teresa had been a member. But first she wanted to make sure that her conversion was not too painful for her mother. Therefore, she spent months with her mother, attending both synagogue and a local church. She then returned to work, teaching school for a number of years. Finally in 1934, the year after Adolph Hitler became chancellor of Germany, Edith entered the Carmelite Order and received the religious name Teresa Benedicta of the Cross.

Edith's intellectual writings continued to receive much attention in the universities of Europe. One Polish seminarian who encountered her work would later become a philosophy professor himself and eventually Pope John Paul II. But in the climate of the time, it was her Jewish heritage and not her mind that was viewed as a threat to Nazi power. In 1941, she was called into Gestapo headquarters. Saluting and shouting out "Heil Hitler!" might have spared her, but instead she cried out, "Praise to Jesus Christ!" Within a month she was in Auschwitz concentration camp where she became one of the 4 million people, mostly Jews, who died in its gas chambers.

Celebrating Morality

Opening Prayer: Lord Jesus, our journey is long and winding, and our need for you is great. Fill us with the power of your Spirit so that in our choices we may echo the wisdom and love that you embodied when you walked the earth as one of us.

Response: Amen.

Meditation #1: Jesus, by living among us you have opened our eyes to the depth of your Father's love which surrounds us. Help us see others with your eyes so that we may see their pain and seek ways to relieve it, appreciate their concerns and share them, know their joy and feel free to join in it.

Response: Lord, open our eyes.

Meditation #2: Jesus, you treated friend and foreigner, the powerful and the powerless, old and young, the healthy and the sick as beautiful and precious. May we stretch our point of view so that we may find alternatives to hatred and shortsightedness. Help us consider ways that our actions can serve others.

Response: Lord, open our hands.

Meditation #3: Jesus, when you gathered your friends around a table and left them the message, "Do this in memory of me," you reminded us that we are to journey together and seek one another's help. May we learn from one another, find inspiration from the wisdom of the past, and seek direction from Church leaders and from fellow Christians past and present.

Response: Lord, open our minds.

Meditation #4: Jesus, we bring to the decisions that we face a jumble of feelings, a history of successes and failures, and values acquired from many sources. We feel pushed and pulled in many directions. When we search for guidance, may we look deeply enough to discover a course of action that is faithful to you.

Response: Lord, open our hearts.

Meditation #5: Jesus, our faith assures us that apart from you we can do nothing, but with you we can move mountains. May every decision that we make become a prayer to you and with you, as we say, " . . .not my will but yours be done" *(Luke 22:42).*

Response: Lord, open our souls.

(Offer individual prayers at this time.)

CONCLUDING PRAYER:

Lord, grant me the serenity to accept the things I cannot change, the courage to change the things I can, and the wisdom to know the difference. Amen.

At her canonization Pope John Paul II told young Christians that Saint Teresa Benedicta of the Cross had an important lesson for them:

"Listen to your heart! Do not stay on the surface, but go to the heart of things! And when the time is right, have the courage to decide! The Lord is waiting for you to put your freedom in his good hands."

As quoted in *John Paul II's Book of Saints,* Matthew, Margaret, and Stephen Bunson, Huntington, IN: Our Sunday Visitor Publishing, 1999, page 22.

Chapter Overview

- God's gift of the Decalogue to the Israelites is also a gift to us.
- The first commandment affirms the importance of adoring the one, true God and rejecting false gods.
- The second commandment calls for speaking and acting with reverence toward God.
- The third commandment reminds us to set aside the Lord's Day for prayer, worship, rest, and recreation.

We began our course affirming God the Father's love in Jesus Christ his Son as the starting point of Catholic morality. Now that we have come to the second half of our course, *Catholic Morality Applied*, we again start out with our relationship with God. In this chapter we will examine implications for moral living in the first three commandments. But first we will situate the commandments within the context of their origin as told in the biblical story of the Exodus.

1. Read and think about the first three commandments. Describe attitudes and actions that would reflect the message of each of them. Then when you have read through this chapter, address this same question in light of its content.

Let us pray...

We adore You, O God, and we praise you for helping us navigate through life's difficult waters. We thank you for giving us the Ten Commandments to guide us through troubled waters. All-powerful, loving, and liberating Father keep us afloat when we feel we are sinking and send us the grace of your Holy Spirit to lead us safely home to you. Amen.

The Ten Commandments

Decalogue—
literally "ten words,"
refers to the Ten
Commandments

"Keep the commandments of the LORD your God, and his decrees, and his statutes that he has commanded you. Do what is right and good in the sight of the Lord, so that it may go well with you, and so that you may go in and occupy the good land that the LORD swore to your ancestors to give you, thrusting out all your enemies from before you."

Deuteronomy 6:17–19

Over three thousand years ago a group of people, enslaved for generations, suddenly found themselves free. The two things they had in common were their slavery and their covenant with God. Many of them traced their lineage back to a heritage and a homeland known only from stories kept alive from the time of their ancestors. Moses, the man whom God called to be a leader of their liberation, made it clear that he was merely an instrument, a mouthpiece for the true God.

Once freed, they set out in search of their ancestral lands but found themselves wandering endlessly in a vast desert. They implored God to remember the covenant he had made with their ancestors. He heard their cries and provided them with enough food and water to survive. Nonetheless, they had no law, no common culture, and no guidelines to help them in their covenant relationship with him. Without these, they were in danger of violating the covenant and falling into a new kind of slavery—sin, lawlessness, unbridled license, and the "might makes right" oppression that they thought they had left behind.

Leaders among them realized that they must adhere to the covenant God had made with their ancestors, for without the covenant they would neither survive nor thrive. Only divine intervention could:

- fashion them as a people,
- guide them on the right path,
- clarify proper relations among them,
- preserve their covenant faithfulness to their God.

Only clear guidelines, a set of rules that apply to everyone, could achieve these goals. Moses asked God to provide laws to guide the newly formed community. His prayers were answered when, while on a mountain in the desert, Moses received two stone tablets on which were written God's laws. Today we know them as the **Decalogue** (ten words), or the Ten Commandments. Over half the world's population accepts these words as being of divine origin. The Ten Commandments tell us the way to live our lives free from the slavery of sin. In fact, the Decalogue is for us a path of life.

In the Decalogue, the Israelites, as they were known, were not trading in one form of slavery for another. The tablets were regarded with great reverence by the Israelites who realized that the commandments spelled out their way to freedom. During their time of slavery they possessed very little freedom or responsibility. As slaves, they did only what they were told. With freedom came responsibility. The commandments guided them in their freedom and directed their newfound responsibility.

In Judaism the commandments are a summation of a much larger body of law—the "Law of Moses." The Law

> **"**The law. . . is not designed to be a yoke, a curb, a straitjacket for human action. Above all, the Torah asks for love: thou shalt love thy God; thou shalt love thy neighbor. All observance [of the law] is training in the art of love. **"**
>
> Abraham Heschel, *Between God and Man* (New York: The Free Press, 1965), page 162

summed up in the commandments spells out how the Israelites should observe the covenant by loving God and showing care and concern for one another. Living faithfully to their laws marked them as members of the family of God.

Jesus knew the Law. Moreover, he invites us to reflect by our lives the deepest meaning of the commandments. Notice how Jesus responds to the question, "which commandment in the law is the greatest?" "'You shall love the Lord your God with all your heart, and with all your soul, and with all your mind.' This is the greatest and first commandment. And the second is like it: 'You shall love your neighbor as yourself.' On these two commandments hang all the law and the prophets" *(Matthew 22: 36–40)*. Thus, Jesus tells us that love is the way to live the commandments.

We would do well to follow Jesus' advice and search for ways to make the Decalogue meaningful words for our lives. In the remaining chapters of this book, we will look at some of the moral issues facing us today in light of the commandments. **A**

Activity

Read Exodus 20:1–17. In a short essay, explain what God wants from the Israelites and from us.

The Ten Commandments

1. I am the Lord your God: you shall not have strange gods before me.
2. You shall not take the name of the Lord your God in vain.
3. Remember to keep holy the Lord's Day.
4. Honor your father and your mother.
5. You shall not kill.
6. You shall not commit adultery.
7. You shall not steal.
8. You shall not bear false witness against your neighbor.
9. You shall not covet your neighbor's wife.
10. You shall not covet your neighbor's goods. **G**

For Review...

1. What is the literal meaning of "Decalogue"?

2. What was the condition of the Israelites when they received the Decalogue?

3. Why did leaders of the Israelites realize that they needed the laws God gave them?

4. Besides freedom, what human characteristic did the Israelites lack while in slavery?

5. How did the law help the Israelites in their relationships with one another?

6. What did Jesus say about the commandments?

Group Talk

The remaining chapters of this book are centered on the commandments. You may know more about them than you realize. To help you test your own knowledge of the Ten Commandments, list three ways to observe each commandment.

The Ten Commandments and the Kingdom of God

"I am the Lord your God, who brought you out of the land of Egypt, out of the house of slavery; you shall have no other gods before me."

📖 *Deuteronomy 5:6–7*

The kingdom of God is the truth and peace and joy of the Holy Spirit *(Romans 14:17)*. It is everything for which we most deeply long—love, cherishing, a life of happiness, and security. It is life: life here and now that is deeply joyful, life that continues after death, and life forever with God. The kingdom of God, then, is not a place but rather a relationship between God and human beings; it is a participation in his life.

Jesus likened the kingdom of God to a magnificent pearl. The merchant who finds this "one pearl of great value" sells all that he owns and buys the pearl *(Matthew 13:45)*. One day a young man asked Jesus "what good deed must I do to have eternal life?" Jesus replied, "If you wish to enter into life, keep the commandments" *(Matthew 19:16–17)*. If we want the "one pearl of great value," that is "to enter into life," the commandments provide us the path that leads there.

The Ten Commandments are not extraordinary obligations imposed upon us by a distant God. On the contrary, they are expressions of the natural law, that interior social contract that he has planted within us. They flow naturally from that which is best within us. The Ten Commandments are a reminder of God's voice within us, telling us of our essential duties toward him and toward our neighbors. By obeying the commandments in our decision making, we will be truly alive both now and forever.

Jesus also said, "I am the vine, you are the branches. Those who abide in me and I in them bear much fruit, because apart from me you can do nothing" *(John 15:5)*.

By believing in Jesus, committing ourselves to him through the Church and the sacraments, and keeping the commandments, Jesus comes alive in us by the grace of the Holy Spirit.

Another way to say this: "What God commands he makes possible by his grace" *(Catechism, #2082)*. **R**

Reflection

1. Describe specific ways that being committed to Jesus might impact the following areas of your life:

   —social life   —school life

   —recreational life   —life goals

   —economic life (accruing and using money)   —your view of political issue

2. Complete the following sentence:
   Some things I do or could do to ensure that Jesus helps guide my life are . . .

The First Commandment

"You shall love the Lord your God with all your heart, and with all your soul, and with all your mind.**"**

📖 *Matthew 22:37*

God's first commandment is a call "to believe in God, to hope in him, and to love him above all else" *(Catechism, #2134)*. We do this by prayer: praising him, lifting our hearts and minds to him, spending time with him, being grateful to him for everything that comes our way,

and placing our needs before him. We believe in, hope in, and love him by worshipping him as our Creator and Lord.

From everything that God has revealed about himself we learn that he is all-powerful, liberating, and loving, as well as kind, merciful, trustworthy, faithful, and unchanging—and that is just the short list. By revealing these qualities about himself, what difference does God want to make in our lives? Part of the difficulty we have in answering this question is that he always exceeds any explanation we might make about him. Words about him do not exhaust all that he is for us. Nonetheless, we have Scripture and Tradition and most importantly the person of Jesus to help us understand the one true God and to guide us in our response to him.

All-Powerful. God single-handedly and freely created the universe. With the Son, his Word, and the Holy Spirit, the giver of life, God the Father keeps it in existence. Given the fact that God is all-powerful, we might wonder why he permits moral and physical evil to exist in the world and bad things happen to good people. This mystery is illuminated by God the Father's sending his only Son into the world to vanquish evil.

By affirming that God is all-powerful makes a statement about us as well as about him. We are not in charge; he is.

"[N]othing will be impossible with God" *(Luke 1:37)*. And his presence surrounds us. In the desert the Israelites gathered manna and other foods that kept them alive. They knew, however, that whatever water and food they found came from God. His all-powerful nature is grounds for our hope. It's a recognition that God is saying to us, "It's okay. It will all work out. It's in my hands." Even our capacity for hope is a gift from him.

Loving. Many films and stories explore the theme of love and freedom. For instance, the Broadway play "The Phantom of the Opera" is about a man with a disfigured face who tries to force the woman he loves to love him. He can force her to obey him, even to marry him, but not to love him. This is the paradox of a loving God. "Loving" and "all-powerful" appear contradictory. A lover wants love freely given; forced love is not love. The God we meet in the Bible endlessly demonstrates his love and apparent powerlessness as he awaits our response. Once again, identifying the characteristic "loving" with God makes a powerful statement about both him and us.

God's love can be seen in his creation of the world and of the human race and in his plan for our salvation. "In this is love, not that we loved God but that he loved us and sent his Son to be the atoning sacrifice for our sins" *(1 John 4:10)*. In fact "God proves his love for us in that while we were still sinners Christ died for us" *(Romans 5:8)*. And while Jesus was in the world, his whole life—his preaching, his gestures, his every action, his healings and other miracles, his death and Resurrection—revealed the depth and dimensions of his love for humanity.

Liberating. Believe it or not, there are still instances of slavery in the world today. Surely the young children sold by their parents who are chained all day to their workstation making silk or other cloth are slaves. Even in the United States there are people, usually undocumented immigrants, who are forced to work to pay off endless debts and have no say in their working conditions. The very idea of enslaving human beings is abhorrent to God and a sin against human dignity.

God creates us to be free from all forms of slavery. Jesus frees all people from slavery and sin. He rewards our faithfulness with the promise that we will know the truth, and the truth will set us free. *(See John 8:31–33.)* Jesus sends us the Holy Spirit; and "where the Spirit of the Lord is, there is freedom" *(2 Corinthians 3:17)*.

However, it's important to keep in mind the allure of slavery. When times got rough out in the desert, many of the Israelites longed to return to Egypt and slavery. At least there they were fed. God wants to free us from every kind of slavery, not just physical. To live the message of the first commandment, then, we need to be attentive to forms of enslavement that keep us in chains as well as to the false gods that lure us and try to control our lives. Only the true God wants our freedom. **A**

Activity

1. Neither the Jewish nor the Muslim tradition allows imaging God. On the other hand, Catholics honor sacred images but reserve adoration to God alone. Draw an image for each of the characteristics of God: all-powerful, loving, and liberating. Then try to draw a fourth picture that would combine these three together in some way. Discuss what you see each of your images saying about God.

2. Besides the three qualities for God that we have from Exodus, what other adjectives would you use for God?

3. Besides physical enslavement, what other types of slavery might people today be subject to? For instance, are addictions slavery?

How Can We Stray from the First Commandment?

There are two major ways to stray from the first commandment.

- On the one hand we can minimize God's importance. We can be indifferent to him, deny his power, ignore his invitations to love him and others, refuse to pray, dismiss religion as a waste of time, and ridicule the Church and its members as hypocrites. We can neglect God by being ungrateful to him for all his gifts to us; we can neglect ourselves as Temples of the Holy Spirit, and we can neglect others in whom Jesus dwells.

- On the other hand we can give ourselves over to distortions of God—false practices and false gods. We can become involved in superstitions like taking seriously such things as tarot cards and palm reading and other practices that take us away from trusting in God.

The first commandment enjoins us to love God with everything we've got. It stands to reason, then, that we sin against this commandment by violating this love. We can do this in a variety of ways:

- Indifference. We ignore God, refuse to spend time in prayer, neglect his love by not loving others, or deny his power.

- Ingratitude. We know that God is the source of the many gifts we enjoy, but refuse to thank God in prayer or in our generosity to others.

- Hatred of God. We curse him for our problems or for the state of the world. We harden our hearts against him and refuse to believe in his love for humanity.

There is also another way to dishonor God—apathy. The traditional word for this apathy is **acedia**, which means not caring, listlessness, laziness, and boredom. A visual image for acedia is someone slouching in a corner while a lively discussion is going on around her. Another image is someone who is too lazy to get up and go to Mass on Sunday. It's easy to see how acedia applied to religion can be deadly. Acedia refers to a lack of "the joy that comes from God" *(Catechism, #2094).* That is, we are made for joy; but we settle for less, or we don't even try to pursue the joy God offers.

acedia—
not caring, apathy, boredom

If we feel listless and bored with school, we won't have much energy for schoolwork and our grades may suffer. If we don't keep up with schoolwork, then we likely will feel bad about ourselves and consequently become even more listless and bored. The same dynamic comes into play in our relationship with God. At any point where we can break the cycle of acedia, God is there waiting to offer us the joy he gave the Israelites when he freed them from slavery.

Despite everything that promises us pleasure, many of us feel sad and depressed to the degree that we can do little more than go through the motions of life. Many factors underlie a lack of enthusiasm for and engagement with God and life. Nowadays we have a better sense that some depression and distracting anxiety result from chemical imbalances. We are blessed with many medicines that can help with clinical depression. Beyond whatever other steps we take to help us with feelings of indifference and acedia, acknowledging God's love and responding love-for-love are the medicines that bring about the ultimate cure.

Adoration is a starting point toward a cure, "the first act of the virtue of religion" *(Catechism, #2096)*. All the problems named in the Catechism under the first commandment represent a turning in upon ourselves. Adoration takes us out of ourselves in an act of reaching out to God in praise and exaltation.

Raising our hearts and minds to God in prayer is one of the highest forms of adoration. God the Father, to whom prayer is primarily addressed, constantly calls each of us to encounter him in prayer. Jesus instructs us in the life of prayer. And the Holy Spirit reminds us with his grace of all that Jesus has taught us about prayer. The Holy Trinity thus inspires us to praise and adore God, bless him, entrust our needs to him, ask his intercession for ourselves and others, and give him thanks in our daily prayers.

Although we offer our prayers and adoration to God, we are actually the ones who gain from them. Prayer and adoration set us on a course away from listlessness and toward joy. The God of love invites us to turn to him and enjoy his blessings. **R**

> **▪▪**Joy has the power to open our hearts, remove fear, instill hope, and foster healing. Joy leads us to wisdom because it connects us to all we are—our mind, heart, power, and spirit. Joy stimulates our immune system, increases our energy, and gives us mental clarity. It helps us heighten our level of consciousness so we can more readily tap our inner wisdom. . . . As our joy expands we feel deeply connected to ourselves and to something bigger than ourselves.**▪▪**
>
> Charlotte Davis Kasl, *Finding Joy* (New York: HarperCollins), 1994, page xv.

Reflection

1. Name three other images that could symbolize acedia. Acedia violates the first commandment when it is a matter of choice. Acedia is also influenced by personal and social factors. Explain.

2. If you were to write a book titled, "Ten Ways to Joy," what recommendations would you include? Do you feel as though your suggestions reflect loving God with your whole heart, mind, and soul called for in the first commandment?

3. Name ways that you could show appreciation to God and for his gifts in your life. Try doing one of these ways you've never done before and write about it.

4. Write a paragraph reflection on the following statement by Rabbi Abraham Heschel *What we lack is not a will to believe but a will to wonder. (Between God and Man* [New York: The Free Press, 1965], page 41)

The Distortion of Religious Practice

- An actress always says, "Break a leg!" before going on stage.
- A baseball player makes the sign of the cross before stepping into the batter's box.
- A girl cautions her friend, "Don't walk under that ladder. It's bad luck."

Are these examples of superstition? It depends upon the intentions of the individuals. We perform many rituals that express our belief in God, give us grace, and bring us closer to him. We step over the line into **superstition** and magic when we attribute divine power to external actions and not to God. In other words, magic attempts to control him and to make things happen despite him.

Good ritual helps us to be in touch with God and invites him into our lives. We might light a vigil candle in a church as a ritual accompanying our prayers for a sick friend. If we light candles believing that through such actions we force the issue and bring about a friend's cure, then we have stepped over into superstition. The Sign of the Cross is a rich, meaningful ritual that Catholics perform. Conceivably someone could treat it magically rather than prayerfully. Horror movies often use Catholic symbols in magical ways. (For example, using a cross to ward off a vampire.) **A**

superstition—attributing magical power to certain practices (i.e. rubbing a rabbit's foot, carrying a lucky coin) or things (i.e. crystals, tarot cards, statues). "Reliance on such power, rather than trust in God, constitutes an offense against the honor due to God alone, as required by the first commandment" (*Catechism, Glossary*).

Activity

1. Describe positive and negative uses of religious symbols.

2. Explain in your own words the following statement: "The veneration of sacred images is based on the mystery of the Incarnation of the Word of God. It is not contrary to the first commandment" (*Catechism, # 2141*).

Atheism and False Gods

We offend against the first commandment by tempting God, sacrilege, and simony. We tempt God when we ask him to prove his power and his providential love as a condition for believing in him. We commit sacrilege when we profane or treat with disrespect, "the sacraments and other liturgical actions, as well as persons, things, or places consecrated to God. Sacrilege is a grave sin especially when committed against the Eucharist" *(Catechism, #2120)*. Simony is buying and selling spiritual things—such as God's forgiveness in the sacrament of Penance—which have God alone as their owner.

Atheism rejects or denies God's existence. Atheism can refer to a variety of false beliefs:

- *practical materialism*, that the material world is all that exists;
- *atheistic humanism*, that man is, "'an end to himself, and the sole maker, with supreme control, of his own history' [GS 20 § 2.]" *(Catechism, #2124)*;
- *social atheism*, that religion, of its very nature, deceives people, gives them false hope, and discourages them from working for a better life.

When some of the Israelites lost faith in God in the desert they built a golden calf, which they then adored. We slip into idol worship when we honor and revere anyone or anything as God. The false gods we are most in danger of worshipping today are not made of gold or clay. We are more likely to value other things over faithfulness to the one true God. We may not even be aware of how much we adore these things in ways that lead us astray from his path. The Catechism lists the following as potential idols for people today: power, pleasure, race, ancestors, the state, and money. **G**

For Review...

1. What is the first commandment?

2. How does someone create a false god?

3. Give an example to illustrate that someone proclaiming faith in the one, true God may be worshiping a false god.

4. What three characteristics does Exodus associate with God?

5. Why does "loving" appear to be contradictory to "all-powerful"?

6. Give an example of slavery in the world today.

7. Name three terms that describe ways we can stray from the first commandment.

8. What does the Catechism say is the starting point to curing acedia?

Group Talk

1. Besides the six listed in the Catechism, are there other "false gods" that people might follow today?

2. Decide whether or not each of the following statements is an example of idol worship. If so, explain why. How could each statement be interpreted that would make it more or less idol worship?

   1. Members of that race are devils.

   2. I have a right to drive a gas-guzzling, polluting vehicle.

   3. My goal in life is to make the most money I can.

   4. I'm willing to cheat if it helps me get to the top.

   5. I'm proud of my country. It's the best in the world.

   6. My priority during weekends is to have as much fun as I can.

   7. During times of war or conflict, I'm more concerned about the lives of my countrymen than those of others.

3. Discuss: Does the following statement describe worshipping a false God?

I was brought up by my parents to give due respect and honor to adults. ... In particular I was always directed to carry out the wishes or directives of my parents, the teacher, pastor, in fact of all adults including household servants, without hesitation, and allow nothing to deter me. What such persons said was always right. These rules of conduct have become part of my very flesh and blood. ... [I] was brought up to obey every command without question, to be neat and orderly in all things, and to keep scrupulously clean.

—Rudolf Hess, director of the Auschwitz concentration camp from May 1940 to November 1943. (quoted in Dorothee Soelle, *Creative Disobedience* [Cleveland, OH: The Pilgrim Press, 1995], pages 7–8)

The Second Commandment

"You shall not make wrongful use of the name of the LORD your God, for the LORD will not acquit anyone who misuses his name."

Exodus 20:7

blasphemy—
speech or action that shows disrespect or contempt for God or persons or things dedicated to God

The second commandment requires us to have respect for God's name. As we learned from the first commandment, God's name is sacred and meant for adoration. Therefore, we are not to speak his name except to bless, honor, and praise him. Uttering obscenities involving his name, cursing someone using the name of the Lord, or employing God's name in crude language defile and cheapen that which is most sacred to our faith.

Does our use of speech deserve to be ranked the second of the commandments? In fact, isn't it true that our speech reflects whether or not we have a sense of the sacred? Without a sense of the sacred, all the other commandments are groundless. (For example, killing is wrong because human life is sacred.) Indeed, if we spoke reverentially about God and his creatures we would be contributing greatly to the spirit of holiness without which our world could not survive. In a sense, all of our speech either witnesses to or mocks God.

A major way that we violate this commandment is expressed by the word **blasphemy**. "Blasphemy is the use of the name of God, of Jesus Christ, of the Virgin Mary, and of the saints in an offensive way" (Catechism, #2162). Blasphemy involves directing toward God words or gestures of malice, hostility, or dishonor. When we consider someone or something to be sacred, whether it is our grandmother, our nation's flag, or a revered teacher, we are deeply offended and outraged when others speak disrespectfully about them. The second commandment demands from us a similar sense of outrage when the name of God, the saints, our Church, or other sacred things are defiled in word and action. **G**

Group Talk

1. Restate the second commandment in positive terms.

2. What does it mean to say that our speech either witnesses to or mocks God?

3. Do you believe that speaking with reverence is essential to human survival?

4. Some magazines, comedians, and television shows focus on poking fun at what we hold sacred. This can be helpful when they expose our idol worship as misguided. It's another matter when it shows disrespect for that which is truly holy. Give examples to illustrate the difference between exposing false gods and disrespecting the true God.

Speaking the Truth

Human speech is either in accord with or in opposition to **God** who is **Truth** itself.

✝ Catechism, #2151

The second commandment highlights the sin of perjury. We commit perjury when we make a promise under oath and either do not intend to keep it or simply fail to do so. Perjury is an offense against the second commandment because of the nature of an oath. Taking an oath is swearing, with God as our witness, to the truth of what we say. By making such an oath, we are employing the Lord's name and truthfulness as a pledge of our own truthfulness.

We are literally, then, taking the Lord's name in vain when we make a false, deceptive, or dishonest oath. By making a false oath, we are calling upon God to be a witness to our dishonesty.

Jesus talked about the second commandment when he said, "Again, you have heard it said to those of ancient times, 'You shall not swear falsely, but carry out the vows you have made to the Lord.' But I say to you, Do not swear at all. . .Let your word be 'Yes, Yes' or 'No, No'; anything more than this comes from the evil one" *(Matthew 5:33–34, 37)*. Jesus' statement does not prohibit us from taking oaths for serious and right reasons, such as in court. Jesus wants our honesty to be such that no one need ever doubt it or have a need to put it to a test. **A**

For Review...

1. What does it mean to say that a sense of the sacred underlies all the commandments?

2. Name a way we would violate an oath.

Activity

1. Write a poem or a story that illustrates either the sacred use of speech or a misuse of speech.

2. What is your school's policy on cheating? How well is it followed by students? Imagine that your school initiated an "honor code" policy whereby every student would pledge not to cheat. If tests were administered in an unsupervised setting, would all, most, very few, or no students cheat? Would you? Why or why not?

The Third Commandment

"Remember the sabbath day, and keep it holy. For six days you shall labor and do all your work. But the seventh day is a sabbath to the LORD your God; you shall not do any work."

Exodus 20:8–10

Can anyone question that human beings need rest? Just as certainly, we have a need to praise and acknowledge God. Rest is most refreshing when we establish a rhythm to it. Similarly, our worship needs a rhythm and regularity. The children's book, *The Little Prince*,

provides this important adult lesson: it's important to keep rituals. Diet and exercise are more effective when we keep to a pattern. American college students who find themselves abroad in late November find it very jarring that no one is celebrating Thanksgiving.

The third commandment enjoins us to be attentive both to our worship and our leisure. For instance, Sunday is the Lord's Day. Saturday is the Jewish Sabbath commemorating the day God rested as told in the creation account beginning the Bible. Sunday is the New Creation or the eighth day of creation. That is, initially the world was created in seven days. By rising from the dead on Easter Sunday Christ brings

creation to fulfillment. Thus Sunday is the eighth day of creation. Accounts we have of the early Church indicate that they gathered for the Eucharist most especially on Sunday.

We keep Sunday holy by participating at Mass on that day (or on the preceding Saturday night) and by abstaining from activities or work that hinder us from the spiritual observance of the Lord's Day. We live the spirit of Psalm 118:24 that exclaims, "This is the day that the Lord has made, let us rejoice and be glad in it."

Because Sunday is the primary holy day of obligation in the Catholic Church, members are required to participate in Mass. Participation at Sunday Eucharist is an opportunity to remember and praise God in Christ Jesus. However, it is not for us as individuals alone. Through Sunday Eucharist, we strengthen one another's faith. Even beyond that, a community gathered at Sunday Eucharist testifies to all humanity that God is good, worthy of praise, and the hope for the world's salvation. By participating in Sunday Eucharist we are adding our voices to a great chorus praising God throughout the world.

Holy Leisure

On Sundays and other holy days of obligation, the faithful are to refrain from engaging in work or activities that hinder the worship owed to God, the joy proper to the Lord's Day, the performance of the works of mercy, and the appropriate relaxation of mind and body. [CF. CIC, can. 1247]

✝ **Catechism, #2185**

St. Augustine, one of the greatest theological writers of all time, spoke of "holy leisure." No doubt he realized that taking time out to enjoy life was an important part of how we worship God, the giver of life. When we play, we imitate God who rested the day he finished the work of creation. Recreation means "re-creation," a creating anew or restoration that comes about both through participation at Mass and through leisure. Leisure helps set our lives in order.

We keep the Lord's Day holy by allowing ourselves a sufficient amount of leisure time to nurture our cultural, social, spiritual, and family lives. Likewise we should be sensitive to the needs of others and refrain from making unnecessary demands on them that would hinder their observance of the Lord's Day. **R**

...Conclusion

Without God's guidance the Israelites would still be wandering aimlessly in the desert. We too can take the divine instruction given in the Decalogue and follow the path that leads home to God, the loving Father. The first three commandments of the Decalogue point directly to our responsibilities toward God. They instruct us to be attentive to how we speak of him. Finally they tell us that if our relationship with God is to remain vibrant we need to keep holy the Lord's Day—the day Christ rose and announced new life for us.

For Review...

1. What two types of activity are included in keeping holy the Lord's Day?

2. Why is Sunday the Lord's Day for most Christians?

3. Why is Sunday Eucharist not for individuals alone?

4. What does St. Augustine mean by the term "holy leisure"?

Reflection

1. What comes to mind when you think about the concept "holy leisure"? How can leisure-time activities be holy?

2. Rank yourself on how well you keep holy the Lord's Day. What could you do differently to enhance Sunday worship and leisure?

3. The Sabbath has been referred to as a day-long meditation. What do you think is meant by that?

Model of Morality

Blessed Kateri Tekakwitha

Pope John Paul II named Kateri Tekakwitha a patroness of World Youth Day 2002. Why did the pope believe a Native American woman who lived three centuries ago to be a model for today's young people? Her brief life holds the answer.

Kateri Tekakwitha

Kateri was a member of the Mohawk tribe of the Iroquois Nation. Her mother belonged to a rival tribe captured during warfare whose life was spared when taken in marriage by the Mohawk chief. She also happened to be Christian. (French missionaries had made converts among some Indians at the time.) Both of Kateri's parents died as a result of a small pox outbreak in her village when she was four. Kateri herself was left with a disfigured face and poor eyesight from the illness. She was raised by her father's brother and two aunts. When a Jesuit missionary visited the village, Kateri was drawn to the message he preached. Perhaps she remembered her mother's Christian prayers and songs from an earlier day.

Kateri's aunts and uncle did not approve of her interest in the "white man's religion" being touted by the "Black Robes." Yet Kateri kept her interest in Christianity despite the rejection and derision she experienced from others of her tribe. At the age of twenty she was baptized. She was mocked for not working on Sundays and for other Christian ways. At the time, however, the Indian population of the area was beaten down badly following the impact of the French. Fur traders introduced Indians to alcohol, and alcoholism was rampant. Along with excessive drinking came other unsavory practices. At her young age Kateri decided to leave her village for another near Montreal where other Christian Native Americans lived. The journey was 200 miles through dense forests and dangerous swampland, but once there she was able to be with others who tried to live a Christian life.

Kateri soon became known for her great piety. She spent long hours in chapel in prayer. When she was in the forest, she would erect a cross of wood and kneel and pray there for hours. She wanted to become a nun but was discouraged from doing so—partially because few Europeans believed that the indigenous people could comprehend the depth of the Christian mysteries. However, by the time she died both whites and fellow Indians recognized Kateri as someone special. Through her constant adoration of God she obviously attained a high degree of spirituality unusual by any standards. Clearly she knew God's love and loved him in return. When she died at the age of twenty-four, word went out that "the saint has died." A number of Frenchmen who saw her immediately after her death discovered that the marks she had on her face since her youth had miraculously disappeared.

In her short life, Kateri met God and dedicated her life to him. She faced unique obstacles. Most of the French felt that as a simple native she was not capable of much of a spiritual life. Most of her fellow Indians derided her for choosing this new way of life, only to realize that she was a spiritual blessing to everyone. No doubt Pope John Paul II wants today's youth to pursue a spiritual life in the face of the many obstacles now surrounding them, just as Blessed Kateri did.

Celebrating Morality

Leader: In adoration of the grandeur of God who loves and liberates us . . .

God of the high and holy places
    where I catch a glimpse of your glory,
    above the low levels of life,
    above the evil and emptiness which
    drags me down,
    beyond the limits of my sense and
    imagination,

All: *You lift me up.*

In the splendour of a sunset,
in the silence of the stars,
in the grandeur of the mountains,
in the vastness of the sea,

All: *You lift me up*

In the majesty of music,
in the mystery of art,
in the freshness of the morning,
in the fragrance of a single flower,

All: *You lift me up*

Awe-inspiring God, when I am lost in wonder and lost for words, receive the homage of my silent worship but do not let me be content to bear your beauty and be still. Go with me to the places where I live and work. Lift the veil of reticence behind which I hide. Give me the courage to speak of the things which move me, with simple and unselfconscious delight. Help me to share my glimpses of glory until others are drawn to your light.

All: Amen.

Jean Mortimer, "Glimpses of Glory"

Leader: Reflect on the following statement by an astronaut about his flight into space: *What I saw was just too beautiful to have happened by accident.*

    —Captain Eugene A. Cernan, Apollo Astronaut

All: Glory to the Father, and to the Son, and to the Holy Spirit. As it was in the beginning, is now, and ever shall be, world without end. Amen.

9

THE FAMILY AND BEYOND

Chapter Overview

- The Catholic family is a domestic church with the Trinity as its model.
- The fourth commandment calls for harmony within families and society by honoring parents, elders, and leaders.
- For the past fifty years, the Information Age has influenced family life and values.
- Computers, video games, and the many forms of information technology impact our moral lives.

The Decalogue recognizes that mutual care and responsibility within families are essential to a thriving community. The fourth commandment reminds us that God does not operate in a realm far above and distant from us. Rather, he is present within families and among those closest to us. Honor and respect are due those immediately responsible for us. From this home base, care and concern flow out to the larger communities to which we belong.

Before we begin...

1. List characteristics of a community that would take seriously the fourth commandment. (Name as many characteristics as possible.)

2. How do the communities to which you belong (family, school, and so on) measure up to these characteristics?

Let us pray...

Dear God, who watches over us like a good mother and father, may our homes and communities be places of mutual respect and harmony. May you—Father, Son, and Holy Spirit—inspire us to make our contributions to family life always caring and loving. Amen.

Family Matters

"Honor your father and your mother, so that your days may be long in the land that the LORD your God is giving you."

 *Exodus 20:12*

For over a century now children have enjoyed the story of Peter Pan. In the story, Peter Pan rules over a band of boys who never grow up. Constant boyish adventures fill their lives. Despite many close calls, they always manage to find their way out of the most harrowing of trouble spots—especially those involving the dastardly but bumbling Captain Hook and his pirates. Nonetheless they are called "the lost boys." They lack parents and a family. Their daily adventures are not enough to quell their longing for a home.

The desire for someone to love us and watch over us is universal. Parents usually fulfill this role as best they can. In this way they point us toward the loving God, and they deserve all the respect we can give them. However, from a Christian perspective it is important to remember that God the Father is the ultimate parent who never lets us down and to whom our prayers are primarily addressed. There are no lost children in God's family.

The family can be referred to as the **domestic church**. This description affirms that families are holy communities where children first encounter God and are educated in prayer. When parents and children treat each other respectfully they are not just upholding the social order, they are serving God. Christ is present in the domestic church as he is present in the larger Church. We can easily miss Christ's presence in our family life because of its ordinariness. Unless something drastic happens, family matters don't make headlines. However, the fourth commandment is the first of the commandments to address how we serve God by serving others. That, in itself, is a statement about how important family matters really are.

A Christian Vision of Family: The Trinity as Model

Holy Trinity—
one God in three
Persons; the Father, the
Son, and the Holy Spirit

Early Christian writers used an interesting Greek word when referring to the relationship that exists within the **Holy Trinity**, one God in three persons— the Father, the Son, and the Holy Spirit. *Perichoresis* means dancing around. (Our English word choir comes from this Greek derivation.) The Holy Trinity, the core mystery of our Christian faith and life, is a God in relationship, swirling around in a dance and making music together. From the Father and the Son comes the Holy Spirit— the same Holy Spirit that Christ the Son promises is within us. Through the grace of Baptism, we are invited to join in the dance and the life of the Trinity. Our families model the Holy Trinity when they are communities of faith, hope, and charity.

What kind of dance is going on in our families? If we're not hidden away in our rooms spending our days on instant messenger, we're coming into contact with our family members on a regular basis. Are our encounters abrasive, aloof, congenial, or loving? *Perichoresis* implies that the Trinity is enjoying itself. This image of God is an invitation to us to make the interactions within our families God-like, that is, loving and joyful. Parents have responsibilities toward children; children have responsibilities toward parents. How those responsibilities are carried out is part of the family dance.

In addition, interaction within families is fostered when families consider the needs of others. The family is where we learn to care and take responsibility for people who could use some help. Sometimes it's an older neighbor who needs help taking out the trash or the parents of an autistic child who could use a break. The movement outward is an important part of the dance, especially toward people who are very young or very old, people who are sick or have disabilities, and people who are poor. **R**

Reflection

The fourth commandment applies to real families, such as your own. Here are some questions to help you explore dynamics in your family right now. (You may not want to share your responses to this exercise with other students or your teacher.)

1. Describe the dance that goes on in your family or in your current living situation. (How do people seek or avoid attention? What are strengths and weaknesses of members of the household? How are they displayed? How do you respond to everyone else? What role do you play in the dance?)

2. Describe the dance of your family when it is at its best. How do you contribute to family cohesiveness?

3. In ten years, do you think that you will dread or look forward to spending holidays with your family? Why?

4. Are there people in your family or neighborhood who would benefit from your help or friendship? If so, do you try to help them? How? If not, how might you help?

Prayer in the Family

The Tradition of the Church proposes to the faithful certain rhythms of praying intended to nourish continual prayer. Some are daily, such as morning and evening prayer, grace before and after meals, the Liturgy of the Hours. Sundays, centered on the Eucharist, are kept holy primarily by prayer. The cycle of the liturgical year and its great feasts are also basic rhythms of the Christian's life of prayer.

✝ **Catechism, #2698**

Traditional Prayer Before a Meal

"Bless us, O Lord, and these Your gifts, which we are about to receive from Your bounty, through Christ our Lord. Amen."

Fifty years ago American Catholics often heard the phrase, "The family that prays together, stays together." There is simple wisdom in this phrase that remains true today, although it is often overlooked. Can you imagine a family today gathering together after an evening meal to say the rosary together? Would a family even take time to read a brief passage from the Bible before a meal each day? Perhaps your family does say grace before meals most days or at least on Sundays and holydays. In speaking about the family, "Daily prayer and the reading of the Word of God strengthen it in charity" *(Catechism, #2205)*. Isn't there truth in this statement? **A**

Activity

1. If your family recites a prayer before meals, what difference do you think it makes? If your family does not say grace before meals and began to do so, what difference do you think it might make?

2. Compose a prayer that you could recite upon awakening and one you could recite at bedtime. Try reciting these prayers for a week and discuss the experience.

Responsibilities

By calling God "Father," the language of faith indicates two main things: that God is the first origin of everything and transcendent authority; and that he is at the same time goodness and loving care for all his children. God's parental tenderness can also be expressed by the image of motherhood, [CF. Isa 66:13; Ps 131:2.] which emphasizes God's immanence, the intimacy between Creator and creature. The language of faith thus draws on the human experience of parents, who are in a way the first representatives of God for man. But this experience also tells us that human parents are fallible and can disfigure the face of fatherhood and motherhood . . . no one is father as God is Father.

Catechism, # 239

The Catechism does not present an idealized image of family life. Rather it states "human parents are fallible and can disfigure the face of fatherhood and motherhood." Every year a number of memoirs are published describing people's experiences of abuse by their elders and parental neglect. It's hard to make it into adulthood without being wounded, even by those responsible for caring for us. Despite human frailty, however, parents have the following responsibilities toward their children:

- educate them in the ways of faith, prayer, and virtue;
- appreciate their children as daughters and sons of God "and respect them as *human persons*" *(Catechism, #2222)*;
- "respect and encourage their children's vocations. They should remember and teach that the first calling of the Christian is to follow Jesus" *(Catechism, #2253)*;
- provide good example;
- create a home in which tenderness, mutual affection, forgiveness, respect, fidelity, and service are the norm. Children also contribute to making a house, a mobile home, or an apartment a real home. **G**

Group Talk

1. Describe each of the five qualities of an ideal home as it applies to families. (For example, in a home tenderness means. ..)

2. Do you think that people planning to marry should be required to take a course on parenting? Why or why not? Similar to a driving test, should engaged couples be refused permission to marry until they pass a basic parenting test?

Responsibilities of Children: Respect and Obedience

"A wise child loves discipline."

📖 *Proverbs 13:1*

"With all your heart honor your father, and do not forget the birth pangs of your mother. Remember that it was of your parents you were born; how can you repay what they have given to you?"

📖 *Sirach 7:27–28*

Growing children can in these ways show respect, obedience, and gratitude to their parents: "anticipate their wishes, willingly seek their advice, and accept their just admonitions" (*Catechism*, #2217). Such demonstrations of respect would certainly foster harmony and good will in families. Modern lifestyles, however, work against following through on these suggestions by limiting the time family members have for interacting with one another. For instance, family members often pass each other in the kitchen on their way to and from school, work, games, and practices. Meals are often some form of fast food gulped down in front of the TV or in the van on the way to sports practice or dance lessons.

The pace and distractions of the contemporary world are not caused by children, but today's children have to deal with the effects of them. For instance, a five-year study at a middle school in Wisconsin found that when students ate a healthful diet for a period of time they ended up behaving better in school. In other words, the price that families pay for meals on the run is not just physical but also behavioral, emotional, and perhaps spiritual as well. An unhealthy diet is just one example of factors that undermine family life today.

The fourth commandment implies developing a spirituality of the home. Our homes can be places where we merely spend time, or they can be holy places.

Following the Golden Rule—treat others as you would have them treat you—is a good starting point for making home a holy place.

Adult children have different responsibilities toward their parents. They continue to respect their parents, but they show it in different ways. Children are to give emotional, moral, and material support to their parents, making sure they have what they need to maintain their lives and their dignity.

Writing down one or two things to do at specific times and posting it in a prominent place would be a good first step in helping at home and in honoring our family. **R**

Reflection

1. Do children owe special respect to their parents simply because they are their parents? If not, what then is the basis for parental respect?

2. One dictionary definition for obedient is: "performing what is required, or abstaining from that which is forbidden" (Webster's New Universal Unabridged Dictionary [New York: Simon and Schuster, 1983], page 1232)
   —Do you believe that this is a fair and adequate definition? Would you add or change anything?

3. Name factors that undermine a healthy home life in today's world.

- Julia is twenty-seven years old. She has been battling drug addiction since she graduated from high school. She has not held down a steady job or stayed in school for an entire semester since then. She began rehab programs twice but never lasted the required time, always ending up returning to her drug habit. Often when she visited home she would steal money from her mother's purse to buy drugs. Her parents kept up her health insurance policy for her and discovered that on a few occasions Julia went to a hospital emergency room for treatment related to her addiction or to fights she had while living on the streets. Now Julia has been arrested for stealing and is in jail in a city one thousand miles from where her parents live. She calls her parents from jail asking them to come there and bail her out.
  —If you were Julia's parents, what would you do?

- Diane is forty-five years old. Her mother is seventy-five. Her mother is a widow who still lives alone in the house where Diane and her brother grew up. Diane now lives with her own husband and two teenage children in a town three hours away from her mother. Although mentally alert, her mother's physical health has recently taken a turn for the worse. She refuses to go to a nursing home, but cannot really manage on her own.
  —What is Diane's responsibility toward her mother? What would you recommend that Diane do?

Obedience and Respect Beyond the Family

The fourth commandment *illuminates other relationships in society.* **In our brothers and sisters we see the children of our parents; in our cousins, the descendents of our ancestors; in our fellow citizens, the children of our country; in the baptized, the children of our mother the Church; in every human person, a son or daughter of the One who wants to be called "our Father."**

 **Catechism, #2212**

The fourth commandment doesn't end with parents and family. It also applies to other relationships in society. Parents entrust their children to a variety of caregivers during the fragile years of their growth. Teachers, coaches, bus drivers, and any number of other people attend to children. They have an important function in children's lives and, by taking on their profession, have serious responsibility as well. Those who hold positions of public authority are obligated to show respect for the basic human rights and work to ensure the conditions that promote the exercise of freedom. There is a delicate distinction to be made regarding children and these public authorities. On the one hand, children should obey their reasonable directions. On the other hand, if a child is convinced in conscience that it would be morally wrong to obey a particular order, the child must not do so.

Besides personal caregivers, parental figures exist within the broader community to whom people of all ages owe obedience. When a police officer motions the driver of a car to pull over, he or she should do so. (The authoritative nature of this profession indicates why "impersonating an officer" is such a serious crime.) One way that citizens are responsible for one another is to elect government officials who uphold the common good of society. To this voting responsibility we must bring the light of the gospel, otherwise, as history has frequently demonstrated, our society can easily become tyrannical and dictatorial. Therefore, voting and other forms of participation in public life are duties that fall under the fourth commandment. **R**

For Review...

1. What universal human longing underlies the Peter Pan story?

2. 2. What does it mean to call the family a domestic church?

3. In what sense is the Holy Trinity the model for family life?

4. What does it mean to say that the Catechism does not present an idealized image of family life?

5. Name responsibilities parents have toward their children.

6. Give an example of how modern lifestyles work against wholesome family life.

7. Name two guidelines for making a home a holy place.

8. What subtle distinction exists regarding children and persons in authority?

9. Name two duties citizens have.

Reflection

1. Obeying people in authority has been more or less emphasized during different time periods. (For instance, during the 1950s "Father knows best" was accepted wisdom. By contrast, for a few years during the late 1960s "don't trust anyone over thirty" was a popular slogan among the young.) What do you think is the prevalent attitude among young people toward authority today?

2. If you were arrested for underage drinking at a party where others were drinking but you only had a few sips of beer, what would your reaction be?

___ I broke the law and deserve my punishment.

___ I shouldn't have been there in the first place.

___ Boy, do I have bad luck.

___ The system is unfair.

___ I wonder if my dad can get me off somehow.

___ I learned my lesson.

___ Everybody does it.

___ Other.

3. Will you vote in elections as soon as you are eligible? Why or why not? What steps are you taking now to be an informed, responsible citizen?

Family in the Information Age

The genius of humankind, especially in our times, has produced marvellous technical inventions from creation, with God's help. Mother church is particularly interested in those which directly touch the human spirit and which have opened up new avenues of easy communication of all kinds of news, ideas and directives. . . .

Mother church knows that if these means are properly used they can be of considerable benefit to humanity. They contribute greatly to relaxation, the enrichment of people's minds and the spread and consolidation of the kingdom of God. But the church also knows that they can be used in ways which are damaging and contrary to the Creator's design. Indeed, she grieves with a mother's sorrow at the harm all too often inflicted on society by their misuse.

"Decree on the Mass Media," # 1–2, in *Vatican Council II, the Basic Sixteen Documents,* edited by Austin Flannery, O.P. (Northport, NY: Costello Publishing Company, 1996).

Technological and social developments have transformed family life from what it was just a few decades ago. For example, the fourth commandment states that parents are to be the primary teachers of their children. However, where does most of our education take place—from parents, in school, or in front of a television or computer? What are some of the lessons—both the obvious ones and the more subtle ones—that we have learned from listening to music or watching television? What education are we receiving from the constant barrage of images on the Internet? When a young boy shoots a gun at lifelike figures on a screen at a video arcade, is his activity the moral equivalent of throwing baseballs at milk bottles during a carnival? Family life exists within a social context. The various forms of media we have are important but subtle shapers of modern-day life, including our family life.

When television first became a common fixture in U.S. households, many people proposed that it would be a boon to family life. For some, the image of family members sitting around a television for an hour or so at night was perceived as enhancing family time together. Some people made the same observation when VCRs became popular. Instead of going out to movies, families could watch a movie together in the comfort of their home. Later, the Internet and cell phones offered the means for families to keep in touch even at great distances.

Certainly much good has come from modern information technologies. However, all forms of mass communication deserve moral scrutiny. Such scrutiny—determining their impact on individuals, families, communities, and the world—is difficult since it is so new and ever-changing. **A** (p. 170)

Activity

Before reading about moral issues related to mass communications, answer *Agree, Disagree,* or *Uncertain* to the following statements.

1. On school nights I would restrict television viewing for school-aged children to one hour or less.

2. I would want a child of mine to have a computer and a phone with a private line in his or her room.

3. I see no point in discussing computers and other technology in relation to family life.

4. If someone comes to our home to visit, the television is always turned off.

5. In our home the TV often remains on even if no one is watching it.

6. If nothing on TV particularly interests me, I always stop watching and do something else.

7. In general, I believe that a home should have only one television and one computer located in a family room.

8. I would restrict computer use on school nights to educational purposes only.

9. Because computer skills are very important, I would introduce my children to computers at an early age and encourage their use.

10. Use of chat rooms and instant messenger services has no moral implications.

11. Playing video games is a harmless and healthy recreational activity.

12. I would not allow a child under twelve to play video games featuring violence.

13. If I had a young child, I would strictly limit the amount of time he or she spends playing video games.

14. If I had children over the age of ten, I would purchase a cell phone for each of them with a family plan so that we could be in touch regularly.

15. I would allow my son or daughter to listen to music or watch TV while doing homework.

16. I would allow my son or daughter to go to bed at night listening to a CD player.

Television—A Journey through the Looking Glass

Today's adolescents were born into "the television age." During the advent of TV, Pope Pius XII declared Clare of Assisi to be the patron saint of television. As a saint of the Middle Ages, Clare knew nothing of NBC's Thursday night line-up of shows, Saturday morning cartoons, or MTV. Clare was accustomed to attending daily Mass. One morning she awoke too sick to get out of bed and attend Mass. Mysteriously, the Mass appeared on the wall of her bedroom, just as if she were actually attending it. Because of this experience, the pope decided that Clare would serve as an appropriate patron saint of this new invention, television.

Why did Pope Pius XII conclude that television should have its own patron saint? Perhaps he wanted to caution its users that this new technology could be used for good or for ill. Certainly it represented a great leap forward in the ongoing march of human progress. However, like any new invention, it opened the door to new challenges and to new possibilities of misuse. Not only did television deserve a patron saint, indeed it needed a patron saint to remind people to oversee its use so that it would continue to be an instrument for good. Television viewing can be relaxing, a pleasant diversion, entertaining, culturally enriching, and even educational. There's nothing wrong with watching TV of itself. (Remember, it even has a patron saint.) In this section, however, we will look at certain cautions we should bring to our television viewing.

Television Viewing—A Growing Addiction

In the western world today people are spending between a third and a fifth of their waking lives watching television. . . . In the United States, first graders will spend the equivalent of one entire 24-hour day per week watching television, more time than they spend in the classroom. For most people in the United States, viewing television has become the third most common activity after sleep and work.

Jeremy Murray-Brown, "Video Ergo Sum," in *Video Icons and Values*, edited by Alan M. Olson, Christopher Parr, and Debra Parr (Albany: State University of New York Press, 1991).

Some evening when you're not watching television, take a walk through your neighborhood. As you walk around, notice the number of distinctive glares from wide-screen color televisions lighting up most homes. It's fair to say that many Americans are addicted to television. A question is whether TV addiction is a more benign form of addiction—like drinking coffee—or more hazardous to our health—like smoking cigarettes. **R**

Reflection

1. If your school decided to sponsor a "No TV week," would you participate? On a scale of 1 to 10, how challenging would it be for you not to watch television for a week? What was the longest period you ever went without watching television? Did the experience have a positive, negative, or neutral effect on your life?

2. If you were in charge of creating guidelines for "Making TV a Choice, not a Habit," what would you include in the plan? Make suggestions as specific as possible.

3. List possible reasons why it's a good idea not to watch television.

Seeing the World as a More Hostile Place

Before discussing what is typically shown on television, it is important to think about the effects of TV viewing itself. George Gerbner, a prominent researcher into the effects of television, finds that *the more people watch TV the more they tend to view the world as a hostile, dangerous place.* He calls this unintended side effect of television viewing the **mean-world syndrome.** In other words, our watching television affects our view of other people—especially our view of strangers. Also, while we usually watch TV to relax, increased television viewing actually tends to make us feel more anxious, insecure, and angry. More time spent viewing television means less time visiting people and becoming socially involved. Other leisure activities, even solitary ones such as reading and listening to music, tend to push us out into community involvement. Watching television is a cocoon-like activity. Today, the average American home has one more television in it than it has people living in it. As a result, watching television often takes place apart from other family members.

Sexuality and Violence on the Tube

A second moral implication of TV viewing has to do with the content of most shows. Television shows, even news

programs, stay on the air by attracting an audience. Two activities that have been titillating from time immemorial are sexuality and violence. Films and television make frequent use of both to lure and hold an audience, sometimes even juxtaposing sexuality and violence together.

If you watch TV regularly, you are probably receiving a steady diet of sexually related material. Especially in the United States, television also regularly serves up programming featuring murder, rape, and other acts of violence. This characteristic of television has been studied more than any other—especially the effects on children of watching violence on TV. Most studies agree that watching violent programs does have a negative impact on children.

Tonight on TV—The Make-Believe World of Prime Time

The greatest impact that television has on our moral perspective is subtle and indirect. In large measure, television strongly influences our understanding of what's "in" and what's "out" in regards to looks, clothing, ways of talking and relating, lifestyles, and values. Most television shows stick to a relatively safe and familiar formula. For instance, studies indicate that white males in the prime of their life far outnumber other groups depicted on television. Women are 50 percent more likely to be portrayed as victims than as aggressive in social relationships. Portraying social relationships that involve violence and solving problems through violence fit more neatly into an hour program than other, less dramatic conflicts and resolutions.

One telltale sign that young children are watching an excessive amount of television shows that are inappropriate for their age is that their language is overly mature. By the time the average American child reaches adulthood, she or he has viewed thousands of references—either direct or indirect—to sexual activity by other than married persons. Hardly ever are any possible negative consequences of engaging in sexual intercourse a part of the story line—effects such as unintended and unwanted pregnancies, venereal diseases, a lingering sense of guilt or of being taken advantage of, or uneasiness with physical intimacy unaccompanied by personal bonding. Sitcom sexual activity is portrayed as casual. Real-life sexual intercourse, however, is never casual in its consequences. Many sitcoms with sexually oriented plots air during **prime time** when the largest numbers of children are watching. **A**

prime time—
the evening hours when television viewing is heaviest

Activity

1. A number of years ago two reporters made the following observation about shows on television. Find out whether their observations remain true of prime-time programming today.

   Television. .. has taught over the long haul that the elderly and the poor are unimportant (few are ever shown); that there are far fewer female role models than male ones; and that almost everyone you want to emulate is well off, is white, and often lives in a Manhattan apartment too expensive for average people to afford.

   Stephen Seplow and Jonathan Storm, "How TV Redefined Our Lives," *The Philadelphia Inquirer,* 30 November 1997, page A16.

2. List what you consider to be positive contributions and negative effects of television. Make your list as inclusive as possible.

3. Make a list of five of the most popular shows watched by you and your friends. Rate them on a scale of 1 (very poor) to 10 (very good) based solely on their moral message. Explain your ratings. What conclusions can you draw from this exercise?

4. Do you believe that it is harmful for young children to watch television shows that discuss or depict sexual activity or other adult themes? Why or why not?

Commercials—Selling "the Good Life"

For Review. . .

1. Whom did Pope Pius XII declare to be the patron saint of television? What experience led to her receiving this title?

2. On average, how much time do people in the western world spend watching television?

3. What is the mean-world syndrome?

4. What two types of activities are frequently used in television shows to attract an audience?

5. The American Psychological Association identified three primary consequences of children viewing violence on television. Name them.

6. Name three subtle, indirect messages conveyed by television shows overall.

7. What is a sign that young children are watching television shows inappropriate for their age?

8. What is a primary way that the portrayal of sexual activity on television is usually unrealistic and harmful?

9. What type of television programming tends to be the most creative and professionally done?

For better or for worse, some of the most creative, artistic, and professional material on television can be found in commercials. Ad agencies are often charged with putting together a captivating thirty-second drama that also brings to the public's attention the item and the brand name being advertised. Unlike regular TV programs, commercials are designed to air over and over again, thus making the investment worthwhile. The most successful thirty-second sound bites have created very popular cult figures.

Few people admit that they are influenced by commercials. Companies, however, spend millions of dollars a year on commercials because they have found commercials *do influence* people. Some stations, featuring infomercials and buying clubs, have even gained a portion of the viewer market by running commercials all the time, without noncommercial interruption! Regardless of the success of ads to sell specific products, the constant diet of commercials that TV viewers ingest—on average, over one hundred a day—supports and promotes a particular vision of a consumer culture. In short, more than any specific product, commercials sell values and a version of "the good life." Own this car and you will be happier. Men, use this deodorant and you will become alluring to beautiful women. Women, this is what it means to be beautiful and sexy (for example, the thinner the better). Drink this brand of beer and you're one of the guys. Eating at this fast-food restaurant is as American as apple pie. This brand of soft drink is the choice of a new generation. In other words, people want to be happy, attractive, and one of the crowd. Commercials say, "Buy this product" and you will be all that you want to be.

Is it any wonder that, after TV viewing, one of the most popular pastimes of Americans is shopping? The constant stimulation we receive to buy happiness is a hard sell and extremely hard to resist. Should we even try? Is there a problem in buying and owning lots of stuff? We can't help but consume things, and we have it on the authority of the Bible itself that material things are good. However, one problem with a consumer mentality is that we come to view consumption—buying and owning things—as a cure-all. (For instance, are you bored? Then rent a DVD. Are you depressed? Buying a new outfit or an expensive game will help.) More importantly, an overemphasis on being consumers can prevent us from developing other dimensions of our human existence—being friends and showing love for others, sharing life's goods with those who are truly in need, and recognizing that our dignity cannot be measured by how much we own or by the brand we wear. In a sense, getting caught up in consumption makes us consumer goods!

Commercials are often clever, inventive, captivating, and memorable. Quite possibly you know a number of commercials by heart. The moral concern associated with commercials consists in how much they distract us from, and set us in a direction different from happiness. **G**

Group Talk

1. Name three commercials that are currently popular. Besides the product they sponsor, what values and what image of "the good life" are they selling? Are these values in any way supportive of, in conflict with, or a distraction from the Christian understanding of the good life?

2. Do you agree with the statement "you can't buy happiness"? Does our consumer society promote the opposite message? Is it particularly hard today trying to live out the message that "you can't buy happiness"? If you have taken steps to oppose the notion of buying happiness, how have you done so? What other steps might you take to oppose this notion?

The Impact of Other Media

Computers and the Internet

One of the sad things is that the increase in computer technology does not get you out into the world more, into nature, into the community, dancing, singing, and so on. In fact, as the technology expands, there is more expectation that you will spend more of your life at a screen. . . . The more that the use of computers is demanded of us, the more we shall be taken away from truly deep human experiences.

George Lakoff, in James Brook and Iain A. Boal's *Resisting the Virtual Life* (San Francisco: City Lights Books, 1995).

If you had a child, would you spend money on piano lessons or on computer software? Would you prefer that your child draw with crayons or with a computer program? Would you consider your child's time at a computer to be educational but his or her time playing outdoors to be just for fun? If a young person enters ninth grade with little computer experience, is she or he educationally deprived compared to other students? Has the time you have spent at a computer generally been more beneficial than time spent on other things?

Computers and the Internet hold out great promise for humanity. For no extra charge we can keep in touch with friends in China, make new friends in Europe, and access sources of information worldwide. The same technology that helps make our world a global village can also transform a family into a household of strangers by significantly reducing the amount of time for family interactions.

As the Lakoff quote suggests, the key underlying problem with computers is not so much what we do with them but rather what we don't do because of our time spent on them. In a 1995 survey Americans ranked "computer skills and media technology" third among the skills students will most need in the future. They considered computer skills to be more important than "values," "good citizenship," and "curiosity and love of learning." Our current fascination with computers is misguided if we lose sight of the importance of basic human qualities and values. Using computers need not run counter to concern for other dimensions of human living. However, all use of technology needs to be examined in terms of how it serves personal well-being and the common good. For one thing, we need to be realistic about the limitations of computers. As one computer programmer puts it, "No matter what anyone tells you about the allure of computers, I can tell you for a fact that love cannot be programmed" (Ellen Ulman, in James Brook and Iain A. Boal's *Resisting the Virtual Life* [San Francisco: City Lights Books, 1995]). **R**

Reflection

The 1995 survey found computer skills to be considered very important to Americans.

____ Why do you think such skills ranked so highly in the survey?

____ Do you think this assessment of computer skills has changed today?

____ Where would you place computer skills in terms of "skills young people will need for the future"?

____ What other skills would you also consider to be important?

____ In terms of importance, how would you rank these other skills compared to computer skills?

Video Games: A Different Screen, a Similar Story

"You've watched enough TV. Go do something else." Today when a parent gives this command, it can simply mean that a child goes to another room and begins playing a video game. The essential activity remains the same. A young person sits before a screen. Even though he or she now pushes buttons, time flies by and the same glaze settles over the eyes, as the gaze stays focused on the screen. Video game playing is often a solitary activity, isolating the player from other family members. Additionally, the content of the game most likely includes some form of violence or make-believe destruction. Are video games a problem or a pleasant diversion? As with other technology, it depends on how we use them.

A popular video-game scenario depicts a man traveling through buildings or over the countryside attacking as many "bad guys" as he can. The main variations on this theme center around the type of weapons used, the nature of the victims, and the realism of the destruction portrayed. In some games intended victims are not bad guys at all but rather officers of the law or even innocent bystanders. As the technology improves, the display of violence becomes more and more realistic. Studies indicate that games featuring violence are the favorites of fourth through eighth graders. Following an incident in which two youths who were fond of particularly violent video games entered their high school and killed a teacher and a number of their classmates, one commentator remarked:

Psychologist David Grossman of Arkansas State University, a retired Army officer, thinks "point and shoot" video games have the same effect as military strategies used to break down a soldier's aversion to killing. During World War II, only 15 to 20 percent of all American soldiers fired their weapon in battle. Shooting games in which the target is a man-shaped outline, the Army found, made recruits more willing to "make killing a reflex action."

John Leo, *When Life Imitates Video, US News & World Report*, 3 May 1999, page 14.

This same psychologist refers to violent video games as "murder simulators," functioning in much the same way as computer flight simulators initially train pilots for real flights. If nothing else, he cautions, we as a society need to be attentive to what we are putting into the minds of our young. **A**

Activity

1. Recreation does not need to serve a particular purpose. It is meant simply to be fun. Do you find time spent on video games to be more or less rejuvenating than other recreational activities? Explain.

2. Propose a design for a video game that would not feature violence. Would such a game have any appeal? Why or why not?

3. Research video game use. For example, are boys more likely than girls to play video games? For what age group are games most popular? What kinds of games are most popular?

Information Technology and Youth Culture

The Internet, television, CDs, and DVDs have become an important part of American youth culture. For some parents, video games are the birthday or Christmas gift of choice for that hard-to-buy-for junior high school-aged child. Youth-oriented television and other high-tech products are passive forms of entertainment created by adults to lure youthful consumers. In fact, much that we associate with **youth culture** is really a collection of images and products foisted upon young people rather than created by them. The concept suggests that young people, approximately ages thirteen to eighteen, make up a subgroup that has its own values, its own interests, its own morals, and its own music and other forms of entertainment. If it exists, then this culture is decidedly different from a culture of childhood, adulthood, or old age. In such a scenario, parents, grandparents, and adults in general can be viewed as people who are "out of it" and at worst a necessary evil. Thus the youth culture concept can undermine the fourth commandment.

What does Catholicism contribute to a discussion about culture and cultural conflicts? We have already mentioned Vatican Council II, the most recent worldwide gathering of bishops. The Council took place during the 1960s—the height of modern cultural upheaval and the beginning stages of today's youth culture. At the time, the bishops wrote that they recognized that "in each nation and social group there is a growing number of men and women who are conscious that they themselves are the architects and molders of their community's culture" (*The Church in the Modern World, #55*). The bishops believe that people, including young people, should be the authors of culture and not just passive inheritors of it.

Given this dynamic view of culture, the bishops of Vatican II propose, "one must aim at encouraging the human spirit to develop its faculties of wonder, of understanding, of contemplation, of forming personal judgments and cultivating a religious, moral and social sense" (*#59*). Does spending time on a particular computer video game or watching a particular television program achieve any of these aims? What we do either adds to or detracts from a wholesome culture—and a wholesome family life. What are the culture and the family that we are creating? **G**

youth culture—
the belief that young people have values, interests, and activities distinct from those of other age groups

For Review...

1. According to the text what is the key underlying problem for young people regarding computers?

2. In a 1995 survey how highly did Americans rank computer skills as needed for the future?

3. What type of activity is most popular in video games?

4. According to one psychologist, what effect can "point and shoot" video games have on young people?

5. According to the bishops of Vatican Council II, what role should people play in culture?

...Conclusion

In societies that function well, children honor their parents and elders, and parents and elders oversee the development and welfare of children. The fourth commandment instructs us always to aspire to such a society. Families today must contend with many concerns that can help or hinder their welfare. The young have access to technological marvels that never existed before. How they negotiate the use of these gadgets will help determine their personal and familial lives. In the end, we are not alone in our task. Honor and respect within families mirror the very inner workings of the Holy Trinity.

Group Talk

1. Do you believe that youth culture exists in our country? If so, what are the dominant characteristics of this culture, both positive and negative?

2. Is youth culture created more by entrepreneurs "selling" it or by young people creating it?

3. Are you a participant in youth culture? Explain.

Model of Morality

Mary Powers

An incident that occurred on December 4, 1969, brought a problem to public view that had been simmering for some time—police brutality in Chicago. Police raided an apartment where Black Panther leader Fred Hampton lived. Police fired more than a hundred bullets into the apartment. Only one bullet came from inside. Hampton died; four others were seriously wounded.

Many people in the Chicago area felt that there needed to be greater accountability of police actions to prevent unwarranted deaths in the future. One of those people was Mary Powers. Even though she was a wife and mother of four children living in a Chicago suburb, she knew she had to do something. She joined Citizens Alert, an organization dedicated to stopping police abuse. The Chicago group was made up of political novices like Mary. However, they found out about the Chicago Police Board, which met regularly to oversee police matters. The Citizens Alert group managed to find out when and where the board met, and they maneuvered their way into what had always been a closed-to-the-public meeting.

Mary and her friends did their homework to find out about incidents needing investigation, and they kept showing up at the board's meetings. In time, the board didn't just rubber-stamp the police superintendent's recommendations as they had always done. Under the watchful eyes of informed citizens, board members began to listen to the stories of possible brutality by police. Four years after Mary's initial visit to its meetings, the board established an office made up of thirty full-time civilians empowered to investigate police misconduct.

Since joining Citizens Alert in 1969 Mary has stayed active. In 2003, at the age of eighty, she stepped down as its executive director. Nonetheless, she remains an active member, working on a number of related projects. Thanks to her initiative, Citizens Alert organizations have been formed in a number of communities, and Mary has established a national organization dedicated to investigating and stopping police brutality.

The fourth commandment has to do with respect, and respect includes not turning our backs on people who need us. Mary Powers is a model of someone who has a family, but does not limit her care and concern to her immediate family alone. Like Jesus himself, Mary expanded her family circle to include people who would otherwise be forgotten or overlooked. Those involved in law enforcement have a difficult task. Most of us would like nothing to do with them until we need them. Even more so, when it comes to those who find themselves on the wrong end of encounters with law enforcement, we would like to dismiss them with, "they get what they deserve." Mary questioned, examined, and discovered that at times people were mistreated or hurt unjustifiably. Isn't this expansion of familial concern what Jesus has in mind for all of us?

Based on Robert J. McGrory's "Faith and the Power of Persistence," National Catholic Reporter, 39:34 (18 July 2003), pages 9–10.

Celebrating Morality

Opening Prayer: Holy Family of Nazareth, guide us in our own struggles to be family. May our homes be places where we can say that Christ is truly present. Help us be attentive to all the little things that make a home a safe, nurturing, life-giving, and loving place. And may we, inspired by the Holy Spirit, go forth from our own families to care for others. Amen.

Reading: 1 Corinthians 13

Litany for the Family: (Respond to each statement with: "Christ is with us."

- When we greet other family members and ask about their day. . .

- When we struggle to say what we mean even when it is difficult. . .

- When we listen and try to understand. . .

- When we celebrate birthdays and holidays and make room for family days. . .

- When we restrain from anger even if we believe we're judged unfairly. . .

- When we share with others what's going on in our lives. . .

- When we place the good of another above our own. . .

- When we adhere to family ground rules. . .

- When we ask for forgiveness, accept apologies, admit when we're wrong, and say I'm sorry. . .

- When we pray for and with one another. . .

- When we do what's expected of us. . .

- When we do more than what's expected of us. . .

- When we say, "I love you". . .

Concluding Prayer: Jesus, our brother, by being human you entered into life within a family where you grew in wisdom and age and grace. Fill us with your own vision of an ever-expanding family circle so that we may recognize our place in the one human family in union with you, the Father, and the Holy Spirit. Amen.

10

CHERISHING EACH PERSON:
Abortion, Euthanasia, and Respect for Life

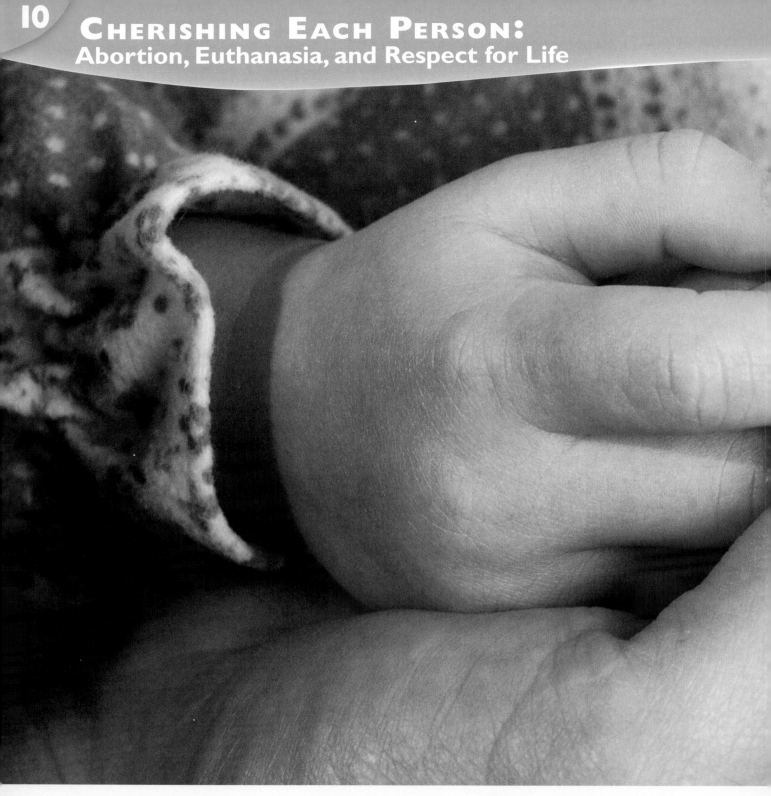

Chapter Overview

- The fifth commandment mandates us to respect the life of the unborn.
- Respect for life is a principle that guides us in caring for those who are sick or who are near death.
- The fifth commandment forbids intentional euthanasia.
- Church teaching addresses the issues of life support and physician-assisted suicide.

The fifth commandment lays out our basic obligation regarding human life in very direct language: Do not kill. In positive terms it means treat human life in all its manifestations and in all stages of its development with the special care that it deserves. Abortion and euthanasia are two affronts to a spirit of reverence for human beings. Both are hotly contested issues charged with strong emotions. As with all matters where human life lies in the balance, we are asked to step back and evaluate these practices in light of their impact on the dignity of the human person.

Before we begin...

Under the topic of respect for life are many issues that are being hotly debated today (e.g. partial-birth abortion, stem-cell research, to name just a few).

1. Name as many specific issues as you can that are related to respect for life.

2. Which issues are related to abortion?

3. Which issues are related to euthanasia?

Let us pray...

God our Father, Creator of the universe, support us in our continuing attempts to know your will and to follow it. Even in the midst of constant change and new challenges, may we compassionately join together with others in a search for truth. In our deliberations about matters of life and death, may we never forget the dignity and worth of each person. Amen.

Respect for Life

"When I look at your heavens, the work of your fingers, the moon and the stars that you have established; what are human beings that you are mindful of them, mortals that you care for them? Yet you have made them a little lower than God, and crowned them with glory and honor."

Psalm 8:3–5

One version of the medieval legend of Sir Launfal has the knight leaving his castle heading out in search of the Holy Grail. As he leaves his castle he passes a beggar, a leper with his arms outstretched asking for a bite to eat. Launfal, eager to find the Grail, hurries by and soon begins a series of adventures that in time leave him beaten down and destitute. He makes

his way back to his castle. He is on foot now since he has no horse. His clothes are in tatters, and his only sustenance is a hardened, stale piece of bread. When he arrives outside of his castle, lo and behold the same beggar sits beside the road. Launfal takes out his morsel of bread,

breaks it in half, and shares it with the beggar. He then breaks the ice on a nearby lake and gives the man a drink. As he does so, an amazing thing happens. The beggar now stands beside Launfal tall and erect. He is Jesus Christ! After all his efforts to attain the Grail, the cup used by Christ at the Last Supper, here was Christ right outside his castle in the guise of a needy, overlooked human being.

Perhaps you know other stories with a similar theme. Jesus went to great lengths to tell us the same story. Human life is sacred for two reasons: God created us; therefore we have a special relationship with him. Jesus takes this notion even further. Humans are holy because they are creations of God, made in his image and likeness. Thus, Jesus wants us to be attentive to the needs of those who are most vulnerable and unable to care for themselves.

Murder is wrong because all human life is precious in God's eyes. The fifth commandment enjoins us to consider all the ways that human life is under attack. It also requires us to think creatively about how we can foster a culture of life so that human beings view one another with the spirit of reverence that Jesus asks of us. With Sir Launfal, we are asked to look at those who are fragile and needy within our own society that too often promotes death or neglect rather than cherishes every life.

Abortion and Respect for the Unborn

For more than thirty years, no moral issue has been more divisive and controversial than abortion, the deliberate cessation of prenatal human life. If we polled a group of North Americans and asked them to name the first moral issue that came to their minds, the vast majority would probably answer "abortion." The emotional intensity surrounding abortion often clouds any attempt at an open exchange of viewpoints on the issue. Discussions about the rightness or wrongness of abortion often focus on peripheral rather than central questions. For instance, abortion debates often center on a woman's right to privacy, a woman's right over her own body, or on the acceptability of abortion in certain circumstances but not in others.

From its conception, the child has the right to life. Direct abortion, that is, abortion willed as an end or as a means, is a "criminal" practice (GS 27 § 3), gravely contrary to the moral law. The Church imposes the canonical penalty of excommunication for this crime against human life.

(Catechism, #2322)

A Single Mother's Story

When Elisha became pregnant in her junior year of high school, she initially felt as though her life was over. She was certain about one thing: No matter what anybody else thought or said, she would never have an abortion. She managed to have her child, a healthy baby boy, and to make it through high school. Now she works and also takes college courses part time. Life has been a struggle for Elisha these past few years. She would caution other young people not to engage in premarital sex. Raising a child as a single mother has been an unending struggle. Sometimes she doesn't think she will make it. She had to grow up fast and learn to be responsible as she provides for herself and her son. However, every night when she hears about her son's day at kindergarten, she is thankful for the beautiful gift that her child continues to be in her life. **G**

Group Talk

Abortion is a much-debated issue in religious, political, and social circles. No doubt you have heard many viewpoints on it. List all the different arguments and opinions that you can think of regarding abortion. As you read through this section, keep this list in mind. Then write a response to each argument and opinion in light of Church teaching on the subject.

When Does Human Life Begin?

The central question in the abortion debate is *When does human life begin?* More precisely, when in the course of the continuing development from fertilized egg to newborn infant does a human person exist? Disagreement on this pivotal question leads to disagreement even about what abortion actually involves.

Someone who believes that a human person does not exist until later stages of prenatal development sees respect for life primarily in terms of concern for the life and health of the pregnant woman. In other words, if no human person exists until sometime late in pregnancy or only at birth, then denying a pregnant woman an opportunity to terminate her pregnancy is denying her access to a medical procedure that she may consider benefits her and harms no one.

In January 1973 the U.S. Supreme Court ruled on the legality of abortion in its famous *Roe v. Wade* decision. The majority on the court ruled that a woman could not be denied her "right to privacy," which includes a right to abortion. They did determine that privacy is not an absolute right. Therefore, the state could intervene when an unborn child reaches "viability"—the ability to live outside the womb. However, even then the health and well-being of the mother supercedes the right to life of the unborn, with some stipulations, even up to birth itself.

Despite the Supreme Court's ruling, the inherent dignity and rights of any unborn child are not up for debate. Human life is to be respected and protected from conception. Human beings must be recognized as possessing the rights of a person from the very beginning of life. The paramount, inviolable right of every being is the right to life itself.

The Beginning of Life

In 1974, soon after the *Roe v. Wade* decision, the Vatican's *Declaration on Procured Abortion* taught about the moral evil of abortion.

Concerning the beginning of life, the document states:

From the time that the ovum is fertilized, a life is begun which is neither that of the father nor of the mother; it is rather the life of a new human with his own growth. It would never be made human if it were not human already. . . . Modern genetic science offers clear confirmation. It has demonstrated that from the first instant there is established the program of what this living being will be: a man, this individual man with his characteristic aspects already well determined. Right from fertilization the adventure of a human life begins, and each of its capacities requires time—a rather lengthy time—to find its place and to be in a position to act. The least that can be said is that present science, in its most evolved state, does not give any substantial support to those who defend abortion (#s 12–13).

The *Declaration on Procured Abortion* makes four essential observations concerning the beginning of life.

1. A new and distinct human life begins at the moment of conception.
2. Information from modern science affirms the statement "Right from fertilization the adventure of a human life begins."
3. Questions about the beginning of life and abortion are not just scientific; they are more properly philosophical and moral. That is, science provides us with intricate information about the physical development of a fetus. However, it is not the role of science to make a judgment about the moral status of a fetus. In other words, we cannot simply step back and expect science to determine when a human person begins to exist. *What constitutes a human person?* is a philosophical and religious question. Sacred Tradition and Sacred Scripture's teachings about what is a human and how a human is to be treated must play a deciding role in answering this pivotal question.

> **"**More than a fifth of all pregnancies around the world end in abortion and unplanned pregnancy remains common. Each year, about 35 of every 1,000 women of childbearing age have abortions. The rates are similar in developed and developing countries, although abortion laws are generally more restrictive in poorer nations. **"**
>
> Beth Gardiner, "Fifth of the World's Pregnancies End in Abortion, Report Says," *The Philadelphia Inquirer*, January 22, 1999, page A28.

4. If we are not sure when, in the course of development, a human person exists, then we should presume that a human person is present at the earliest stage. This statement is addressed to people who say, "How can we be certain when a human person first exists? If we can't be sure, shouldn't the decision be a matter of choice?" From the document's teaching, it can be concluded that, in case of doubt, we must always decide in favor of the belief that the unborn fetus is a human person. To deliberately decide otherwise violates the fifth commandment's injunction against taking human life.

Abortion and Values in Conflict

People who argue that abortion is morally acceptable raise many questions. Their arguments often demonstrate sensitivity to the difficulties that can accompany pregnancy and having children:

- What about in the case of rape—isn't abortion permitted then?
- How about if we know that a child will be seriously deformed—shouldn't that be considered?
- Shouldn't the physical and psychological health of the pregnant woman be considered?

The *Declaration on Procured Abortion* recognizes that women seek abortions to prevent physical, psychological, financial, or other hardships to themselves or to their unborn child. It also recognizes that circumstances leading a person to contemplate abortion are often difficult, at times even tragic. However, the declaration calls people to consider the fundamental value of life that underlies an abortion decision. The right to life itself, once conceived, outweighs all the other values and concerns involved. **R A**

The gravity of the problem comes from the fact that in certain cases, perhaps in quite a considerable number of cases, by denying abortion one endangers important values which men normally hold in great esteem and which may sometimes even seem to have priority. We do not deny these very great difficulties. It may be a serious question of health, sometimes of life or death, for the mother; it may be the burden represented by an additional child, especially if there are good reasons to fear that the child will be abnormal or retarded; it may be the importance attributed in different classes of society to considerations of honor or dishonor, of loss of social standing, and so forth. We proclaim only that none of these reasons can ever objectively confer the right to dispose of another's life, even when that life is only beginning. . . . Life is too fundamental a value to be weighed against even very serious disadvantages. (# 14).

For Review...

1. According to the text, what is the central question in the abortion debate? What are the two dominant positions people have on this question?

2. List the four key points made about the beginning of life in the *Declaration on Procured Abortion.*

3. What stand does this document take regarding the many difficulties that pregnancy can cause for some people?

Reflection

One commentator draws the following analogy to dramatize the position that, in the face of doubt about the status of a fetus, abortion is wrong: If a hunter hears a rustling noise behind some bushes and he or she is uncertain whether it's a deer or a human, the hunter is not justified in firing a gun in that direction.

- What point is the analogy trying to make?

- Is it a valid analogy for helping us understand the abortion debate?

- Write your comments on this analogy.

Activity

Write a Respect for Life prayer, focusing on some concerns raised in this chapter.

Moral Issues at the End of Life

The story of the suffering, death, and Resurrection of Jesus holds out hope for all of us faced with death. It also brings a vision of reverence for life to the many moral issues surrounding death and dying. Today, death and dying have become more complicated than people would ever have envisioned even a half-century ago. For the end of life as for its beginning, each new medical or technological advancement brings with it new moral dilemmas. As with all areas of medical ethics, the dignity of the human person and respect for life are the principles underlying evaluation of proper care and treatment of those who are sick, near death, or dying. **R**

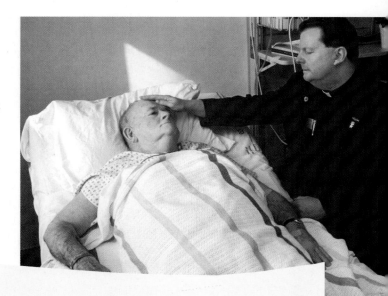

Reflection

Before reading this section discuss and write up a response to the following questions.

1. Over the past few decades, what developments have shaped moral discussion about death and dying?

2. In our tradition there is a patron saint of a "happy death"—Saint Joseph, who was blessed to die in the presence of Mary and Jesus. Describe the role, if any, that each of the following would play in fostering a happy death. What are some policies and practices that could help people experience such a death? If you were to arrange this list so that it reflects your own concerns, what would the list look like?

• a minimum of pain and suffering

• the presence of caring family and friends

• a deep faith and hope in God's love

• being in God's grace

• reception of the Anointing of the Sick and holy viaticum (Holy Communion for the dying person)

• presence of a Catholic priest or chaplain

• a sense of being "right" with God and other people

• a firm belief in an afterlife

• a sense of personal accomplishment

• strong ties with family and friends

• knowledgeable and compassionate healthcare providers

• the ability to make choices

What is Death?

Death, friend or foe? Because of hope in an afterlife, should we actually approach death serenely or even welcome it? Does our view of death and dying

help us in responding to specific moral challenges brought on by modern medical advances?

At the very start of history, the first man and woman were immune from death. Original sin changed that and now we must all suffer death. No one escapes. Even Jesus died and, by doing so, conquered death and reversed the damage done by the sin of our first parents. Jesus told us, *"I am the resurrection and the life. Those who believe in me, even though they die, will live, and everyone who lives and believes in me will never die. Do you believe this?"*

John 11:25–26

We learn that "all of us who have been baptized into Christ Jesus were baptized into his death" *(Romans 6:3)*. Through Baptism, then, we have already died with Christ and are on a pilgrimage to a new life. Death is the end of that pilgrimage, because it is the portal to eternal life with God. As Saint Teresa of Ávila said, "I want to see God and, in order to see him, I must die" *(quoted in Catechism, #1011)*.

Death, nonetheless, inspires some of our worst fears. Despite what we have learned from Jesus, Scripture, and the Church, we may still believe that death is a journey into an unknown darkness. Additionally, death is often identified with tragic endings, the sadness of losing friends and family members, weeping, pain, and helplessness. But the suffering often associated with dying should not blind us to the blessings Jesus gave us through his own suffering, death, and Resurrection. His suffering and death led to resurrection—for himself and for us who believe in him. In other words, death is an enemy, but an enemy overcome.

As we look at specific moral issues related to death and dying, it is important to keep in mind this balance that Catholic teaching gives us. For instance, we are concerned about pain relief and compassionate care and comfort for the dying. Jesus said, "Cure the sick!" *(Matthew 10:8)*, and the church strives to do so by caring for the sick and interceding for them in prayer. Additionally, the Church is very concerned about how we can best enable one another to die a happy death. On this point it is important to recall that the root of the word health is the same as that for salvation. In the end, therefore, being healed means not avoiding death but being saved—life with Christ after death. If we don't distinguish between our concern for healing and Catholic teaching about death and resurrection, we can end up with simplistic but misguided positions on some important moral dilemmas. **A G**

The Catechism on Suicide

—Everyone is responsible for his life before God who has given it to him. . . . We are stewards, not owners, of the life God has entrusted to us. It is not ours to dispose of. *(#2280)*

—Suicide . . . offends love of neighbor because it unjustly breaks the ties of solidarity with family, nation, and other human societies to which we continue to have obligations. Suicide is contrary to love for the living God. *(#2281)*

—Grave psychological disturbances, anguish, or grave fear of hardship, suffering, or torture can diminish the responsibility of the one committing suicide. *(#2282)*

—We should not despair of the eternal salvation of persons who have taken their own lives. By ways known to him alone, God can provide the opportunity for salutary repentance. The Church prays for persons who have taken their own lives. *(#2283)*

—Suicide is seriously contrary to justice, hope, and charity. It is forbidden by the fifth commandment. *(#2325)*

Activity

1. Fold a piece of paper in half. On one side of the paper, draw a symbolic representation of life. On the other side, draw a symbolic representation of death. Open up your paper so that both drawings are visible. What do they suggest about your view of death?

2. What are the prevailing views toward death and dying present in our contemporary society? How are they similar to or different from what you believe to be a Catholic view toward death and dying?

Group Talk

Do you agree that it is important not to reduce "dying well" merely to dying a painless death? What else might be involved in dying well?

The Quality of Life

- Everything changed for Laurie the day she received the diagnosis. In fact, everything changed for her family, her friends, and her classmates as well. The tumor was cancerous. Surgery to remove it provided some relief, but the cancer itself had already spread. She began aggressive treatments immediately. Side effects were not pleasant. Laurie continued attending school, but she no longer looked seventeen.

  Her classmates didn't know what to do. Usually it was Laurie who set them at ease and calmed their fears. Even though it was "business as usual" at school, everyone had it in the back of their minds: Laurie, our friend, is sick; she may be dying. Not surprisingly, Catholic teaching about life and death took on special meaning during liturgies and religion classes at Laurie's school. Although some students questioned and got angry with God, Laurie's faith grew stronger. She sustained her classmates and inspired everyone with her courage and trust in God.

  Laurie strengthened her spirit by receiving the Sacrament of the Sick and Holy Communion. She fought the spreading cancer as best she could, but her body grew progressively weaker even while her spirit remained strong. Appropriately enough, Laurie's death came shortly after Valentine's Day, a day when Laurie was showered with love. The funeral was tear-filled and sad but also uplifting. Death claimed victory; but those gathered in the church celebrated that a greater victory had been won for Laurie—the victory of eternal life in Christ.

- It happened suddenly. While vacationing in Florida Tanya collapsed in front of her husband Bill. Without warning she lost consciousness and stopped breathing. Bill called immediately for medical assistance, and paramedics arrived in just over fifteen minutes. They were able to revive Tanya's breathing and rushed her to a nearby hospital.

  After stabilizing her condition and completing a series of tests, doctors notified Bill that Tanya, his beautiful and energetic sixty-seven-year-old wife, was now over 90 percent brain dead. Artificial nutrition and hydration along with the oxygen she was receiving could keep her functioning at this level indefinitely, but barring a miracle she would never regain consciousness.

  Bill gathered with other family members to ponder the best course of action. Both Bill and Tanya had written a living will—a statement about what they wanted done if such an event occurred. The medical staff treating Tanya explained to the family available options and potential consequences of each one. Through their sadness the family talked and prayed over what to do. They consulted their parish priest for advice about the Church's teaching. They were in a dilemma: They didn't want to let go of their wife and mother, but they also wanted rest and peace for her.

- Now forty-one, Mack has been a paraplegic since the crushing block he received while playing football in his senior year of high school. For the past twenty-some years, he has maintained a steady level of activity, even though his condition makes even simple tasks burdensome. Fortunately, Mack has received help from some family members who assist him on a regular basis and from home-care workers paid for by insurance. Lately, his pain has increased, and he has been wondering if it's all worth it. Wouldn't everyone be better off without him? What does he really have to live for? Does he contribute anything to those around him other than added hardship? Can he take living like this much longer? He has decided that he wants to consider all the options available to him. **A**

Activity

Today, in addition to priests, laypeople also make up hospital ministry teams. Imagine that you are a member of such a team. For the three persons mentioned above—Laurie, Tanya, and Mack—write a prayer that would be appropriate to say if they ended up in your hospital.

Euthanasia

When we move from a general discussion about Catholic views on death and dying to specific moral issues related to the topic, we come quickly to the topic of euthanasia. Just as moral discussion about abortion centers on the question of when human life begins, so the morality of euthanasia is complicated by questions about when human life ends. In life, our lungs automatically inhale life-giving oxygen, our heart pumps blood throughout the body, and our brain serves as a control center for all

the conscious and unconscious activities that keep the body functioning. When a person is dead, these essential life systems no longer function. Thus, the threshold between life and death would seem to be clearly defined. Yet, more and more we are hearing of instances in which this threshold is not so clear. Because of

increased complexity in the dying process resulting from improved medical technology, important new moral decisions face us.

Church teaching makes a distinction between allowing a person to die and euthanasia. "Allowing a person to die" means "discontinuing medical procedures that are burdensome, dangerous, extraordinary, or disproportionate to the expected outcome" *(Catechism, #2278)*. We will discuss this later in the chapter.

Euthanasia has come to mean mercy killing—mercifully putting to death someone who is dying or who is experiencing extreme suffering, as we might put to death a dying beloved pet. Pope John Paul II gave the following definition: "Euthanasia in the strict sense is understood to be an action or omission which of itself and by intention causes death, with the purpose of eliminating all suffering" *(The Gospel of Life, #65)*. Since it is an act that is directly contrary to the dignity of the human person, euthanasia is a violation of the fifth commandment. In a word, it is murder. However, to understand the moral issues surrounding euthanasia today we need to distinguish among a number of actions and inactions that sometimes are identified with the term.

euthanasia—
"an action or an omission which, of itself or by intention, causes the death of handicapped, sick, or dying persons—sometimes with an attempt to justify the act as a means of eliminating suffering" *(Catechism, Glossary)*.

Euthanasia in the Strict Sense

Notice that Blessed Pope John Paul II referred to "euthanasia in the strict sense." In other words, he recognizes that sometimes people use the term to refer to actions that are not, strictly speaking, euthanasia. He also is pointing out that the same action may or may not fall under this strict definition of *euthanasia* depending on the kind of act involved, the intention behind the action, and the circumstance surrounding the action. Here are terms used in moral discussions about euthanasia today.

Active or direct euthanasia means taking deliberate steps to end the life of a suffering and incurably ill person. This is what the pope means by "euthanasia in the strict sense." This action may happen with (voluntary) or without (involuntary) the consent of the patient. Regardless of whether the euthanasia was performed at the request of the suffering and dying person or decided upon by another, active euthanasia involves the direct and intentional taking of life.

Passive or indirect euthanasia means deliberately not taking steps to prevent a sick person's death, precisely with the desire and intention that this withholding will lead to or cause his or her death. An example would be refusing a relatively minor, almost always successful, stomach surgery for a Down's syndrome newborn because he or she is a person who is developmentally disabled and the parents would prefer the child not to survive. In this instance, although it involves an action not taken, the intention—just like active euthanasia—is to take a life, however well- or ill-meaning the intention. Like active euthanasia, this action may happen with or without a patient's consent. Passive or indirect euthanasia, like active euthanasia, is wrong because the intention is the taking of a life. **R**

Reflection

In 1968 Harvard Medical School first listed criteria to indicate when a person is "brain dead." In 1981 a presidential commission updated these criteria. Find a recent statement that specifies what factors are used to determine if a person could be declared dead. (Such a determination carries many ramifications. For instance, defining what constitutes the moment of death is important because of the quick decisions that must be made in cases of organ donors.) Write a report on the factors that in recent decades have made the criteria for determining death more and more complicated.

Allowing Death to Occur Is Not the Same as Killing

If you visited a hospital that features the latest medical equipment, you would notice the array of machines, monitors, and other apparatus available for seriously ill or injured patients. This array of medical technology can cause some people to fear that, if their health becomes seriously impaired, the decision about whether to live or die will be out of their hands. They imagine with dread the possibility of being kept alive without any hope of serious recovery. With all the medical treatments and equipment available today, the dying person can be forgotten. Keeping the body functioning even at minimal levels can become the driving force behind treatment.

For instance, the body functions of a comatose person with no medical hope of recovery can remain operating indefinitely with the help of machines and artificial nutrients.

The Declaration on Euthanasia addresses this problem by stating, "When inevitable death is imminent in spite of the means used, it is permitted in conscience to take the decision to refuse forms of treatment that would only secure a precarious and burdensome prolongation of life" *(#4)*. This statement acknowledges that at times modern medical technology and medical practices will not cure a person but will only delay death indefinitely. In such cases, medical treatments that do no more than prolong life at great expense or with excessive burden may be discontinued. Such a decision is not "mercy killing" or euthanasia in the strict sense, since it allows the natural dying process to occur. Thus, the focus is on foregoing excessively burdensome treatment, not on killing the patient. It must be pointed out that such "over-zealous" treatment is unnecessary, as long as the intention is not to directly take life *(Catechism #2278)*.

Medical personnel who work with dying patients often find themselves faced with decisions that rely on these subtle but important distinctions. For instance, what is acceptable when a frail and

incurably ill person is experiencing pain and has been prescribed medicine to relieve the pain? At some point,

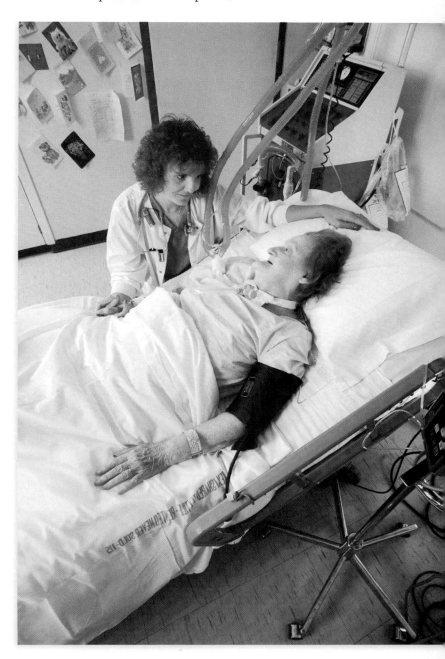

increasing the dosage of certain pain medications might inadvertently hasten or contribute to death. In this situation it is important to recall Pope John Paul II's definition of euthanasia in which he reminds us that the intention behind an act must be considered.

Further Medical Issues

ordinary means of life support— medical procedures that offer sufficient or reasonable benefits without excessive or undue burdens to the patient or his or her family

extraordinary means of life support— medical procedures that offer little hope of benefit and which cause undue or excessive burdens to the patient or his or her family

Around fifty years ago when modern medical technology was making great advances, Pope Pius XII made a distinction between taking ordinary means of preserving life versus taking extraordinary means. He indicated that extraordinary means of life support need not be taken. Since then Church leaders have further clarified the difference between **ordinary (necessary) means** and **extraordinary (unnecessary) means**. The important distinction here is not so much a matter of what is done, as it is a matter of the burdens and benefits of available procedures. In other words, the questions to ask are: *(1) What are the emotional, physical, and financial costs and the risks—the burdens—of a particular procedure on a patient, the family, and the community? (2) What are the likely results—the benefits—of performing the procedure?* Thus, life-support measures that can reasonably be expected to improve a seriously ill person's condition are ordinary means.

Likewise, nutrition and hydration are ordinary means. On the other hand, procedures that merely delay death temporarily but that offer no real hope of reversing the dying process tend to fall into the category of extraordinary means.

Defined in these terms, the same medical interventions can be labeled ordinary in one situation and extraordinary in another. For example, if an otherwise healthy person suddenly stops breathing, putting that person on a ventilator would be expected and necessary if at all possible. Timely use of a ventilator could lead to recovery and avoid death. However, if a person were already near death due to complications from cancer and then stops breathing, a ventilator might be an extraordinary life support, optional rather than necessary. Depending on circumstances and intention, withholding treatment may or may not be euthanasia.

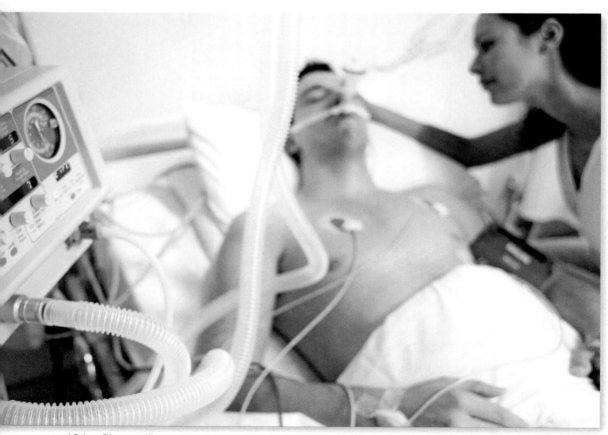

- A seventy-year-old woman suffers her third stroke in five years, leaving her paralyzed on her left side and unable to raise herself from her bed without assistance. She notifies the nursing home staff that if she stops breathing she would like not to be revived.

- A sixty-five-year-old man discovers that he has colon cancer. His father died of this disease many years ago, and the man fears undergoing the same suffering. He plans to take a lethal dosage of painkillers before the condition gets much worse.

- A couple's daughter is born with severe mental retardation and also with a major blockage (requiring extensive surgery) in her intestines preventing her from taking in regular nourishment. Since the parents do not want their child to live with the degree of retardation that doctors indicate she suffers from, the couple refuses to sign papers allowing doctors to remove the blockage. Without this operation the child will soon die.

- An eighty-five-year-old woman is hospitalized with numerous ailments. She suffers from pneumonia, and persistent coughing has weakened her considerably. She complains of chest pain and is prescribed morphine that is administered intravenously to help ease her pain. During the night she calls for a nurse and requests additional pain medicine. According to the patient's medical chart, her doctor permits an increase in morphine as requested. The nurse knows that with the woman's already terminal condition, the amount of morphine being prescribed might indirectly hasten her death. Nonetheless, the nurse does increase the dosage. **G**

Group Talk

Determine whether the above decisions fall under Pope John Paul II's definition of "euthanasia in the strict sense." Explain your decisions.

Physician-Assisted Suicide

A fairly recent addition to the euthanasia debate is the question of **physician-assisted suicide**. This practice is really a form of active-voluntary euthanasia, since it involves a seriously ill person seeking out a physician to assist him or her in ending his or her own life. Until recently, the question of medical professionals either killing or helping in the killing of their patients wouldn't even have been considered. Such actions go against longstanding professional principles of health care. The role of the physician is to heal, as well as to provide comfort and care, not to kill. Now physician-assisted suicide has become a matter of national debate. As might be expected, the impetus for legalization of this practice originates within the same concerns that lead some people to advocate euthanasia in general. That is, they hope that the availability of a doctor's assistance in ending their life will free them from needless pain, physical and mental debilitation, and undue prolongation of the death process. Part of their hope may be that by killing themselves they will not become a burden to their loved ones or deplete their family's financial resources.

Physician-assisted suicide seems to reflect the quick-fix mentality that permeates our society. Relying on physician-assisted suicide rules out seeking alternative approaches to meeting the fears and concerns of seriously ill persons. It also fails to see possible benefits that can be achieved from time spent undergoing the natural dying process and preparing for death, both for the patient as well as for his or her family and friends. In his encyclical *The Gospel of Life*, Pope John Paul II called this practice an instance of "false mercy." He asks, what does a person who seeks assistance in ending his or her life really want? He suggests the following: "The request which arises from the human heart in the supreme confrontation with suffering and death, especially when faced with the temptation to give up in utter desperation, is above all a request for companionship, sympathy and support in the time of trial. It is a plea for help to keep on hoping when all human hopes fail" *(#67)*.

The pope recognizes that advocating physician-assisted suicide can arise from positive motivations, from a caring and compassionate human heart. However, he asks people to look behind such a request. Every suicide is a plea for help. The pope sees physician-assisted suicide as a plea for companionship, sympathy, and support. It is a cry for help in attaining the hope beyond human hope that the Catholic message provides. He points out that taking a life, even one's own and even during difficult times, attacks the fundamental respect for the dignity of human life that should underlie all decisions about how to view people and how to treat them. That is, human life is precious, even to the very end.

Suffering does not diminish the preciousness of life, nor does imminent death or apparent uselessness. The pope implies that, instead of the false mercy of suicide or euthanasia, we serve human life better when we address the deep concerns that sick and dying persons have. **R**

...Conclusion

Catholic moral teaching calls for respect for human life. Today, due to earthshaking developments in science and technology, the very concept *human life* has been called into question. Legalized abortion has been with us for a number of decades. We need guidance when it comes to decisions accompanying the beginning and end of life. The moral dimension accompanying medical procedures must never be lost amid the high-tech atmosphere that surrounds them. In the midst of the challenges we face, it is important for us always to heed the words of Scripture *(Deuteronomy 30:19)*: "Choose life."

For Review...

1. What experience of Jesus' gives us hope in facing death?

2. Which two views about death are balanced in Catholic teaching?

3. What is the difference between active and passive euthanasia?

4. What is the difference between voluntary and involuntary euthanasia?

5. Which two questions determine whether a life-support measure is an ordinary or an extraordinary means?

6. What is the Catholic teaching regarding extraordinary means to preserve life?

7. Define *physician-assisted suicide*.

8. Why does Pope John Paul II call physician-assisted suicide "false mercy"?

Reflection

Use the Internet or other research instruments to find out the current state of physician-assisted suicide. Is it legal in any countries or states? Is it under consideration in any other countries or states?

Make a case for or against the following statement:

Physician-assisted suicide is the beginning of a "slippery slope." Once active-voluntary euthanasia is accepted, then active-involuntary euthanasia will follow that. In other words, we could be headed toward a society in which people who are deemed noncontributing or burdensome may be gotten rid of.

Model of Morality

Dame Cicely Saunders

In 1948 a thirty-year-old nurse/hospital social worker encountered a dying patient in a London hospital. She was concerned about the way society and hospitals treated people who were dying. Cicely Saunders decided to do something about it. She realized that she first needed a medical degree if she were to have sufficient influence in the medical field, so she set off and became a doctor. There already existed a London hospital dedicated to care for the dying. In 1879 the Irish Sisters of Charity opened Saint Joseph's Hospice in East London, founded specifically for people who are poor and destitute, and who were terminally ill. Cicely Saunders wanted to design an approach to help all those who were terminally ill.

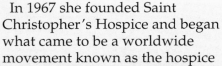

Dame Cicely Saunders

In 1967 she founded Saint Christopher's Hospice and began what came to be a worldwide movement known as the hospice movement, or palliative care. The Queen of England recognized her for her contributions by naming her a Dame of the British Empire.

The word *hospice* is taken from the word hospitality. Those who travel far from home know how important hospitality is. Travelers need people to welcome them and to assist them on their journey. Hospice recognizes dying as the last and perhaps the most important journey that people will take. Hospice offers an intense, multifaceted treatment for people with a fatal illness. Hospice refers not to a place but to an approach to being with

and caring for dying persons. Hospice care incorporates a wide variety of services, all designed for people who have weeks or at most months to live.

Medical professionals, who saw themselves as healers, were not clear how to help patients who were dying since they could no longer heal them. The hospice movement proposes that it is precisely at this time that all the resources of a society should come into play to help make the journey to death as painless, as comfortable, as meaningful, and as communal an experience as possible. When people are nearing death, then health-care workers should join with family members, social workers, representatives of religious organizations, and concerned volunteers to offer hospice—support and companionship for the final journey in life. The hospice movement has a strong Christian component to it. Hospice care for dying persons takes place within a network of family and friends and as part of a spiritual community.

Hospice does not try to hasten or postpone death. Instead it seeks to help people live as fully and as comfortably as possible during the last days of their lives. Before the hospice movement, family members often did not talk openly about death or dying when one of their numbers was nearing death. Everyone tried to spare everyone else the painful reality that someone close to him or her was dying. Hospice rejects a "let's not talk about it" approach to dying. Unlike earlier perspectives, hospice realizes that pain and suffering associated with dying have social and spiritual dimensions that must be talked about and brought to closure before the family member dies.

Leader: Gracious God of life, may we savor all the moments of our own lives and provide comfort for those dear to us whose lives are ending. May we show to all persons, born and unborn, the care that you have for us. Through your son, Jesus Christ, may we find meaning in life, consolation in suffering, and faith in the world to come. Grant us peace, now and at the hour of our death.

All: Amen.

Reader:

"For it was you who formed my inward parts; you knit me together in my mother's womb. I praise you, for I am fearfully and wonderfully made. Wonderful are your works; that I know very well. My frame was not hidden from you, when I was being made in secret, intricately woven in the depths of the earth. Your eyes beheld my unformed substance. In your book were written all the days that were formed for me, when none of them as yet existed."

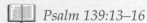 *Psalm 139:13–16*

Reader:

"Can a woman forget her nursing child, or show no compassion for the child of her womb? Even these may forget, yet I will not forget you. See, I have inscribed you on the palms of my hands . . ."

Isaiah 49:15–16

Leader: Reflect silently on reverence for human life.

Concluding Prayer:

Let us pray. . .

Father, God of all consolation, in your unending love and mercy for us you turn the darkness of death into the dawn of new life. Show compassion to your people in their sorrow. . . .Your Son, our Lord Jesus Christ, by dying for us, conquered death and by rising again, restored life. May we then go forward eagerly to meet him, and after our life on earth be reunited with our brothers and sisters where every tear will be wiped away. We ask this through Christ our Lord.

All: Amen.

From the Catholic funeral service, in *The Rites of the Catholic Church,* (New York: Pueblo Publishing Co., 1976).

Chapter Overview

- We are called to counteract violence in its many forms, both explicit and hidden.
- Church leaders have declared capital punishment an unnecessary affront to the dignity of human life.
- The Church promotes alternatives to war and calls for restriction of warfare as much as possible.
- The moral issues of nuclear weapons and the arms race, terrorism, and non-violence challenge us to follow the gospel of Christ.

The fifth commandment serves as the centerpiece of the biblical exploration into the meaning of respect for human life. This pivotal theme brings us to questions related to violence and warfare. Is the deliberate taking of life ever justified? Does taking a life always diminish the human family? When people are being killed, is it justifiable to execute the killers? If so, under what circumstances? In this chapter we will look at a number of key moral issues related to violence and peace. No country is immune from violence, and the United States has a particularly high rate of violent crime. The United States also continues to sanction capital punishment—a practice opposed by Church leaders as unnecessary in practically every circumstance today. In our world, leaders of many nations still rely on acts of war to achieve their ends. As with all moral matters, a Catholic looks deeply and lovingly at these issues, seeking always to determine: *What would Jesus have me do?*

Before we begin . . .

Answer *Agree*, *Disagree*, or *Uncertain* to the following statements. Explain your responses.

1. Violence is a particularly serious problem among young people today.

2. Incidents of violence occur more frequently in the United States than in other Western countries.

3. I would feel safe walking alone at night in most neighborhoods I know.

4. The best way to decrease violent crime is to enforce stiffer punishments for crime.

5. The best way to decrease violence is to address deep-seated social problems such as poverty and economic inequality.

Let us pray . . .

Jesus, we praise you as the Prince of Peace. You left us a message that still rings true today: How blessed are your peacemakers. Instead of a world divided, may we see a world united in your love. Where this world is broken, may we be your peacemakers—resetting breaks, reconnecting disjointed parts, and healing the hurts that lead to violence. May we always move beyond anger, hatred, and vengeance—even in the face of the new kinds of violence we face. Make us channels of your peace. Amen.

Where Does Violence Begin?

The following scenarios depict situations that could easily turn violent.

- Matt's fascination with guns began at an early age. Matt's father, an avid hunter, did not discourage this interest. Matt's favorite picture of himself is the one of him at age eleven wearing army fatigues and holding the first gun his father bought him. Unfortunately, this "macho" pose did not translate into kind treatment by or popularity among his schoolmates. To the contrary, classmates often picked on him. This was so common an occurrence that he often imagined people making fun of him even when they weren't. During target practice, Matt began to imagine that he was shooting at the boys and girls at school who taunted him the most. These moments were the ones that gave him the greatest satisfaction. *If they're not careful, I'll show them who's the tough guy,* he often mused.

- Once again Michael was spending the night at his regular street corner with a few friends from the neighborhood. Even though the night air was chilly, he felt more at home here than he did at his house where his father was, as usual, sprawled out on the sofa, half sleeping, half watching TV. Since his father didn't care and his mother was too distracted by other things to pay much attention to him, Michael left the house as much as possible.

Meanwhile, tensions were heating up between Michael's crowd and the group of kids who hung out at the pizza place a few blocks away. This night, two of his friends showed up with baseball bats. They claimed that a carload of kids from the other group had yelled obscenities at the girls on Michael's corner, and they were going over to the pizza place to teach them a lesson. Michael didn't want to get involved, but he didn't want to go against his crowd either. *Maybe I'll just go along and watch,* he thought.

- Scott first learned about the group from the Internet. They spoke out against the ways American society is being taken over by foreigners, non-Christians, and non-whites. Their views made sense to him. Scott saw nonwhite superstars making millions in the sports, music, and motion-picture industry. He saw a lot of nonwhites living off the government—not working at all—while he and his family were following the rules, paying taxes, but just scraping by. The government was no help. Actually, it was part of the problem. The group posted guidelines about what people who shared their views could do about affronts to a true, pure American culture. They described how bombs could be made from materials available at hardware and feed stores. When they announced that a convention was to take place in a nearby state, Scott decided he would attend. Finally, he felt as though he had found an outlet for the anger and hatred that had been welling up inside him. **A**

Activity

Look for an account of violence that occurred sometime over the past year. Make a list of factors that might have contributed to the violence. Describe possible changes that might have prevented the violence or lessened its damage.

Violence

The fifth commandment forbids the intentional destruction of human life. Because of the evils and injustices that accompany all war, the Church insistently urges everyone to prayer and to action so that the divine Goodness may free us from the ancient bondage of war. [Cf. GS 81 § 4.]

✝ Catechism, #2307

The fifth commandment's condemnation of murder does not cancel out our right to self-defense. In defending ourselves, we have the right to incapacitate an aggressor, even if that includes delivering a lethal blow. "'The act of self-defense can have a double effect: the preservation of one's own life; and the killing of the aggressor. . . .The one is intended, the other is not'" (St. Thomas Aquinas, STh II-II, 64, 7, *corp. art.*] *(Catechism, #2263)*. To take self-defense one step further: Elected leaders, police officers, military personnel, and all those who have responsibility for the lives of others have a grave duty to defend those who are entrusted to them and to ensure the common good.

Culture of Death

In 1995 in an encyclical called *The Gospel of Life*, Pope John Paul II wrote about his concern for what he called a "culture of death"—the violence that disfigures our human community. Here is what the pope had to say about our violent culture of death:

And how can we fail to consider the violence against life done to millions of humans, especially children, who are forced into poverty, malnutrition and hunger because of an unjust distribution of resources between peoples and between social classes? And what of the violence inherent not only in wars as such but in the scandalous arms trade, which spawns the many armed conflicts which stain our world with blood? What of the spreading of death caused by reckless tampering with the world's ecological balance, by the criminal spread of drugs, or by the promotion of certain kinds of sexual activity which, besides being morally unacceptable, also involve grave risks to life? It is impossible to catalogue completely the vast array of threats to human life, so many are the forms, whether explicit or hidden, in which they appear today!(#10)

Interestingly, Pope John Paul II did not mention stories of violence that typically make newspaper headlines. Instead, he speaks mostly about broader social issues, such as hunger, the violence of poverty, and the violence of unjust distribution of resources. He distinguished between **explicit violence**, in which people are physically harmed or killed by the direct actions of another, and **hidden violence**, in which people are harmed or killed indirectly because of various social factors. He wanted us to recognize that allowing a child to go hungry is as much an expression of a culture of death as beating a child would be. "Peace is the work of justice and the effect of charity [Cf. Isa 32:17; cf. GS 78 § § 1–2.]" *(Catechism, #2304)*. In other words, we don't simply work for peace. Rather, when we create justice, peace follows. On the other hand, peace is always absent in a society where justice is lacking. Working for justice is peacemaking; injustice is a form of hidden violence.

The Gospel of Life— 1995 encyclical by Pope John Paul II about the value and sacredness of human life

explicit violence— a situation in which someone is physically harmed or killed by direct action

hidden violence— a situation in which someone is harmed or killed indirectly, because of various social factors

Underlying Causes of Violence

skepticism—

in general, a doubting and questioning attitude. As defined by Pope John Paul II, a lack of belief that there are fundamental truths, dismissing any sense of right or wrong

In *The Gospel of Life*, Pope John Paul II also identified what he considered to be four factors accounting for the violence that stains our world. The first factor he names is one of attitude—**skepticism**. By skepticism he means disbelief, in this case dismissing the idea that there are clear standards of right and wrong. This kind of dismissal of standards leads to an "anything goes" philosophy of life. Instead of crying out against violent behavior and social conditions, a skeptic in this narrow sense of the word looks the other way since he or she has no basis upon which to condemn violence and no hope that things can change for the better.

Second, John Paul II attributed the increase of violence to the breakdown of family and community life. He points out that today many individuals and families are left alone with their problems. Living in our modern world is difficult enough even with a great deal of support. Instead, too many people are forced to face challenges alone, causing pressure to build up, which can bring on violence.

Third, John Paul II listed social and economic problems, the many forms of hidden violence that easily spill over into explicit violence. Here again he places poverty first. Besides being a form of violence in itself, poverty creates anxiety and pressure which, in turn, fosters other types of violence. The pope also included violence against women as a social problem that the world community must address.

Finally, Pope John Paul II saw a dangerous trend in the way people view each other. Namely, many people are denying their solidarity with everyone else. This denial leads to "a war of the powerful against the weak" *(Gospel of Life, #12)*. In such an atmosphere, the comfortable and self-sufficient treat those who are weak and have special needs either with indifference or as being the enemy to be ignored, resisted, or eliminated. **A**

Activity

1. Name three examples of hidden violence as Pope John Paul II understood the term. Explain how each is a form of violence in itself and also how it might spill over into more explicit violence.

2. Pope John Paul II identified four underlying causes as central to the problem of violence. Give examples that might support his position. Can you name other key causes of violence?

3. Do you believe that it is an added burden to be poor in a predominantly affluent country compared to being poor in a predominantly poor country? Why or why not?

4. Do you agree or disagree with the following statements: Most wealthy people don't realize the difficulties that people who are poor must face. If they did, they would do more to help those who are poor.

Anger and Hatred

Jesus takes the fifth commandment to its core: "You have heard that it was said to those of ancient times, 'You shall not murder'; and 'whoever murders shall be liable to judgment.' But I say to you that if you are angry with a brother or sister, you will be liable to judgment" *(Matthew 5:21–22)*. Scandal is a form of murder. It is an action that draws another to do evil. Those who are guilty of scandal can murder the virtue and integrity of others and lead them toward spiritual death.

In his statement about murder, Jesus urges us not to allow our hearts to become breeding grounds for violence. Anger and hatred happen. The question is *What do we do about them?* We can be either creative or destructive with our anger. For instance, anger and hatred are destructive when we carry them around and at the slightest provocation allow them to burst forth in hurtful ways. Seeking ways to get revenge is also destructive. Hurtful, destructive anger is also called "murderous anger" *(Catechism, #2302)*.

There's a two-sided dimension to anger when it is destructive. The victim of murderous anger is, of course, the person against whom such anger is directed. However, the victim is also the person harboring and expressing fierce anger. Both are harmed. We may presume that anger and hatred come naturally to us humans. Whether or not that is true, we still have the capacity and the responsibility to control anger rather than to allow it to control us. Saying, "I was so angry I couldn't help myself" will get us into trouble sooner or later. Jesus, who expressed righteous anger himself, offers us a better way: "But I say to you, Love your enemies and pray for those who persecute you, so that you may be children of your Father in heaven" *(Matthew 5:44–45)*.

For Review...

1. What was Pope John Paul II's term for the violence that disfigures the human community?

2. What is the difference between explicit and hidden violence?

3. Define skepticism as Pope John Paul II defined the term. How did he see this brand of skepticism contributing to an acceptance of violence?

4. According to John Paul II, what three other problems lead to violence in our culture?

5. What addition to the fifth commandment does Jesus make?

6. In what sense is the harm of murderous anger two-sided?

Capital Punishment

Capital Punishment and Scripture

The first murderer in Scripture was Cain (*Genesis 4:1–16*). When Cain murdered his brother Abel, did God put him to death or order his execution? The answer is *no!* Cain was punished but not executed. In fact, God said, "Whoever kills Cain will suffer a sevenfold vengeance" (*Genesis 4:15*). God, then, placed a mark on Cain, so that anyone seeing the mark would know not to kill him.

God the Father reveals himself fully through his Son and, in doing so, provides us with even greater insight into the issue of **capital punishment**. Jesus never offers violence as a solution for correcting the ills of society. On the contrary, Jesus reveals God's unconditional love for all persons, regardless of their crimes or worthiness. Jesus does not desire the death of sinners but rather that they convert and attain eternal life.

Jesus' focus on mercy is seen when a woman caught in adultery is brought before him (John 8:1–11). The religious leaders point out that in the law Moses commands that such women be stoned to death. The leaders want to know what Jesus thinks about this. He bounces the challenge back to the woman's accusers by saying, "Let anyone among you who is without sin be the first to throw a stone at her" (*John 8:7*). One by one her accusers walk away until only Jesus and the woman are left alone. Jesus then tells her, "Neither do I condemn you. Go your way, and from now on do not sin again" (*John 8:11*).**R**

> **"**Jesus often shifts focus of judgment to a higher court, a court where there is no need for polygraph, where there is absolute knowledge of evidence, of good deeds and of evil, of things private and things public; a court where there is justice and mercy, both law and grace, wrath and tenderness. **"**
>
> Bishop Sean O'Malley, OFM Cap., "The Gospel of Life vs. The Death Penalty" Pastoral Letter on Capital Punishment, February 25, 1999.

Reflection

Answer *Agree*, *Disagree*, or *Uncertain* to the following statements.

1. I believe that the death penalty should be used more frequently and more publicly.

2. Executing criminals violates the principle of respect for life.

3. Statistics indicate that the threat of the death penalty cuts down on violent crimes.

4. Capital punishment in our country is administered fairly, disregarding differences such as race or locale.

5. Someone who claims to be a follower of Jesus should oppose the death penalty.

Does Capital Punishment Help Society?

In 1972 the U.S. Supreme Court declared the death penalty as practiced in individual states to be unconstitutional. At the time, the country was moving toward the position of most other Western nations who determined that capital punishment was ineffective, unnecessary, and immoral. However, in 1976 the Supreme Court declined to disallow new state laws and procedures, thus making it possible for thirty-eight states to have legalized capital punishment.

The death penalty is acceptable only when society has no other means of defending itself *(The Gospel of Life, #56)*. Pope John Paul II stressed that the existence of high-security prisons makes capital punishment unnecessary and immoral in modern societies. Today cases for which no effective alternative exists to capital punishment are "practically non-existent [John Paul II, *Evangelium vitae* 56]" *(Catechism, #2267)*.

The United States Catholic bishops addressed the issue of capital punishment most thoroughly in a 1980 document titled *Statement on Capital Punishment*. Before speaking to the issue itself, they let it be known that they were concerned about security within society, about the victims of crime, and in a special way about members of law enforcement whose lives are endangered through crime. However, they don't want these concerns to result in a misguided search for simple solutions to the complex problem of criminal justice. Capital punishment does not automatically make our society safer,

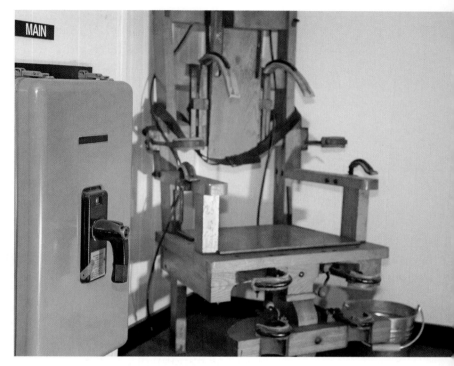

nor does it relieve the pain of crime victims and their families. In their statement, the bishops review capital punishment in light of the three justifications traditionally advanced for punishment—deterrence, rehabilitation, and retribution. **G**

Group Talk

List as many arguments as possible for and against capital punishment. Give possible pros and cons to each argument. Which arguments do you believe are more convincing? Which arguments do you believe reflect a Catholic perspective? Explain.

Does Capital Punishment Lessen Crime?

deterrence— punishment or fear of punishment can help prevent crime

Deterrence means that punishment or fear of punishment can help prevent crime. *Particular* **deterrence** means that an individual who committed a crime in the past is deterred from committing any future crime. Obviously, capital punishment can serve this purpose. However, alternative forms of punishment such as life imprisonment without the possibility of parole can also serve as a particular deterrent. *General deterrence* means that fear of punishment inhibits people in general from committing certain crimes. On the effectiveness of capital punishment as a general deterrent, the bishops report what many studies have indicated: "Empirical studies in this area have not given conclusive evidence that would justify the imposition of the death penalty on a few individuals as a means of preventing others from committing crimes" *(Statement on Capital Punishment, page 3).*

Rehabilitation

rehabilitation— programs aimed at training and reforming wrongdoers so that they no longer commit crime

For about three centuries, our society has relied on imprisonment as its principal means of dealing with wrongdoers. From its beginning, the modern prison system had as a primary goal the **rehabilitation**, or reform, of a wrongdoer. Prisons were penitentiaries—that is, places to do penance, to see the error of one's ways, and to return to society a reformed person.

The bishops realize the difficulties of helping people to reform. Nonetheless, they urge us to be mindful of Jesus' message of forgiveness and conversion. Capital punishment shuts the door to any possibility of reform and reintegration into society.

Retribution—What Is Just Punishment for Crime?

Retribution is the third justification for punishment of criminals. It means restoration of order by ensuring that wrongdoers atone for their deeds. Retribution seeks to restore order through punishment of wrongdoers in such a way that everyone in a society knows that criminal behavior is totally unacceptable.

The bishops teach that retribution does justify punishment, but that society's methods of punishment are not meant to satisfy instinctual urges to lash back at people who offend us. "An eye for an eye" must be tempered with "Love your enemy." "Thus we would regard it as barbarous and inhuman for a criminal who had tortured or maimed a victim to be tortured or maimed in return" (*Statement on Capital Punishment*, page 4). In other words, retribution must be distinguished from revenge. **R**

retribution— restoring the social order by punishing wrongdoers, thus declaring that certain behaviors are not tolerated in society

Why the Bishops Are Against Capital Punishment

In the *Statement on Capital Punishment* the bishops call for abolition of capital punishment. They do so on the basis of four Christian and human values.

First, abolition sends a message that we can break the cycle of violence, that we need not take life for life, that we can envisage more humane, hopeful, and effective responses to violent crime.

Second, abolition of capital punishment is a manifestation of our belief in the unique worth and dignity of each person from the moment of conception, a creature made in the image and likeness of God.

Third, abolition of the death penalty is further testimony to our conviction, a conviction that we share with the Judaic and Islamic traditions, that God is indeed the Lord of life.

Reflection

Look for reports on programs that actually exist whose aim is rehabilitation of prisoners. Based on these reports and on your own creativity, design a program aimed specifically at the rehabilitation of eighteen- to twenty-five-year-old prisoners. Why would you choose this model?

Fourth, we believe that abolition of the death penalty is most consonant with the example of Jesus, who both taught and practiced the forgiveness of injustice and who came "to give his life as a ransom for many" [Mark 10:45].

The bishops conclude their *Statement on Capital Punishment* with the observation that the death penalty makes our society neither safer nor better, as much as we might like it to. Instead, it provides the illusion of a final solution when in fact it is not. **G A**

For Review...

1. According to official Church teaching, what circumstance would make capital punishment acceptable?

2. Explain the difference between particular and general deterrence.

3. According to the U.S. Catholic bishops, has capital punishment been successful as a general deterrent to crime?

4. What was a primary goal of instituting the modern prison system?

5. Define *retribution*. How is it different from revenge?

6. Name the four arguments of the U.S. Catholic bishops about why capital punishment should be abolished.

Group Talk

1. Review the U.S. Catholic bishops' statement against capital punishment. What is most compelling in the Church's teaching?

2. Do you agree that capital punishment represents a quick-fix mentality that does not consider either long-term consequences or Catholic principles? Why or why not?

Activity

A major reason the Supreme Court in 1972 refused states the right to execute criminals was that the court found that the death penalty was not being administered equally and without bias. Do research to create a profile of prisoners who are executed in the United States based on race, income, education, state, and gender. According to your findings, is the death penalty currently employed without bias? Explain.

War and Respect for Life

Life is sacred. The Church's moral teaching applies to the question of war the same principles it applies to the question of abortion, euthanasia, capital punishment, and other issues in which human lives are at stake. We are to respect life itself as well as the lives of individuals. We are believers in a God who is Creator and Father of all and who has given into our hands the stewardship of the earth and the duty to love others as we love ourselves. War is an assault on human life and brings with it suffering and death. Jesus invites us to be peacemakers. To do this, we must struggle for peace, which is always a struggle for life.

In an address to the diplomatic corps (13 January 2003), Pope John Paul II said: *War is not always inevitable. It is always a defeat for humanity. . . . War is never just another means that one can choose to employ for settling differences between nations. As the Charter of the United Nations Organization and international law itself reminds us, war cannot be decided upon, even when it is a matter of ensuring the common good, except as the last option and in accordance with very strict conditions, without ignoring the consequences for the civilian population both during and after military operations.*

The past century was scarred by many wars. Given the high stakes involved in modern warfare, upholding clear principles regulating war on the part of the entire world community is absolutely necessary if the coming century is to be less bloody. A thoughtful and thorough statement of Christian teaching on war is the 1983 pastoral letter of the United States Catholic bishops, ***The Challenge of Peace: God's Promise and Our Response***. The letter discusses the morality of war. It enunciates general principles about war and suggests some specific applications of those principles to our contemporary world.

The Challenge of Peace—
1983 pastoral letter of U.S. bishops addressing issues of war and peace

The Challenge of Peace acknowledges that the use of violence in war is a complex moral issue. For example, the pastoral letter says that: "Even a brief examination of war and peace in the Scriptures makes it clear that it does not provide us with detailed answers to the specifics of the questions which we face today" *(Challenge of Peace, #55)*. Although the Bible does not give us definitive answers about war, it does aim us always in the direction of peace. The pastoral letter points us in the same direction when it offers us the following as a first principle regarding war: "Catholic teaching begins in every case with a presumption against war and for peaceful settlement of disputes" *(Challenge of Peace, Summary, A1)*.

According to the bishops, in defending and working for peace, there are two legitimate options: to resist bearing arms or to bear arms. Nonetheless, it's important to keep in mind that both of these options, while in disagreement on means, do agree on the goal—a just resolution of conflict accompanied by the least possible harm to all parties involved. Given this understanding of means and ends, the bishops accept the idea that war is permissible when entered into for defensive purposes. However, it is subject to rigorous restrictions that have been spelled out since the early centuries of Christian history. Decisions on war are prudential judgments on the application of the Church's principles to concrete reality. The bishops remind us that "the possibility of taking even one human life is a prospect we should consider in fear and trembling" *(Challenge of Peace, #80)*. **A**

Activity

Attitudes toward the morality of war can fluctuate with time and with changing circumstances. On a scale of 1 to 10 (1 means being totally against any form of war and 10 means being totally accepting of war), rate the attitude toward war that currently exists in our society. Explain your rating.

The Just-War Tradition—
Principles to Restrict and Regulate War

The bishops describe traditional principles called the **just-war principles** that can guide us in deciding when war is justified. The bishops consider modern war such a horror that, "a decision [to engage in war], especially today, requires extraordinarily strong reasons for overriding the presumption in favor of peace and against war" *(Challenge of Peace, #83)*. Therefore, the just-war principles "seek to restrict and reduce its horrors" *(Challenge of Peace, #83)*. In other words, the bishops are reminding us that there is no good violence. There is only justified, regrettable violence when all else fails. Violence is not an instrument to bring about victory rather than defeat. Resorting to violence itself is defeat, a defeat of the sacredness and communal nature of all human life.

A listing of the just-war principles clarifies the teaching that warfare, with its frequent wholesale destruction of life, is morally acceptable only in rare instances. **G**

> **just-war principles—** a set of principles outlining conditions when use of violence would be acceptable

Just-War Principles

Just Cause: War is permissible only to confront "a real and certain danger. . ."

Competent Authority: War must be declared by those with responsibility for public order.

Comparative Justice: Every party to a conflict should acknowledge the limits of its "just cause." Do the rights and values being defended justify the loss of others' lives?

Right Intention: During the conflict, right intention means pursuit of peace and reconciliation (not, for instance, increased economic power in a region).

Last Resort: . . .all peaceful alternatives must have been exhausted.

Probability of Success: With a fair degree of certainty, intended results are likely to be achieved.

Proportionality: .. .the damage to be inflicted and the costs incurred by war must be proportionate to the good expected by taking up arms.

The United States Catholic bishops, *The Challenge of Peace: God's Promise and Our Response*, 1983, #s 86–99.

Group Talk

Consider a recent episode when military force was used by a particular nation. Using each of the just-war principles, make a case that war was or was not justified.

Based on your evaluation, how can just-war principles be valuable instruments for determining whether military force should be used in international conflict situations?

nuclear deterrence—
the proposition that
when two nations pos-
sess the ability to inflict
nuclear damage on each
other, then neither
nation is likely to use its
nuclear weapons in the
first place

nuclear
proliferation—
any increase in the
number of nations
that possess nuclear
weapons or that
have the capability
to build them

The bishops' document, *The Challenge of Peace*, also offers some helpful guidelines regarding specific issues related to war and peace. Their pronouncements mirror the strong criticism of modern warfare that has been voiced by Church leaders especially since Vatican Council II in the 1960s.

Nuclear Weapons and the Arms Race

"The arms race is one of the greatest curses on the human race and the harm it inflicts on the poor is more than can be endured."
The Church in the Modern World, #81

Remember that the U.S. bishops wrote *The Challenge of Peace* during the period known as the Cold War when tensions were great between the two major world powers of the time, the United States and the Soviet Union. The bishops did not condemn the U.S. government for maintaining its arsenal of nuclear weapons. It recognized their potential as a deterrent against all-out warfare between the two superpowers. **Nuclear deterrence** means that if two nations possess the ability to inflict nuclear damage on each other, then neither nation is likely to use its nuclear weapons in the first place. Concerning nuclear weapons, the bishops condemn:

1. Initiation of the use of nuclear weapons.
2. Further buildup of nuclear weapons by any nation. (In part, the bishops see money spent on nuclear weapons as taking away from money available for helping people in need.)

3. Nuclear proliferation (the spread of nuclear weapons to other nations).

The arms race is a grave evil and a curse on the human race. In this race, nations seek to possess more powerful, more sophisticated, and a greater amount of weapons than potential enemies. It's a deadly game of keeping up with one's neighbor. This trend is counterproductive and dangerous for the following reasons *(Catechism, #2315)*:

1. It doesn't ensure peace.
2. It aggravates the causes of war.
3. It impedes efforts to help people in need.
4. It thwarts development.

In other words, over-armament increases fear and tension between nations, relies on violence or its threat to provide security, and takes resources away from peaceful efforts to eliminate the causes of war.

Responding to Terrorism

Politicians and moralists have recently debated whether just-war criteria can be applied to a war against terrorism. Determining what is a justifiable response to terrorism is much more complex than the forms of warfare we usually think of. For instance, terrorist acts are not done in the name of a country but of a cause. Many people might share sympathies with the cause but do not participate or even condone the violent methods used to attain the goal. Separating combatants from noncombatants is difficult. Also, "success" against terrorism is not easily measured. For one thing, since terrorists operate outside of the accepted arrangement of separate nation-states, toppling a government and replacing it with another only brings limited success.

One part of a response to terrorism is to apply Pope John Paul II's four pillars of peace: truth, justice, love, and freedom.

Truth *will build peace if every individual sincerely acknowledges not only his rights, but his own duties towards others.* Justice *will build peace if in practice everyone respects the rights of others and actually fulfils his duties towards them.* Love *will build peace if people feel the needs of others as their own and share what they have with others, especially the values of mind and spirit which they possess.* Freedom *will build peace and make it thrive if, in the choice of the means and the ends, people act according to reason and assume responsibility for their own actions.*

World Day of Peace, January 1, 2003 **A**

> **"**Terrorism is built on contempt for human life. For this reason, not only does it commit intolerable crimes, but because it resorts to terror as a political and military means it is itself a crime against humanity. There exists therefore a right to defend oneself against terrorism, a right which, as always, must be exercised with respect for moral and legal limits in the choice of ends and means. The guilty must be identified, since criminal culpability (blame) is always personal and cannot be extended to a nation, ethnic group or religion to which terrorists may belong. **"**
>
> Pope John Paul II, Message for the Celebration of the World Day of Peace, January 1, 2002.

Activity

Apply the four pillars of peace to a war on terrorism.

Nonviolence—A Practical Alternative to Violence?

nonviolence— conflict-resolving techniques that do not rely on physical or psychological injury of an opponent

conscientious objector— one who for moral or religious reasons is opposed to serving in the military

Jesus teaches and exemplifies the truth that unjust violence is a contradiction of our faith in God, the Creator of all people, who cares for all of his children. Such violence runs counter to our faith in Jesus, who teaches us: "if anyone strikes you on the right cheek, turn the other also" *(Matthew 5:39)*. Unjust violence, then, contradicts the teaching of the Church and is contradictory to our faith in God.

Besides its history of wars, the twentieth century is also notable for progress made in developing nonviolent techniques to help us deal with conflicts. Mahatma Gandhi of India helped his country achieve independence from England without relying on violence, bloodshed, or even hatred. The United States has also been home to a number of nonviolent movements. The civil rights and anti-war movements, especially during the 1960s and 1970s, featured leaders like Martin Luther King Jr. who were dedicated to meeting conflict with nonviolent resistance. The bishops would like to see further exploration into **nonviolence** as an alternative to violence and war as a means of resolving conflicts:

Nonviolent means of resistance to evil deserve much more study and consideration than they have thus far received.

There have been significant instances in which people have successfully resisted oppression without recourse to arms *(Challenge of Peace, #222).* **R**

Principles of Nonviolence

1. Nonviolence is a way of life for many people. It is active nonviolent resistance to evil.

2. Nonviolence seeks to win friendship and understanding. The goal of nonviolence is redemption and reconciliation.

3. Nonviolence seeks to defeat injustice, not people. Nonviolence recognizes that evildoers are also victims.

4. Nonviolence holds that suffering can educate and transform. Nonviolence willingly accepts the consequences of its acts.

5. Nonviolence chooses love instead of hate. Nonviolence resists violence of the spirit as well as of the body. Love restores community and resists injustice.

6. Nonviolence believes that the universe is on the side of justice. The nonviolent resister has deep faith that justice will eventually win.

Reflection

1. Give examples when nonviolence would require courage.

2. According to principle #2, what is the aim of nonviolence? What is the aim of violence? How are the two different?

3. What does principle #3 mean by saying that "evildoers are also victims"? Give examples.

4. Both violence and nonviolence can result in suffering. Is there a difference in the suffering that each entails? Explain.

5. Give examples of "violence of the spirit."

6. We might think of violence as "natural" and therefore as unavoidable, whereas nonviolence runs against the nature of things. In the "Principles of Nonviolence," principle #6 raises the discussion to a spiritual, cosmic level. It proclaims that in the "big picture" love, justice, and nonviolence are indeed more fundamental than hatred, injustice, and violence. Do you agree?

7. If you were to read a book titled *Alternatives to War*, what strategies do you think would be described in it?

Conscientious Objection

According to the definition used by the Selective Service Agency, which oversees military registration for the U.S. government, a **conscientious objector** is one who on the grounds of moral or religious principles is opposed to serving in the armed forces or bearing arms. The government does require eighteen-year-old men to register for military service. The laws in place overseeing this registration do allow individuals to apply for conscientious objector status, in which case if a draft were instituted these people would perform non-military service rather than military service. Being a conscientious objector is a legal position. Not registering for the draft or simply refusing induction into the military (popularly known as being a draft dodger) is illegal.

The bishops have called for another category to be instituted: selective conscientious objection. A **selective conscientious objector** is one who believes that the particular war in which he or she would be called to fight is against his moral or religious principles. While there is currently no legal status for such a position, the bishops state that: "We continue to insist upon respect for and legislative protection of the rights of both classes of conscientious objectors" *(Challenge of Peace, #233).* **G**

...Conclusion

Respect for life is a fundamental Catholic moral principle. Reflecting on the fifth commandment as expanded by Jesus, Church teaching cautions against the use of violence and the culture it helps create. In Catholic teaching, violence, even if it's justifiable, used against any persons diminishes the dignity that human life deserves. Violence fosters a culture of death. Seeking ways of cutting back on violence in all forms helps nurture a culture of life. Since injustice is a root cause of violence, true peace comes only when we are sensitive both to explicit as well as to hidden expressions of violence. Creating a culture of life means finding alternatives to reliance on the death penalty, to the use of warfare, the recourse to nuclear weapons, and the tragedy of terrorism. In the spirit of Jesus, the Church calls upon us to view violence with remorse and regret.

Group Talk

The bishops took a controversial stand regarding the U.S. government and nuclear weapons—that it is all right to possess such weapons but not to use them. First as a citizen of the United States, and then as a citizen from another nation, debate the positives and negatives of the United States possessing nuclear weapons.

1. What first principle regarding war do the U.S. Catholic bishops state in *The Challenge of Peace?*

2. According to the bishops, in working for peace what two options lay open to Christians?

3. Name the seven principles of the just-war theory.

4. Explain deterrence as it applies to nuclear weapons.

5. Concerning nuclear weapons, what three things do the bishops condemn?

6. What are Pope John Paul II's four pillars of peace?

7. What was the major achievement of modern nonviolent movements?

8. Name two U.S. movements that have employed nonviolent techniques.

9. What position do the U.S. Catholic bishops take on nonviolence?

10. What is a conscientious objector?

11. What is the legal status of a conscientious objector in the United States?

12. What is selective conscientious objection? What is the U.S. Catholic bishops' position on both types of conscientious objection?

Model of Morality

Dr. Takashi Nagai

On August 9, 1945, the second and last atomic bomb ever used in warfare fell upon the most Catholic city in Japan.

The immediate death toll in Nagasaki was nearly 80,000 people. A few orders of Catholic nuns lost all their members in the blast.

Coincidentally, Nagasaki was not the original target that day. Heavy clouds over the intended target led to the switch. Nagasaki was home to the Mitsubishi Iron Works factory, which supplied materials for the war. Again, however, cloud cover obscured the factory and instead the pilot set his sights on the Catholic cathedral in the heart of the Catholic district as a more visible target. Adding another ironic twist to the story, the pilot of the plane that dropped the bomb that day was an Irish Catholic young man from Boston.

Dr. Takashi Nagai, dean of radiology at the University of Nagasaki, was in his office that day when the bomb fell. After having his own wounds attended to, he set about helping as many people as he could. When he returned home, he found that his two children had survived but that his wife had died, clutching rosary beads in her hands. Dr. Nagai realized that the destruction from the blast was so great that he needed to take a broader view if he were to find any meaning in it. He had converted to Catholicism nine years earlier, so naturally he turned to his faith to help him through this catastrophe. His thoughts immediately turned to the cross.

Catholics in Japan knew well the mystery of the cross and that suffering and death can lead to new life. When Catholicism was first introduced into the country, the emperor and other officials viewed Japanese who became Catholic as a threat to the state. Crucifixes and other objects of Catholic devotion were placed on the ground. Those who refused to stamp on them were killed immediately.

Catholics of Nagasaki brought this history of martyrdom to bear on their experiences of the devastation that occurred less than a week before the war ended. The deaths of so many of their brothers and sisters were another form of martyrdom.

As a leader of the Catholic community, Dr. Nagai addressed the crowd gathered for a large outdoor Mass held a few days after the dropping of the bomb. Dr. Nagai spoke about the event not in the narrow terms of the suffering it caused the people of his city. Instead his words addressed the deep-seated blight on the soul of all humanity that accompanied this war: "Joyfully we have hated one another; joyfully we have killed one another". Just as Christ had done on the cross, so the people of Nagasaki paid the price of the great affront to the human family that was the war. At the time his words upset many others.

Suffering the effects of radiation both from his work and from the blast, Dr. Nagai lived as an invalid until his death in 1951. In time he realized that the lesson of Nagasaki would be lost unless humanity would throw off its reliance on war when conflicts arise. Instead, people must learn to love and work together:

Men and women of the world, never again plan war! . . . From this atomic waste the people of Nagasaki confront the world and cry out: No more war! Let us follow the commandment of love and work together. The people of Nagasaki prostrate themselves before God and pray: Grant that Nagasaki may be the last atomic wilderness in the history of the world.

Based on Robert Ellsberg's, *All Saints* (New York: The Crossroad Publishing Co., 1997), pages 12–13

Leader: Jesus, you rejected violence but died a criminal's death. Help us to realize that in the end there is no good violence. Before your death you gave us a simple but awesome task, to be neighbors to everyone. You taught us that every human life is sacred and every unjustified act of violence an affront to the human spirit. May we pause and reconsider your message to us when voices echo a culture of death. Keep us faithful to you as we face conflicts at home, in our communities, and in our world. Amen.

Reader #1: Matthew 5:23–24

All: Lord Jesus, help us to live your word.

Reader #2: Matthew 5:43–48

All: Lord Jesus, help us to live your word.

Reader #3: Revelation 21:1–4

All: Lord Jesus, help us to live your word.

Leader: You have given all peoples one common origin, and your will is to gather them as one family in yourself.

Fill the hearts of us all with the fire of your love and the desire to ensure justice for all our brothers and sisters.

By sharing the good things you gave us may we secure justice and equality for everyone, an end to all divisions, and a human society built on love and peace.

Concluding prayer from the "Prayers of the Mass for the Progress of Peoples," in Novena for Justice and Peace (Washington, D.C.: Campaign for Human Development, 1983), page 15.

12 SEXUALITY AND MORALITY

Chapter Overview

- Sexuality is more than physicality; it is a drive toward fruitful union and a reaching out to others.

- Catholics are called to follow Jesus, the model of chastity.

- Marriage is the naturally ordered context for sexual expression.

- Catholic moral teaching based on the sixth and ninth commandments provides guidance for decision making in areas of sexual behavior.

The sixth and ninth commandments bring us to an examination of the wonderful gift God has given us—sexuality. We were created out of love, through love, and for love. Like all good things, however, misuse and manipulation of sexuality can cloud its beauty and goodness. The decisions that we make regarding our sexual capacities can enrich or dehumanize us. In this chapter we will look at how our culture has perceived sexuality. We will explore fundamental principles about sexual morality that reflect our Catholic faith. Finally, we will look at some specific cases to help us explore our own attitudes related to sexual morality.

Before we begin . . .

Answer *agree*, *disagree*, or *uncertain* to the following statements.

1. Most sixteen-year-olds cannot have a deeply loving sexual relationship.

2. If I were dating someone, I would expect that person to be my best friend.

3. A double standard about sexuality exists in our society—one for boys and one for girls.

4. The majority of boys will go as far as girls will let them.

5. Boys are more interested in sexual intercourse; girls are more interested in romance.

6. Most guys think that girls owe them something physical after they've gone out for a while.

7. Most girls think that guys owe them something physical after they've gone out for a while.

8. I would be very upset if I were treated as a sexual object.

9. Sexually explicit movies, magazines, and books are harmful and should be illegal or at least highly restricted and regulated.

10. Making sexually explicit materials available on the Internet should be a crime.

Let us pray . . .

We praise you, Jesus, as Word made flesh. You are one with us, a constant reminder that we, too, are holy in spirit and in flesh. May the physical urges we experience lead us to appreciate the awesome wonder of the human body. May we always treat ourselves and others with respect, especially in our sexual behavior, ever conscious that we carry your Holy Spirit within us and share that Holy Spirit through word and touch, smiles and laughter, hugs and handshakes. Amen.

Sexual Expression

- Marci and Frank have been married for fifteen years. They have never gone on a vacation alone since the first year of their marriage. Now they are about to be together without the children for an entire week. They feel like newlyweds—nervous, playful, excited, and yet anxious about how they'll get along without focusing on the children.

- Tracy and Rick, both juniors in high school, were in the school play together when they started dating. Their involvement became more and more intense. They began to spend most of their time alone with each other or talking on the phone. Gradually, Tracy began feeling a need for other people in her life. She wanted to tell Rick, but she didn't want to hurt him. Though their relationship continued, it became uncomfortable and unpleasant for her. She wondered how she could resolve this dilemma without hurting Rick.

- Tom had found a pornographic magazine discarded on a bench weeks before. Since that time he has hidden the magazine amid the sports books in his room. Some nights when he is alone in his room doing homework, he takes out the magazine for a few minutes and pages through it, stopping briefly to look at each woman. Lately, however, Tom has been thinking that he should throw out the magazine. He finds that something just doesn't feel right about looking at these pictures. He feels that he is violating himself and the women in the pictures as well.

- Since Joe became friends with Michele, he has spent little time with his old friends. Joe is happy to spend time with Michele joking and talking about life. From his new-found perspective, Joe finds his old friends' routine very immature. They drink and then act very irresponsibly; they get girls to drink with them and then coerce the girls to have sex with them. Joe thinks about telling his old friends that they should change their ways before any more damage is done.

Sexuality

Definitions and Attitudes

Few topics are as exciting and frightening, as stimulating and alluring as sexuality. If we find that we are talking but that nobody is listening to us, we can change the topic to sexuality and immediately we have an attentive audience. People who produce popular novels, television shows, and movies know that sex in the media will keep their audiences awake and attentive.

Sexuality is a part of our lives that draws us out of ourselves and urges us to seek union with others. When we speak about sexuality, we can mean a great variety of behaviors, feelings, and experiences. Sexual activity includes kissing, flirting glances, holding hands, words of comfort and support, passionate embraces, as well as more intimate forms of sexual expression.

All the incidents on the previous page relate to sexuality. Both the young couple struggling to hold in check the intensity of their sexual expression and the married couple seeking to rekindle the intensity of theirs describe real-life dramas in which sexuality plays a central role. The joys and the problems related to sexuality are not limited by age, culture, social class, or lifestyle.

As with everything human, sexuality has a darker side. Sexuality can seem to control us, or it can be used to exploit us where we are most vulnerable. For instance, Tom's fascination with explicit magazines can easily become an obsession, while Joe's friends exploit others sexually.

Each of the commandments gives us a "God's eye view" of some aspect of our lives. The sixth commandment reminds us to treat our sexuality with reverence and to express our sexuality in responsible ways. **G**

Group Talk

Our attitude toward sexuality is greatly shaped by our culture. List at least five messages that various segments of our popular culture communicate to you about sexuality. Analyze the messages you wrote down by answering the following questions about each one:

• Is the message positive or negative?

• Does it help us appreciate ourselves and our sexuality better?

• Does it provide helpful guidance for decision making regarding sexual morality?

Defining Sexuality: Sexuality Is More Than Our Bodies

> *"... sexuality ... is by no means something purely biological, but concerns the innermost being of the human person as such."*
>
> Pope John Paul II, On the *Family*, number 11.

When it comes to describing what it means to be human, our language fails us. We may say, "I have a body" and "I have a soul." Such use of language is just a manner of speaking, an attempt to capture in words the richness and the subtlety of the human condition. In fact, as we live our lives, we cannot divide ourselves into such clear-cut physical and spiritual dimensions as "body" and "soul." Similarly, our sexuality is not something that we have—as if our sexuality were merely something non-essential added onto who we are.

We are sexual creatures through and through, from our innermost being to the surface of our skin. Sexuality, then, is the way that we express ourselves as physical-spiritual creatures. Sexuality is a psychological, spiritual, and physical reality. These interlocking dimensions of our identity cannot be isolated one from another. As sexual beings, we are drawn out of ourselves to seek connections and fulfillment with others as well as to "be fruitful and multiply" *(Genesis 1:28)*.

Sexuality is a way for us to create. It is a reflection of the creative power of the Holy Trinity. The love of the Father, the Son, and the Holy Spirit created the heavens and the earth. This act of creation was the first proclamation of God's "plan of his loving goodness" *(Catechism, #315)*. God is love and his being is a mystery of loving community. By creating human beings in his image, God imprinted in them the vocation, the ability, and the responsibility to reflect the creative love of the Trinity. To help us achieve this vocation to love creatively, God gave us the gift of sexuality. With this gift, we share in God's creative love by forming bonds with other people. Reflecting the Creator, the gift of sexuality finds its fullest expression in the lifelong committed union of marriage from which flow the procreation of children.

Therefore, every marital act must be open to the transmission of life. **A**

For Review...

1. What are the sixth and ninth commandments?

2. Explain the statement, "As with all aspects of our humanity, sexuality has a darker side."

3. How does sexuality reflect the creative love of the Trinity?

Activity

Write a prayer of gratitude to God the Father, the Son, and the Holy Spirit, who has created out of love the earth and all that is in it.

Our sexuality draws us out of ourselves to seek union with another. Besides physical union, what are some ways that we can develop closeness with others?

Catholic Teaching and Sexuality

Our sexuality is a blessing from God. He created us in his image as sexual beings and our fundamental vocation is to love him and others. By creating human beings in his image, "male and female he created them" *(Genesis 1:27)*, God gave personal dignity to both genders. He crafted men and women with differences that complement each other and that orient them toward marriage and the growth of families.

In our very flesh we have a capacity for communion, generosity, and **fecundity**.

These are positive and powerful descriptions of this awesome capacity we have as sexual creatures. In other words, Catholic teaching about sexuality is good news. Jesus Christ is both true God and true man, the Word of God made flesh. As a man, Jesus too was a sexual being. His sexuality like ours is part of God's good news. Out of love for us, God has revealed himself and given himself to us. He created us out of love. He created us to love one other, and our sexuality is a vital way for us to love others.

However, saying that the Catholic message about sexuality is "good news" does not mean that the message is easy or simple to follow. "Integrated sexuality" is called for. That is, we are to express ourselves sexually in ways that reflect our integrity as physical-spiritual beings made in God's image. The word for such expression is **chastity. R** (p. 226)

fecundity—
fruitfulness; bearing children

chastity—
integration of sexuality reflecting our unity as body and spirit; responsible sexual expression

Qualities of Chastity

We can look to Jesus as the model of chastity. By being baptized into the life of Jesus, we are called to lead lives of chastity, whether we are single or married, laity or consecrated to the religious life as nuns, brothers, or priests. Here are qualities that are associated with this important virtue of chastity.

Self-mastery. The practice of chastity trains us to be truly free. We can either control our passions and find peace, or we can let our passions control us and become enslaved by them. We can give into our blind impulses and lead lives worthy of a soap opera; or we can consciously and freely choose what our conscience tells us is right and realize lives of harmony and holiness.

Ways to achieve chastity. To fulfill our baptismal promises and resist sexual temptation, we are encouraged to obey God's commandments; exercise the virtues of prudence, justice, fortitude, and temperance; heed the teachings of the Church; and be attentive to the Holy Spirit in prayer.

Patience. The self-mastery involved in chastity is a lifelong endeavor. It requires discipline at all stages of life and a redoubling of effort at certain stages, particularly during adolescence.

Grace. Remember, chastity is a moral virtue. We acquire chastity, as all other mortal virtues, through education, deliberate actions, and perseverance. Grace purifies our efforts and heightens the virtue within us.

Reflection

Each of the following comments has been made in reference to sexuality. However, some of the statements reflect a chaste outlook on sexuality; others do not.

For each statement decide:

- Which statements do you agree with or disagree with?

- Which statements more clearly reflect the attitude toward sex of your peer group?

- Which statements do you think reflect the virtue of chastity?

1. If it feels good, do it.

2. Our sexuality is a treasure to be cherished.

3. How do you know what it's like until you've tried it?

4. Our bodies are sacred and sacramental signs of the holy.

5. It's okay to have sexual intercourse as long as you don't hurt anybody.

6. Any level of sexual activity is a sacred trust—to be shared honestly, caringly, and responsibly.

7. Enjoy it now; worry about the consequences later.

8. Sexual intimacy is sharing on a very deep level. Physically, it symbolizes psychological and spiritual intimacy of equal depth. Hence it is reserved for married couples.

9. When we did it, we agreed there would be no strings attached.

10. Sexual involvement with another person represents a serious commitment.

11. If two people truly love each other, then it's okay to have sexual intercourse.

12. Sometimes love means saying "no."

13. Everybody does it. If I don't, then there must be something wrong with me.

14. I feel a lot of pressure to experience sexual intercourse, but I value that intimacy far too much to give in to the pressure.

15. Nowadays it's expected that teens have sexual intercourse. If I have a chance, why should I be any different?

Violations of Chastity

...among the sins gravely contrary to chastity are masturbation, fornication, pornography, and homosexual practices.

✝ **Catechism, #2396**

Concupiscence is an intense form of human desire and is particularly targeted by the ninth commandment. St. Paul identifies concupiscence with the rebellion of the flesh against the spirit. Often it is associated with lust, a craving for sexual gratification without regard for boundaries, morality, or harm to others. Lust disregards the principle that God intends sexual relationships for the procreation of children and the sharing of love within the union of marriage. We combat the power of lust by keeping our hearts pure and by practicing modesty. We purify our hearts by aligning our minds and our wills to the pursuit of holiness, charity, and truth. We practice modesty by respecting our bodies, being patient in our relationships, clothing ourselves in a decent manner, and talking carefully about sexuality.

Masturbation is the erotic stimulation of the genital organs achieved by means other than sexual intercourse. As such, masturbation is an act that violates the intended purpose of God's gift of sexuality. Sexual intercourse is meant for marriage and for the expression of the mutual self-giving and procreation that are a vital part of marriage. It is not meant for our personal and selfish pleasure.

Fornication is sexual intercourse between an unmarried man and an unmarried woman. Once again, the gift of sexual union is meant for the benefit of the married couple and the generation of children. Fornication clearly falls outside of that realm and is, thus, an act that violates chastity.

Pornography is the display of erotic behavior in written or pictorial form for the purpose of sexual excitement. It violates chastity by perverting the gift of sexuality with the sole motivation of sexual arousal. Pornography is an assault on human dignity. It demeans the dignity of everyone involved—the actors, the sellers, and the public—and thus constitutes a grave sin.

Prostitution is the practice or the act of engaging in sexual relations for money or other forms of profit. Those who pay for sexual intercourse sin against themselves, and those who sell themselves violate their dignity by making themselves into mere objects of pleasure. As a people created by a loving God, we have reason to grieve as we see men, women, adolescents, and even children selling their bodies in order to profit monetarily or in other ways. This is especially sad when they sell their bodies to obtain food, clothing, and other necessities of life. **R**

Later in this chapter the issue of rape and the challenges of homosexuality will be discussed.

Reflection

1. How has your religion helped you appreciate sexuality to a greater degree? What are some ways to integrate the virtue of chastity into your daily life?

2. Analyze the following statement: Chastity is against pleasure.

Marriage

Marriage is so important that it is one of the Church's sacraments—the sacrament of Matrimony. Matrimony symbolizes the loving union that Christ has for his Church. The sacrament imparts to the husband and wife the grace to love each other with the depth of love with which Jesus loves the Church. And just as Jesus' union with the Church is unbreakable, the union between a wife and her husband is also indissoluble.

Engaged couples must enter into the marriage covenant with their eyes wide open. By expressing their consent before the Church, the husband and wife mutually confer on each other the sacrament of marriage. Couples, then, should be well prepared to give this consent and thus give themselves, each to the other, in a lifelong covenant of faithfulness and self-sacrifice. Couples should be aware that their love must be open to fertility. And with the gift of children they have the opportunity to transform their home into a "domestic church," in which their children will first learn the truths of faith, the ways of prayer, and the virtues exemplified by Jesus.

Since marriage launches the couple's public life in the Church, it is appropriate that the marriage ceremony be a public celebration. This means that couples should avail themselves of the beautiful liturgy of the Church, pledging their love before the Church's minister, the witnesses, and "the assembly of the faithful" *(Catechism, #1663)*.

Marriage is a vocation, a calling to live life and to encounter God in a particular way. Through marriage a couple forms an "intimate partnership of life and love [GS 48 § 1.]" *(Catechism, #2364)*. Out of their commitment to each other comes the married couple's "mission to transmit human life and to educate their children [GS 50 § 2.]" *(Catechism, #2367)*.

Sexuality in Marriage

Sexuality in marriage serves the following four goals:

- Physical-sexual activity is intimately linked to bearing and raising children. In fact, each and every marital act must be open to the gift of life.

- Physical union represents full and complete sharing of life in love between two people. That is, sexuality in marriage is both life giving and love giving, an expression of mutual commitment to each other and to family life.

- Sexuality finds meaning in relation to community. In other words, our sexuality is not for ourselves alone. In marriage, the "community" involved is at least two people and potentially a third—namely, a child who could be born as the result of sexual union. In addition, sexual activity has an impact on a larger community. A goal for Catholics is to become more caring individuals, people more sensitive to others' needs. Sexuality and marriage cannot be divorced from these community goals. A happy and wholesome outlook on sexuality can help married couples love life and share themselves more lovingly with others *(Catechism, #1534)*.

- Marriage between two baptized persons who are free to marry, carried out in accordance with the Church's laws, is a sacrament. In Matrimony a couple can experience their God and can serve as a sign of his presence to each other and to others. God, who is their Creator and who loves them, is present in every aspect of the life of a married couple—including their outlook on sexuality.

Violations of Marriage

Marriage is a total, lifelong, indissoluble, and exclusive commitment between a man and a woman. Marriage is naturally intended for the good of husbands and wives and for the procreation and education of children (*Catechism, #1601*). The following acts violate this understanding of marriage.

Adultery, expressly forbidden by the sixth commandment, violates the dignity of marriage. Adultery is "[m]arital infidelity, or sexual relations between two partners, at least one of whom is married to another party" (*Catechism, Glossary*). Adultery is an act of injustice against one's spouse and against the sanctity of marriage. Jesus did not mince words when speaking about adultery, condemning even the desire to commit adultery (*Matthew 5:27–28*).

Divorce tears apart that which God has joined together. In fact, divorce spreads its damage in many directions: toward spouses who have truly attempted to maintain their marriage commitment but have been abandoned by their spouse; toward children whose loyalty to both of their parents has been undermined; and toward the good ordering of society that is built on the stability of marriage and family. Jesus said that divorcing one's spouse and marrying another is adultery and that marrying a divorced person likewise is adultery (*Luke 16:18*). In itself, divorce may not be sinful. It is objectively sinful to remarry after divorce if no annulment has been granted by the Church. Thus, "the remarriage of persons divorced from a living, lawful spouse" (*Catechism, #1665*) violates the law and plan of God. Nonetheless, the Church still embraces those who are remarried; and even though they cannot receive the Eucharist, they are encouraged to lead Christian lives and educate their children in the practice of the faith.

Polygamy is having more than one spouse at the same time. It violates the dignity of marriage, which God intends to be an exclusive commitment between one man and one woman. In the United States, polygamy is against civil law.

Incest is defined as sexual relations between people who are so closely related that the law forbids them to marry. The practice of incest corrupts the values that strengthen families. An issue often related to incest is the sexual abuse of children and adolescents by adults. This is an act that is both criminal and deeply evil. Such abuse causes inestimable damage to its victims, who are among the most vulnerable and innocent members of society.

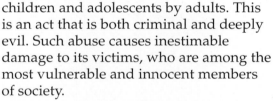

Methods of artificial contraception—such as condoms, birth control pills, tubal ligations, and vasectomies—separate the sexual act from the act of procreation and thus are morally unacceptable. Artificial methods of birth control run counter to the nature of marriage in which sexuality must be open to both the sharing of mutual love and the procreation of children. The link between sexual activity, love, and child-bearing was established by God. Human beings cannot break this link. **A**

Activity

1. Read John 8:2–11. What can you learn from Jesus' treatment of the woman caught in adultery?

2. Read John 4:7–30. What can you learn from Jesus' treatment of the woman at the well?

Sexuality Outside of Marriage

In today's society there are voices pressuring us to believe that it is acceptable to have intimate sexual expression apart from marriage. What does sexuality communicate when it is detached from marriage? Here are three alternative views of what sexuality may communicate as advocated today.

Recreational Sexual Intercourse

recreational sexual intercourse— morally wrong sexual activity as the pursuit of pleasure with no constraints other than mutual consent

Only the most insensitive person would consider sexual intercourse to be a form of communication equal simply to a handshake or a phone call. On the other hand, there are those who recommend that engaging in sexual intercourse for the fun of it is reason enough, even though it is a grave offense against marriage. **Recreational sexual intercourse** says, "If it feels good, do it." The only prerequisite is mutual consent—both parties agree that "whatever happens, happens. I am not responsible for you; you are not responsible for me."

Emotional-Relationship Sexual Intercourse

emotional-relationship sexual intercourse— morally wrong sexual activity presumed as being acceptable when the two people involved feel love for each other

The second perspective on sexuality as language is "If two people feel as though they truly love each other, then intimate sexual intercourse is a natural and acceptable way to express those feelings." In contrast to recreational sexual intercourse, **emotional-relationship sexual intercourse** takes the quality of a relationship into account.

Two people who have established a relationship add sexual intercourse to the ways they relate to each other. Supposedly, they engage in sexual intercourse with a sense of mutual responsibility and respect. However, the responsibility ends as soon as circumstances change, such as when one of the two no longer feels love for the other or a relationship with someone else starts growing. Surprisingly, what the couple plans to do if the woman becomes pregnant is an issue often not addressed. Rules underlying sexual intercourse in such a relationship are unwritten and subject to change. For instance, sex that begins as a desire to express love can continue even after love dies. In this case, it becomes sexuality for convenience rather than sexuality as an expression of love. It is easy to see how emotional-relationship sexual intercourse violates the plan of God.

Almost-Committed Sexual Intercourse

Today, long engagements are more the rule than the exception. There are those who suggest that an "almost total commitment" makes intimate sexuality acceptable and even beneficial. "Almost total commitment" situations might include a couple who are living together, who are planning on getting engaged sometime in the future, or who are already engaged. However, if you talk to any married couple, invariably you will hear from them that "living together" or being engaged is not the same as being married. There is something total and transforming about the union of two people in marriage.

Full physical sexual expression communicates more than just pleasure, more than just a serious relationship, and even more than an almost total commitment between two people. Rather the fullness of sexuality is meant for the fullness of marriage. Only married sexual intercourse combines the recreative (pleasure-sharing) with the unitive (love-expressing) and the procreative (life-giving) characteristics of sexuality. These three qualities together manifest what the fullness of sexual expression is meant to communicate. **R**

almost-committed sexual intercourse— morally wrong sexual activity that presumes that it is acceptable when the two people have expressed a degree of commitment to each other, such as during engagement

For Review...

1. What are the qualities of chastity?

2. What are ways that chastity can be violated?

3. List the four goals of marriage as put forth in recent Church teaching.

4. Name some ways that people can violate the dignity of marriage.

5. Name and describe the three types of sex-as-language described in the text.

Reflection

— For each of the types of sexual expression listed above, write a paragraph describing what message it communicates. Begin the paragraphs:

Recreational sexual intercourse says . . .

Emotional-relationship sexual intercourse says . . .

Almost-committed sexual intercourse says . . .

— Based on your paragraphs, why do you think the Church says that sexuality finds its rightful place in the context of marriage?

Specific Situations

Just fifty years ago most of society knew what was allowed and what was forbidden in regard to sex and other moral activities. The vast majority—including television, popular songs, books, and movies—generally upheld the same standards of conduct as those advocated by the Church. Today, young people experience a great barrage of conflicting opinions and viewpoints about sexuality. At times, it may feel as if Church leaders and teachers are leading Catholics in one direction while much of popular culture is pointing them in another. Meanwhile, young people must contend with intense and newly awakened emotions and physical feelings with the prospect of marriage quite a distance off.

Sexually transmitted diseases (STDs), the availability of birth control options, the epidemic of unwanted teenage pregnancies, the availability of abortion, and the lack of guidance from many elements within society create the need for us to develop a thoughtful, careful, and responsible sexual morality. Self-control, restraint, saying "no," and concern for more than immediate gratification continue to play a much-needed role in our decisions about sexuality. Moreover, we need guidance from more than television talk shows and magazines sold at supermarket checkout counters. In other words, decisions about our sexuality are so important that they deserve our fullest effort and attention.

How Should We Respond to Our Sexual Urges?

Jim and Joann's relationship began slowly. They met at a party and started to seek each other out at social gatherings. Eventually, they started dating and spending most of their time together.

For the entire next year, Jim and Joann dated each other exclusively. Although they didn't talk about sexual intercourse directly and although sexuality has not been the major focus of their relationship, Jim and Joann have become increasingly intimate physically. During the times when they are alone together, they have held to an unspoken rule about "how far to go." Neither Jim nor Joann takes their physical involvement lightly. Whenever they step beyond the boundaries that they unconsciously set for themselves, they feel uncomfortable and find themselves pulling back.

With the junior prom just a few weeks away, Jim and Joann want the night to be special. It seems to be an appropriate time to show how much they love each other; and, with a little planning, the opportunity for privacy will be available. Without discussing the matter with each other, both Joann and Jim wonder if prom night would be the perfect occasion to overstep the boundaries that they have established for themselves. **R**

Reflection

1. Name two television shows and two movies of today that deal in some way with sexuality or relationships. What messages do they communicate? How do they communicate these messages?

2. Compare and contrast these shows with television programs popular in the past.

The story about Jim and Joann is too brief to capture all of the subtleties that are present in a relationship. However, let us consider some questions that this young couple might ask themselves.

Imagine that the prom night arrives, and, after the planned festivities, Jim and Joann steal away and have sexual intercourse for the first time. What effect would this experience have on them individually and on their relationship? What are possible far-reaching effects the experience might have? Or imagine that before prom night arrives, Jim and Joann talk to each other about their desires and decide that they will refrain from becoming more intimate physically—especially on prom night. What effect would this decision have on them and their relationship? Which decision would more likely lead to personal growth and more clearly reflect concern for each other?

A decision to engage in full physical-sexual intimacy outside of marriage is an offense against the sixth commandment and usually leads to an experience of sexuality that is less satisfying, maturing, and loving. Additionally, unnatural sexual stimulation, such as oral sex, is also gravely contrary to natural law. Intimate physical-sexual activity among teenagers never solves problems and frequently makes them worse. The following is a list of problems that can develop for sexually active adolescents:

- Experiencing a type of commitment to another without the structures and supports of a marriage commitment
- Violating conscience and the guilt and turmoil that this causes
- Breaking parental trust
- Changing the focus of a relationship from enjoying each other and growing together to experiencing physical sexuality with each other
- Experiencing a change in other significant relationships, such as with parents and with other close friends of both sexes
- Feeling pressure to continue a relationship which statistically has little chance of ending in marriage
- Feeling more invested in and committed to the relationship than either person originally intended
- Feeling pressures resulting from deep physical intimacy and self-giving, unmatched by total intimacy and self-giving
- Attempting to separate intercourse from a committed relationship open to children
- Risking an unintentional pregnancy **G**

Group Talk

Look over the reasons listed here why unmarried teens should refrain from engaging in full physical-sexual intimacy. Do you think any of the reasons mentioned should not be included? Are any of the reasons not ones that you had thought about? Can you think of other reasons that you would add to the list? Add your response to the list.

Rape: When Sexuality Becomes Violence

rape—
forcing sex on an
unwilling partner

Rape is the forcible violation of the sexual intimacy of another person. It does injury to justice and charity. Rape deeply wounds the respect, freedom, and physical and moral integrity to which every person has a right. It causes grave damage that can mark the victim for life.

✝ **Catechism, #2356**

acquaintance rape—
forcing sex on someone
known by the assailant

date rape—
rape that occurs in the
context of a date or a
dating relationship

By definition, **rape** is forcing sex upon an unwilling partner, regardless of the circumstances. Rape occurs if forced sex happens when a couple have been dating, when a couple are married, when both parties are drunk, when one party initially appears willing, and in other circumstances.

Both women and men can be raped. Recent studies indicate that a surprisingly large number of men were raped when they were growing up. This revelation is not common knowledge because men, like women, often hide this information even from their closest friends and family members. When a victim knows the person who rapes him or her, it is known as **acquaintance rape**. (One form of acquaintance rape is **date rape**—rape that occurs while two people are on a date.) As the following quote points out, acquaintance rape accounts for the greatest percentage of rapes that occur.

Statistics on rape are notoriously unreliable, but most observers now agree that a conservative estimate suggests that at least one out of three women will be raped or will be the victim of attempted rape in her lifetime.

. . .What is particularly troubling is the context in which rape occurs. . . .Rape is not committed only by strangers. In a study of nearly one thousand women, Diana Russell found that only 11 percent had been raped (or had been the victims of attempted rape) by strangers, while 12 percent had been raped by "dates," 14 percent by "acquaintances," and 14 percent by their husbands.

Karen Lebacqz, "Love Your Enemy: Sex, Power, and Christian Ethics," in Lois K. Daly, ed. *Feminist Theological Ethics* (Louisville, KY: John Knox Press, 1994). **A**

Activity

Do research to find the most recent statistics on rape, including incidents of acquaintance rape. Read about organizations concerned about rape and report on any guidelines they provide concerning precautions to prevent rape and what a person can do if she or he has been a victim of rape. What are the laws of your state regarding what constitutes rape?

To understand the phenomenon of the frequency of rape in American society, it is important to examine our society. At the beginning of this chapter, the point was made that the meaning of sexuality is strongly shaped by our culture. Although it has been challenged recently, one theme that is deeply embedded in our culture is that men should play a dominant role in society. Flowing from such a theme, men should be the aggressors and women either the passive receivers or the resistors when it comes to determining the extent of sexual involvement. In a sense, a case could be made that a culture that emphasizes male dominance fosters rape more than mutuality in sexual activity. On the other hand, emphasizing mutual respect and love above self-seeking and control over another supports an atmosphere that clearly rejects rape.

Homosexuality and Catholic Life

Even in high school, Jackie sensed that she was different. She always had friends, both boy and girl friends. She was a leader in many school activities. But dating never appealed to her much. She preferred group activities and working on projects with classmates. As she grew older and started dating, she was more attracted to girls than boys.

When Jackie entered her state university, she looked forward to continuing her involvement in clubs and activities. One organization that caught her eye during orientation week was the "gay and lesbian students' association." At first she laughed: No such organization existed at the Catholic high school she attended! However, she felt drawn to exploring what the organization and its members stood for. Perhaps she could find out more about why she always felt different from her friends who were into dating so much. Jackie also decided to seek out the pastor of the church she had been attending while at school. Maybe he could help her with her dilemma.

As if sexual morality isn't complicated enough when it involves two adults of different genders, same-gender activity requires an even more sound moral analysis. Frequently young children who watch TV know about **heterosexuality** and **homosexuality**—or at least popular stereotypes of homosexuality. In the past few years a number of television shows featured ground-breaking episodes that revealed the homosexual orientation of

cast members or the characters in the shows. (Homosexual activity is sexual activity engaged in by two people of the same gender; heterosexual activity is female-male sexual activity). On this matter, the Church is clear:

- Marriage is the only context for sexual expression.

- Intimate sexual activity finds its true and complete meaning in a marriage between an adult woman and man who love each other, who are committed to each other and to the possibility of having and raising children.

- Homosexual and non-marital hetero-sexual activity fall outside acceptable sexual expression.

homosexuality— sexual attraction toward persons of the same gender. Homosexual activity is sexual activity engaged in by persons of the same gender.

heterosexuality— sexual attraction toward persons of the other gender. Heterosexual activity is sexual activity engaged in by persons of different genders.

Beyond that, both the Church and society have been grappling with two other questions related to homosexuality:

- How can the Church and society help persons with homosexual inclinations to fulfill their Christian vocation to be loving and life-giving people? (People who are homosexual in orientation are called to chastity along with everyone else.)

- How can the Church and society direct non-homosexual persons to treat persons with homosexual inclinations in loving and just ways? ("They must be accepted with respect, compassion, and sensitivity" *[Catechism, #2358]*).

In other words, the existence of persons who have homosexual inclinations rather than heterosexual ones creates a variety of dilemmas for homosexuals and heterosexuals alike. For instance, some states and nations have proposed that homosexual couples should be allowed to marry. Pope John Paul II said that this would distort and undermine the nature of marriage and therefore is unacceptable.

How can the Church and other institutions provide guidance and set rules about how heterosexual and homosexual persons should live their lives and how non-homosexuals should view and treat homosexuals? For instance, how can the Church help prevent violence in word or deed against people whose sexual orientation is homosexual?

Jesus asks his followers to love their neighbors—especially those neighbors whom others would prefer not to love. The presence of homosexual persons in a predominantly heterosexual society represents another way that Jesus' fundamental commandment is put to the test. For instance, recall once again the story of the Good Samaritan *(Luke 10:25–37)*. When a person is found hurting by the side of the road, Jesus wants us to treat that person as a neighbor regardless of whatever prejudice we might hold against that person. The one who helps another in need is being a neighbor. If within the Church community people with homosexual tendencies and people with heterosexual tendencies do not treat each other in neighborly fashion, then the Church is not following the example Jesus has given us. **G**

...Conclusion

Our sexuality is integral to who we are. Our attitudes, values, and behaviors related to sexuality tell us a great deal about ourselves. Through the creative and responsible ways that we express our sexuality, we celebrate ourselves—body and soul, female and male—as made in God's image and as reflections of his love.

For Review...

1. According to the text approximately what percentage of women are victims of rape or attempted rape? What does the text say is most striking about the context of most rapes?

2. How is official Church teaching regarding homosexual sexual activity similar to its teaching on other forms of non-marital sexual activity?

3. What two problems do the Church and society seek to address regarding persons with homosexual inclinations?

Group Talk

Church teaching about the immorality of homosexual activity must not be viewed as a rejection of homosexual persons. For instance, in the late 1990s the U.S. Catholic bishops wrote a letter titled "Always Our Children" in which they cautioned parents to treat homosexual children with the love and care that all God's children deserve. Why do you think that the bishops felt a need to remind Catholics to love young people who discover that they possess homosexual tendencies? Is persecution against gays a problem in our society? In your community? Explain.

Model of Morality

Jean Donovan (1953-1980)

The virtue of chastity does not mean being morbid or looking down on sexual pleasure and the joys of friendship, intimacy, marriage, and family. Rather, chastity calls for recognizing the fullness of what it means to be human and integrating sexuality in a morally acceptable way into the totality of one's life, regardless of one's calling.

You may know the story of Jean Donovan. Raised in an upper-middle class family in Connecticut, her life ended at age twenty-seven serving poor and displaced persons in faraway El Salvador. She died at the hands of a Salvadoran death squad who viewed helping people who are poor as an affront to the government. Jean's body, along with the bodies of three nuns with whom she worked, was found by the side of the road near their old van.

Jean Donovan

Before volunteering for the dangerous work she undertook in El Salvador, Jean lived what we would consider to be a typical young person's life in America. She held a steady job in the business field. She was known for partying and having a good time with friends. In fact, most people who knew her thought of her as happy-go-lucky and a jokester. She did have her eccentricities, such as driving her motorcycle to work, which was not the standard vehicle in the business world. When she told acquaintances that she had entered a program preparing her for mission work in El Salvador, one of her friends asked her if she were planning on being "Saint Jean the Playful."

When Jean left for El Salvador, she had the "American dream" in sight. She had a good job and was engaged to a doctor.

She wanted her own family and the pleasures of life. El Salvador was a dangerous place to live, which she knew, but she also saw first hand the suffering of the people there, especially of the children. She felt her presence made a difference. However, shortly before her death she wrote:

I'm 26 years old. I should be married. I shouldn't be running around doing all of these things. But then I think, I've got so many things I want to do. It's hard when I see my friends getting married and having babies, that's something I've thought about . . . am I ever going to have kids? Sometimes I wonder if I'm denying that to myself. I really don't want to, but that's maybe what I'm doing. And then I sit there and talk to God and say, why are you doing this to me? Why can't I just be your little suburban housewife? He hasn't answered yet.

(quoted in "Jean Donovan: Except for the Children," Religious Task Force on Central America and Mexico Web site, page 4)

Jean Donovan is a model of chastity because she gave herself in friendship to people, creating relationships with others on an equal level. She also willingly gave herself selflessly to the people in El Salvador who had special needs. Whether in a business office, at a party, or in a Salvadoran barrio Jean exuded joy and spread her joy to others. She integrated the physical and the spiritual in all that she did. In so doing she was living the virtue of chastity. If she had survived the troubled time of El Salvador and returned to the States, no doubt she would have lived a fruitful and joyous life of mutual sharing with others, even if she became a "little suburban housewife."

Leader: Let us pray. Jesus, like us, you experienced bodily pain and pleasure. Like us, you were drawn to other people and others were drawn to you. You touched people, and they were healed. We pray that our bodies and our emotions, the deep well of our physical urges, our capacities for thinking and deciding, and our need for one another may serve as wholesome companions as we seek to know you and to love others throughout our lives.

All: Amen.

Reader #1: Genesis 1:26–31

Reader #2: Mark 10: 13–16

Leader: The Word became flesh . . .

All: and lived among us.

Leader: The Word became flesh . . .

All: and finds delight in people.

Leader: The Word became flesh . . .

All: so that the awesome preciousness of our bodies might be revealed.

Leader The Word became flesh . . .

All: to remind us to care for our bodies.

Leader: The Word became flesh . . .

All: and experienced the challenges of change and growth.

Leader: The Word became flesh . . .

All: to celebrate—touch, taste, sights, sounds, and smells.

Leader: The Word became flesh . . .

All: proclaiming New Life for soul and body.

Leader: The Word became flesh . . .

All: to greet us eye to eye.

Leader: The Word became flesh . . .

All: and is present when we meet in love.

Leader: The Word became flesh . . .

All: to share our pleasure and pain, our grief and anxiety.

Leader: The Word became flesh . . .

All: finding a beauty in us that even we can't see.

Leader: The Word became flesh . . .

All: and calls us out of boredom to delight in the people and things around us.

Leader: The Word became flesh . . .

All: a Word who heals through the power of physical touch.

Leader: The Word became flesh . . .

All: to assure us that our desires rightly channeled lead us to God.

Leader: Jesus, our brother in the flesh, you embodied the way, the truth, and the life for us. May we together, each one of us embodied in our own unique way, give glory and praise to you now and forever. Amen.

13

LIVING THE TRUTH IN LOVE

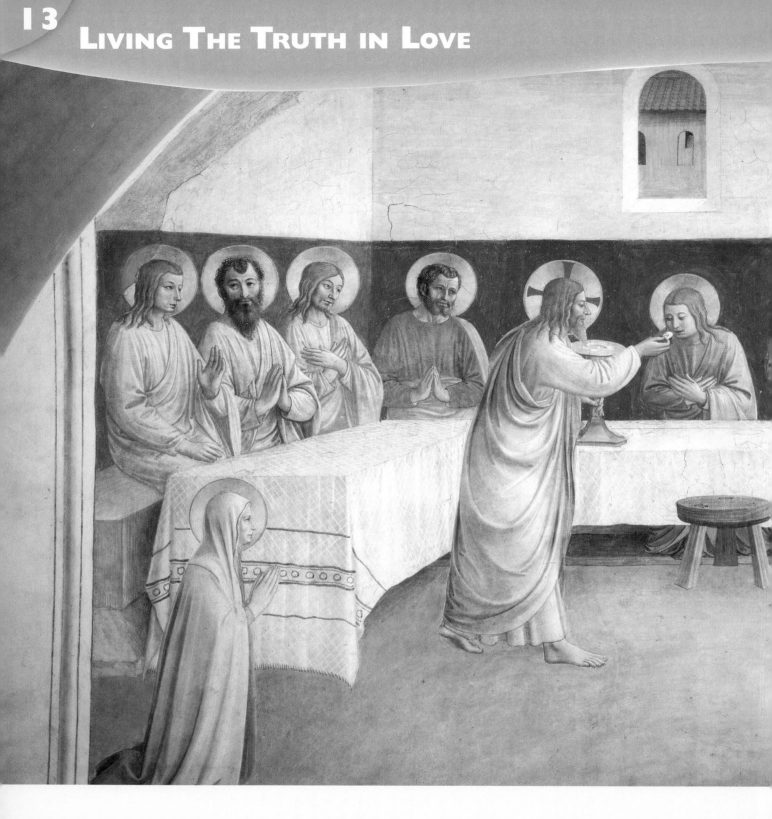

Chapter Overview

- The eighth commandment calls us to respect truth.
- We can abuse speech by what we say or fail to say.
- Disregard for truth leads to a culture of mistrust.
- A truthful society seeks to give all people a voice and to address their needs.

The eighth commandment states:"Do not bear false witness against your neighbor." As with all the commandments, the eighth commandment has broader applications than the narrow meaning of the words. That is, it means much more than simply not speaking falsely about others. The commandment points out that only a life lived with honesty and integrity reflects our dignity as persons created by God and in his image. In short, it obliges us to live the truth in love.

Before we begin . . .

1. "Don't bother with Brendan. He joined the drug crowd. Now he's high all the time."
2. "Do you have Mr. Brown for Spanish class? Everybody says he's gay."
3. "Why is Matt coming along? He's a fat, zit-faced slob. No girls will talk to us now."
4. "Just tell your dad that we're going to the game at school. We'll stop in at the game and then go to the party at Darien's house. That way you won't be lying."
5. "I'd love to be a teacher; I think it's my true vocation. However, I'm going to major in business in college since there's no money in teaching."

—Most of the statements refer to a person or group who is being talked about. Put yourself in that person's or group's place. Would you find the statement hurtful? A lie? An unfair representation of the truth?

—Does every statement involve lying, deception, or harmful speech? If not, name exceptions.

—Do any of the statements involve lying to oneself?

—Is every statement morally wrong to say? If not, what would make some statements acceptable and others not?

—Are any statements stereotyping? Is stereotyping always misleading or falsifying the truth?

Let us pray . . .

Jesus, our brother, guide us as we seek to know the truth and to speak and act according to the truth. Be with us in the decisions we make so that others will see us as persons of integrity. Help us to be honest with ourselves, that we may be beacons of truth throughout our lives. Keep us on the straight path until we find eternal rest with you and the saints. Amen.

Living in the Light of Truth

"For all who do evil hate the light and do not come to the light, so that their deeds may not be exposed. But those who do what is true come to the light, so that it may be clearly seen that their deeds have been done in God.**"**

John 3:20–21

Have you ever been outside when twilight turns to darkness, and you can't quite make out figures in the distance coming your way? It may be a dog or a cat. It might even be a mountain lion! Living in darkness may be thrilling momentarily, but it would become overbearing if that were our only experience. We long for the light. When we lie we contribute to the darkness, fomenting an atmosphere of uncertainty and mistrust around us. Continual lying makes our personality as murky as distant figures in twilight. Lying prevents relationships from blossoming. Relationships can be pretty fragile to begin with. Those built on lies will inevitably crumble or, worse yet, destroy the people who are in them. If you have ever experienced an open, honest, and mutually considerate relationship, then you know the difference. **A**

A directive underlying all of the last six commandments is, "Don't be cruel." Initially, the eighth commandment seems less significant than the earlier ones. On face value it condemns misrepresenting the truth and publicly making disparaging remarks about others. Murder, theft, and adultery seem to be much more cruel than "bearing false witness." This perspective fails to realize the impact of the words we say and of what we communicate in general. Some older adults have wrestled all of their lives with the demon of one derogatory remark made by a parent, a teacher, or a trusted companion during their childhood. Jesus himself does not relegate cruel speech to being a less important commandment. He makes a strong case for the opposite position:

"You have heard that it was said to those of ancient times, 'You shall not murder;' and 'whoever murders shall be liable to judgment.' But I say to you that if you are angry with a brother or sister, you will be liable to judgment; and if you insult a brother or sister, you will be liable to the council; and if you say, 'You fool,' you will be liable to the hell of fire.**"**

Matthew 5: 21–22

Activity

Write a story describing a relationship built upon lies. Then re-write the story as if the relationship were built on honesty. Compare the two relationships.

Bearing Witness to the Truth

Prior to his crucifixion, when he was being interrogated by Pontius Pilate, Jesus stated his reason for coming into the world: "to testify to the truth. Everyone who belongs to the truth listens to my voice" *(John 18:37)*. That is, Jesus' entire reason for being, his entire life, was to be a witness to truth. Interestingly, the word "martyr" means witness. Early Christians who recognized Christ's truth refused to deny him. As a consequence many were killed, proclaiming a message of truth in their very blood. We know these witnesses who kept the light of truth alive as the great martyrs of the early Church.

Jesus calls his followers to be witnesses to the truth. We do this by being truthful. Truthfulness is the virtue by which we are true in what we do and truthful in what we say. We are truthful when we choose not to be hypocrites, liars, double-dealers, or frauds. By acting truthfully Jesus and the martyrs paid with their lives. Today our truthfulness can occasionally exact a heavy price from us, and yet we suffer an even worse fate if we don't align ourselves with truth. Living a lie kills the spirit. Even laziness in the pursuit of truth wounds the soul.

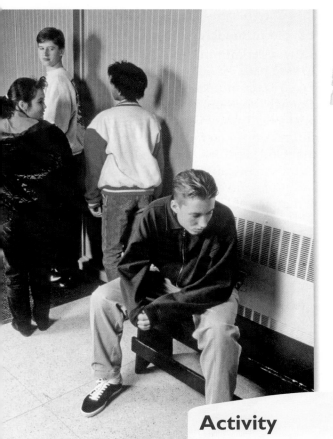

> *"Man is the only animal that blushes. Or needs to."*
>
> Mark Twain

By our very nature, we are inclined toward the truth. Our dignity as human beings requires us to seek the truth and, once we know it, to act in accordance with it. Even though people lie, it's important to realize that truth telling is behavior proper to the human condition. This is why we blush or fidget when we're not telling the truth. In fact there's something wrong with us if we're not uncomfortable lying. Lying without being aware that it is an aberration is sickness, a psychological disorder. **A**

Activity

—Write on an index card what you believe is the basic truth proclaimed by Jesus. Consider carrying the card with you.

—Give examples when living or speaking the truth could be difficult.

—Truth telling is referred to as "uprightness." *(Catechism, #2468)* What opposite image could be used to describe lying? Why would this be an appropriate image?

—The great American writer and humorist Mark Twain often wrote about lying. In *Huck Finn* Twain comments:"You can't pray a lie." Explain what he might have meant.

A Primer on Communication—Four Principles

1. **Verbal and Nonverbal communication.**
Studies indicate that between sixty and eighty percent of what we communicate comes through nonverbal messages. Nonverbals include tone of voice, accent, eye contact, physical proximity and appearance, surroundings, posture and body position, and gestures. Nonverbals refer to everything but the words we say. If we claim (in words) to be interested in what someone has to say but our body language (nonverbals) indicates otherwise, the other person typically responds more to the nonverbal messages. Therefore, if we want to witness to the truth, we need to be attentive not just to what we say but also to how we say it.

2. **We're always communicating.**
We walk into class late and slowly make our way to the back of the room. We shuffle through papers and never look up at the teacher. Whether we like it or not, we're communicating to everyone else in the room. Five people are sitting together at lunch. Two of them do all the talking, and yet everyone of them is communicating in some way. A student is giving a presentation in class and her classmates appear to be bored to death. They are communicating. Such is the human condition. Our lives are a constant give and take. Therefore, to follow the eighth commandment we need to witness to the truth in love in all of our encounters with others.

3. **We are continually participating in "feedback loops."**
Whatever someone communicates to us affects us in some way. In turn our response affects the other person. Communication is always two-way. This dynamic of constant action and reaction during communication is known as a "feedback loop." There is not one who gives and one who takes but rather ongoing give and take. Feedback loops extend beyond the few people immediately involved in communication. We then give to and receive from others who in turn interact with people whom we'll never know. Through our communication we are helping to create the world. It can be harmonious music or a Tower of Babel.

4. **We can't avoid influencing others.**
Since we're always communicating, it's important to step back on occasion to think about what we're communicating. Our ongoing influence on others is an awesome responsibility as well as a wonderful dimension of our humanity. In fact, Christianity proclaims that God "speaks" through us. In the words of the American monk Thomas Merton, "God utters me like a word containing a partial thought of Himself" (*New Seeds of Contemplation, page 37*). That is, every smile or kind word offered to another also gives a hint of him. Likewise, angry and hateful words distort the image of God that we are meant to be. Finally, while he communicates through us, we also must recognize that God communicates to us through others. Therefore, communication includes listening to the word of God spoken through those around us. **R**

Reflection

— Give examples of situations when nonverbals communicate something different from the verbal messages spoken.

— Spontaneity is important in communication. However, it's also helpful to examine how and what we communicate without our awareness. Ask an acquaintance or two to describe your style of communicating.

— Describe the difference it would make if we viewed ourselves and others as "words uttered by God."

Respect for the Truth

Respect for truth means respect for persons. **Lying** is the most obvious offense against the eighth commandment. When we lie, we communicate a falsehood in order to mislead someone. By misleading others or leading them into error, we are showing them disrespect. The seriousness of the lie can be determined "by the nature of the truth it deforms, the circumstances, the intentions of the one who lies, and the harm suffered by its victims" *(Catechism, #2484)*.

Outright lying is not the only way to offend against the eighth commandment. We can violate the commandment even by telling the truth. For example, if a close friend tells us something deeply personal about himself and asks us to keep it a secret, are we duty bound to avoid telling anyone else? If we even find out information about someone that could be damaging, must we refuse to share the information? If we hear a rumor about someone without knowing whether there's any truth to it, can we pass it on?

Knowledge about others is precious. We need "to judge whether or not it is appropriate to reveal the truth to someone who asks for it" *(Catechism, #2488)*. We must also be reminded that, "Everyone should observe an appropriate reserve concerning persons' private lives" *(Catechism, #2492)*. By the same token, we must be judicious about keeping secrets. Certainly the secrets confessed in the Sacrament of Reconciliation cannot be revealed. And when confidences that may harm others are entrusted to us, we are responsible not to divulge them to others.

Respect for the truth requires us to make judgments about what to do with the many truths that we discover. Respect for the truth does not give us permission to be brutally honest. **G**

lying—
"saying what is false with the intention of deceiving one's neighbor" *(Catechism, #2508)*

For Review...

1. What does Jesus say about language that is injurious of others?

2. What is the opposite of "bearing false witness"?

3. What does Jesus tell Pilate his mission is?

4. What does the word *martyr* mean?

5. Are human beings naturally inclined toward the truth or falsehood?

6. Name the four principles of communication.

7. Is it always acceptable to reveal truths about someone?

Group Talk

— Is keeping or revealing secrets always/sometimes/never a good thing? Explain.

— Is it acceptable for parents to read their teenage child's private diary (never/always/sometimes)?

— Can you think of types of information about someone that would be inappropriate to reveal?

— Can you recall a rumor that you heard? Were you quick to believe it or did you reserve judgment? What did you do with the information?

— Name three observations about someone that could be stated in either positive or negative ways.

— Rate yourself on your practice of speaking well of others.

Offenses Against Truth

Four Misuses of Speech

> Respect for the reputation and honor of persons forbids all detraction and calumny in word or attitude.

 **Catechism, #2507**

calumny—
telling lies defaming someone's character

detraction—
revealing personal, derogatory information without sufficient reason

rash judgment—
judging another person unkindly

gossip—
participating in the spread of injurious information about someone

Unless we're particularly jaded, we sense whether or not we are telling the truth in love. Here are some of the ways that we can violate this principle. **Calumny** means telling lies about someone in a way that injures his or her good name. **Detraction** refers to revealing, without sufficient reason, information about someone that injures his or her good name. That is, unnecessarily injuring someone's good name is wrong whether or not what we say is a lie. Revealing information about someone is wrong if our intention is to dishonor or make fun of the person. **Rash judgment** means presuming the worst about another without adequate information to back up our judgment. **Gossip** refers to passing on true or false negative information for no beneficial reason.

These four offenses are assaults on personal dignity since they involve humiliating someone. They also demonstrate how feedback loops operate at their worst. We could steal someone's property and later return it. We can't restore a person's good name once it has been taken away. Belittling remarks about another, whether spoken seriously or in jest, can spread like wildfire. Therefore, the offender in the offense is not just the one speaking but the one who seeks out and readily accepts the comments. In other words, if we harbor a desire to hear about someone's faults then we are fostering an atmosphere simmering with gossip and rash judgment. Such an atmosphere creates a culture of mistrust.

One venue ripe for gossip and rash judgment is the Internet. People can feel comfortable spreading stories about others in Internet exchanges that they wouldn't say about them in person. However, despite the impersonal nature of the Internet, peoples' good names can be injured just as badly. Actually, calumny and detraction via the Internet can be even more harmful than telling lies or revealing secrets to one or two friends. Sharing derogatory stories over the Internet can increase the audience, and the potential harm, a thousand-fold.

> *"The Church's call and God's commandment to reverence the truth teach us that without truth there can be no trust, and without trust there can be no true community. . ."*
>
> Bishop Donald W. Wuerl, *The Catholic Way* (New York: Doubleday, 2001), page 339

The Power of Scandal

Scandal takes on a particular gravity by reason of the authority of those who cause it or the weakness of those who are scandalized.

Catechism, #2285

Scandal—
wrongdoing that serves to disillusion or harm more vulnerable people; "an attitude or behavior which leads another to do evil. . . grave offense if by deed or omission another is deliberately led into a grave offense." *(Catechism, #2284)*

perjury—
lying under oath

"Tax scandal rocks nation's capital." "State police investigated in sex scandal." The term **scandal** here points to an affront against truth and integrity by people who are entrusted with a responsibility to uphold these virtues. Scandal refers to (a) wrongdoing by people who hold some kind of trust and (b) misusing that trust in such a way that it harms and disturbs more vulnerable people. Adults and teens can betray their trust with children through words or examples. For instance, an Australian study found that more than half of young people ages eleven to seventeen had seen some pornography on the Internet. It's scandalous for someone to make sexually explicit material available knowing that a good chance exists that children will see it. Teenage drinking is illegal. Teenagers drinking in front of younger brothers and sisters, presenting it as fun without inherent dangers, adds a dimension of scandal to the behavior. **A**

The most public form of bearing false witness is **perjury**. Someone commits perjury who lies under oath, such as in a court of law. Perjury is a punishable crime because the judicial system depends upon a witness telling the truth.

Activity

Name an incident that represents scandal as described here.

Self-Deception versus Self-Confidence

Me and Them

Better not let them know what I like, they'll think I'm weird.

Better not let them know what I think, they may disagree.

Better not laugh too soon or too long, they may not think I'm cool.

Better not express my feelings, they'll think I'm gay.

I can't seem to make it where it really counts, in the social scene.

"They" won't let me, ready to pounce on any sign of weakness or violation of the unwritten code.

God, let me be free.

Let me be me.

Imagine trying to convince yourself that you really like someone even though you don't anymore. Or telling yourself that everything is okay when you're falling apart. Or trying to impress some classmates by telling them that you went to a particular concert over the summer when you didn't.

The above examples represent lying to others. They also suggest a degree of lying to oneself.

Self-deception is a dangerous game to play. If we have inadequate self-confidence then disappointment with our actual reality can lead to creating a fictionalized reality.

Self-deception may at times be a moral choice, but often it reflects our psychological makeup. Young children can describe things as they want them to be rather than as they are. If we continue this practice past childhood then it's a problem. From a psychological perspective, lying can go both ways. We can try to build ourselves up by putting others down. Or we can try to inflate ourselves unreasonably. When we address our self-deception and come to terms with the truth, we discover the power of the phrase, "the truth will make you free" *(John 8:32)*.

In contrast to lying, the eighth commandment urges us to develop personal qualities that identify us as persons of truth. Being reliable and trustworthy are two such qualities.

Genuineness and honesty are also characteristics of a person of truth. Even though our culture encourages us to be ourselves, we experience many pressures preventing us from doing so. It's good to know that we're not alone in our struggles to be upright persons. Jesus assures us that: "If you continue in my word, you are truly my disciples; and you will know the truth, and the truth will make you free" *(John 8:31–32)*. **G**

Group talk

— Do you believe that self-deception is strictly a psychological problem, not a moral one? Explain.

— How common do you think self-deception is? What are some ways we can work against this tendency?

— On occasion movies explore the twists and turns of self-deception. Describe a film in which self-deception plays a role.

— List characteristics that you associate with a person of truth.

Standing Up for Ourselves and Others

Lying is a form of violence and destruction. It damages our ability to know what is true and what is false and thus affects our decisions and judgments. Lying can plant seeds of discord and discontent that can grow into many forms of evil. Lying can destroy friendships and families and can undermine the trust that is so important to the well-being of our communities. When we commit offenses against truth, we are obliged to make appropriate reparation.

Even revealing factual information about another can be destructive. However, it is also important to realize that we can show disrespect for truth through our silence. At times we are called upon to make our voices heard in the cause of compassion and concern. For instance, when people are bullying a friend or when rash judgments are being hurled against a teacher, a stranger, or a public figure, we need to tell the truth in love. The same principle applies to ourselves.

Standing up for ourselves and others takes courage. For many of us asserting ourselves, even in the cause of truth, is particularly difficult. Whenever we make an attempt to stand up for those who are being put down we are being heroic. We are also aligning ourselves with God who is truth. **R**

For Review...

1. Give an example of each of the following:
   —calumny
   —detraction
   —rash judgment
   —gossip

2. Name two ways the Internet contributes to possible violations of the eighth commandment.

3. Define the terms *scandal* and *perjury*.

4. What psychological factor can lead to self-deception?

5. 5. What does it mean to say that we can disrespect truth through silence?

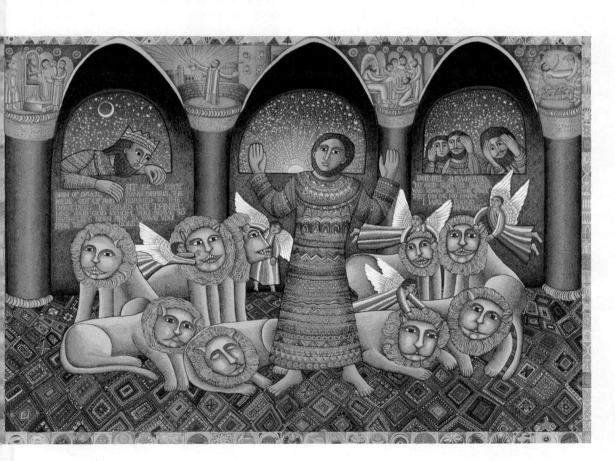

Reflection

Have you personally stood up for or have you observed someone else stand up for someone who was being put down? Describe the incident.

Truthfulness in the Public Arena

Society has a right to information based on truth, freedom, and justice. One should practice moderation and discipline in the use of social communication media.

 Catechism, #2512

spin—
giving a self-serving slant on a news story; manipulation of the truth intended to deceive

Civic leaders have a special responsibility to uphold the truth. Unfortunately, politicians often try to get elected by disassociating themselves from other politicians or from "politics as usual." As campaigns move along, candidates frequently attack one another not on issues but on personal integrity. Such exchanges feed into the mentality that "all politicians are corrupt." While we need to be cautious of statements made by civil authorities, we also need to be cautious about harboring expectations of deception on their part. That is, rash judgment of public figures contributes to a culture of mistrust.

Television has become the primary medium through which citizens receive news of current events. TV lends itself to a particular approach to reporting the news—brief sound bites of information. What we hear from representatives of government and journalists is their **spin** on events. "Spinning" is a relatively new term and has come to mean manipulation of the truth intended to deceive. "Spin doctors" are political commentators or spokespersons who present information in such a way that aspects of the story unfavorable to their view are left out. **G**

We are to form "enlightened and correct consciences" *(Catechism, #2496)*. A well-formed conscience is truthful, that is it makes judgments using sound reason, the wisdom of Church teachings, and the gifts of the Holy Spirit. With the help of a well-formed conscience, we are more capable of sifting through the media's spin and sound bites. Our conscience can lead us to an understanding of what is true and what is false in the world around us.

Group Talk

Are the following statements examples of spinning? What interpretation of each one would make it spinning?

1. "We're winning the war on poverty."

2. "People in that country are better off thanks to our decisive military action."

3. "Our candidate has done more to help the environment than any others."

4. "We have increased one hundred percent the amount of money spent on national security."

5. "Violence among young people today is caused by songs containing constant references to violence."

Media and the Blurring of Truth

Sources of information available to us have multiplied exponentially over the past decade or so. And yet quality information through major media outlets is scarce or seldom explored by most people. Many Americans report getting most of their knowledge of current events from watching late-night talk shows intended to be entertainment. News journal programs are under pressure to be both entertaining and informative. Some news programs feature segments or interviews about other television shows rather than about events that touch people's lives. Even news programs must respond to what people want. "The news" is reduced to a newspaper headline or a two-minute segment of a television program. Extensive coverage of an issue takes place only during major crises. The truth can become blurred or lost, even though we encounter an overwhelming number of images from the media.

According to the Catechism, information from the media should be:

—true

—complete

—honestly and properly conveyed. *(#2494)*

The three terms work together. A quick factual statement may be true but not complete. As mentioned in relation to spinning, true statements can be less than honest if only partial or slanted information is given. When there's pressure to present

stories in a provocative, entertaining way, then they can be improperly conveyed. In relation to advertising, it is wise to remember: "Let the buyer beware." Television news, features, and "docu-dramas" require a similar caution, "Let the viewer beware." **A**

Activity

If an entertainment program runs a segment portraying a celebrity in a negative light, how do you tend to respond?

In 2003 the CBS Television Network decided not to show a mini-series depicting the personal life of President Ronald Reagan during the time he was in the White House. The program portrayed the president negatively. Some people pressured CBS that it was inappropriate to portray a former president in a negative light while he was still alive. Others felt that the negative portrait did not coincide with what they knew of President Reagan.

— Did CBS make the right decision in canceling the program? In answering this question, consider:

— freedom of the press and free speech

— calumny, detraction, and rash judgment

Truth and Art

Michelangelo's "Pietà" portrays the Blessed Mother holding her son Jesus right after he was taken down from the cross. The sculpture beautifully captures the human experience of death and grieving in a powerful way. Under its discussion of the eighth commandment, the Catechism examines the role of art in human life. It seems to be an unusual connection. Art is not about truth, is it? It's about beauty. Doesn't art offer the possibility of departing from truth, bending it in strange and peculiar ways? And yet truth and beauty have traditionally been linked together. (Catechism, #2500)

The beauty of a work of art reveals an otherwise hidden truth and sheds new light on it. Works of art should "give form to the truth of reality in a language accessible to sight or hearing" (Catechism, #2501). Artistic creation is a particular activity since human beings are created in the image of God. Great works of art unveil the beauty of truth in ways that we would otherwise miss. **R**

For Review...

1. What effect can negative campaigning have on voter perceptions?

2. What is *spinning*?

3. How does television blur the presentation of truth?

4. What is the relationship between beauty and truth as exhibited in art?

Reflection

1. To be considered a real work of art, does an artistic piece need to be:

   — well-constructed

   — uplifting

   — truthful

   — comforting

   — a trigger for the emotions

   — a depiction of something pleasant

   — a window into the human condition?

2. Can we say of a work of art:

   — bad art, good moral message?

   — good art, bad moral message? Explain.

3. Name and describe a work of art (any medium) that exposes lies or portrays a truth often overlooked.

4. Ask an art teacher or an artist how they view the relationship between beauty and truth. (You might also look for any statement on the subject from famous artists.)

Uncovering Truth and Falsehood

Every form of social or cultural discrimination in fundamental personal rights on the grounds of sex, race, color, social conditions, language, or religion must be curbed and eradicated as incompatible with God's design.

Gaudium et Spes, #29 § 2. (quoted in Catechism, #1935)

Scripture refers to Satan as "the father of lies" and "deceiver" *(John 8:44, Revelation 12:9)*. In other words, evil is particularly sinister when it passes itself off as the truth. We accept many falsehoods because they are ingrained in our cultural consciousness. We can miss evils around us because they appear to be true. Evil lies and doesn't blush.

The eighth commandment calls for the pursuit of truth. People in our world and even in our communities are hurting in ways that we are barely aware of. Respect for truth means bringing to light ways that people are hurting in our society and seeking ways to help the people of the world who are suffering from discrimination. Certain perspectives on people are deeply entrenched in the group consciousness of our society. Sometimes we overlook the truth because we don't look behind stereotypes.

On the deepest level, we're all children of the same God. He has created us in his image and likeness and looks upon each of us as a person of dignity. We are called to respect that dignity by considering everyone as "another self." We are called to do what we can to "reduce excessive social and economic inequalities" *(Catechism, #1947)* that undermine the dignity of God's children. **R**

> **discrimination—**
> a situation in which people suffer disadvantages simply because they are members of a particular group (for example, age, race, gender)

Discrimination

Discrimination exists when people suffer disadvantages simply because they are members of a particular group— for example, because they belong to a certain socioeconomic class, or to a particular race, gender, or age. When it exists on a societal level, discrimination against members of these groups is categorized as classism, racism, sexism, and ageism.

Reflection

This section categorizes people according to class, race, sex, and age. Does taking note of how different groups of people are faring in our society help us uncover truth? Give examples to explain your position.

Classism

True or false: class differences are not very important in the United States. In our society, we like to downplay the importance of social class. We envision that anyone in the United States can grow up to become president, a millionaire, the head of a corporation, a world-renowned doctor, or a sports superstar. All it takes is talent, hard work, and the right amount of luck. We think that those who make it to the top deserve their rewards or simply happened to luck out, like winning the lottery. On the other hand, those at the bottom should accept the fact that they simply do not measure up to the successful. We look for inspiration to the story of Abraham Lincoln who made the leap from log cabin to White House. We recount stories of immigrants who arrived penniless in our country and later rose to wealth, fame, or power.

Some "rags to riches" stories are true. However, the truth is that the great majority of poor people in our country are trapped in the same spiral of poverty at work worldwide. That is, the richest people in our country have a commanding head start in the competition for quality education, the best jobs, access to the finest health-care facilities, housing in safe and preferred neighborhoods, cultural enrichment, travel, and many other benefits that we equate with success in our society. On the other hand, a child born into a family living below the poverty line is unlikely to obtain a solid preparation for college, will receive inadequate or minimal health care and nutrition, and will not be exposed to much of the cultural enrichment that is commonplace for others. Only the most heroic of efforts and the best of luck will transport this child into the mainstream of American social and economic life. Thus, the vast majority of poor people in our country currently make up an underclass that is trapped and powerless to make economic and cultural advances, at least by following conventional channels.

Racism

racial prejudice—
strong dislike for members of a race other than one's own

racism—
subordination of persons who belong to a particular race due to attitudes, actions, or institutional structures at work in a society

Church leaders have called racism an open wound that still plagues our world. This wound is manifest in our country in ways such as inequality among racial groups in terms of life expectancy, infant mortality rates, unemployment statistics, representation in positions of power, and average income levels. Currently, even though the majority of poor people in the U.S. are white, a disproportionate percentage of the poor are Native Americans, African Americans, and Latinos. Not surprisingly, members of these races also comprise a small percentage of those in positions of power in our society, such as politicians, lawyers, judges, college professors, business CEOs, and so forth.

This last fact points to an important distinction that we need to make: **Racism** is different from **racial prejudice**. Racial prejudice is a strong dislike for members of another race simply because they are members of that race. On the other hand, racism is more than the racial prejudice of individuals. The U.S. Commission on Civil Rights defines racism as "any attitude, action or institutional structure that subordinates a person or group because of their color" (*Racism in America and How to Combat It,* 1970). In other words, racism means that in a society certain groups have more power and others less power because of race. Racism means that members of certain racial groups suffer disproportionately or lack benefits available to others. Like all justice concerns, racism describes society in general and not just individuals.

Racism can be direct, that is, when race is the obvious and intended criterion by which someone suffers injustice. Racism can also be indirect, in which case racial discrimination is not intentional but race is nonetheless a factor leading to injustice. An example of direct racism would be if a real estate company purposely refuses to sell homes in a designated neighborhood to members of a particular race. Indirect racism would be if all brokers of a particular real estate company are members of one race who seek out as prospective buyers only members of their race—not because it represents official policy but simply because that is the way they have always done business. **R**

Sexism

"*Often when speaking about women, their lives and their needs, a member of the audience will confront me with the question, 'How can you be concerned about women when there is so much suffering, so much poverty, so much starvation in the world?' That kind of question, I believe, comes from a habit of thinking of 'the poor,' 'the homeless,' or 'the hungry' as abstractions. When we try to touch the human face of poverty, we will disproportionately discover a woman's face, often a minority woman's face. She will be young and she will be old. Statistically, she ranks among the 'poorest of the poor.' In the United States, two of three adults in poverty are women; worldwide that statistic climbs to over 70%.*"

Maria Riley OP, "Women Are the Poor," in Center Focus [November 1984], Washington, DC: Center of Concern.

The hour is coming, in fact has come, when the vocation of women is being acknowledged in its fullness, the hour in which women acquire in the world an influence, an effect and a power never hitherto achieved.

Pope John Paul II, *On the Dignity and Vocation of Women* [1988], Introduction.

Sexism refers to attitudes, practices, and institutional structures that oppress people solely on the basis of their gender. In two important areas, income and public power, statistics show that women more than men suffer from sexism both in the United States and throughout the world. The vast majority of people who are poor are women and the children dependent upon them. Poor women tend to lack resources available to poor men; typically women carry added burdens that men do not. (For instance, a poor man is more likely to leave family behind to go in search of work or better living arrangements while a woman with children is more likely to place immediate needs of the children above her own economic betterment.)

sexism—

attitudes, practices, and institutional structures that oppress people solely on the basis of gender

Reflection

— Defend your stance on this statement: In my country, class divisions do not exist.

— "The Church and Racism" document from 1988 claims that racism is "a wound in humanity's side that mysteriously remains open." Does this statement still apply today? What kinds of information would support your answer to this question? Find statistics via the Internet that would support or refute your answer.

Even apart from the numbers who are poor, women on average earn less than men do, even in the U.S.

To say that women suffer from sexism does not mean that men are free from pressures and problems because they are men. Our society presents stereotypes about what it means to be a woman and to be a man. As is equally true for women, men can experience great pressure to measure up to a particular image of society's ideal. Over against sexism, justice calls for setting people free to be themselves and providing equal opportunities for people to develop themselves. **G**

Ageism

ageism— discrimination against people solely on the basis of their age

Growing old brings its own pleasures and its pains. However, if difficulties experienced by older people are intensified by societal attitudes and practices, then ageism results. **Ageism**, discrimination based on age, can be a problem for people of any age. No doubt at some time in your life you have felt discriminated against because of your age. However, our society tends to glorify youth. Older people who wish to remain active and vital must fight against cultural stereotypes. Older people who find it more and more difficult to remain active and vital need special care from younger members of society.

As with every other "ism" we have named, justice applied to ageism asks: Are people hurting in any way because of societal values and practices related to age? In one culture, older people tend to be viewed more as a blessing than a burden. In another culture, the opposite attitude can be dominant. When social attitudes and commonly accepted practices add to rather than diminish the trials of biological aging, then injustice results. **R**

Group Talk

A. In American culture are there "lies" about how men and women should look and act? If so, name some.

— Are the cultural images of how men and women should look and act harmful? Do they influence you in any way?

— Do you think that pressures about appearance will be lessened or increased as you get older?

B. Use examples to debate the following statement: In our society, women typically experience more disadvantages than men do.

...Conclusion

We are drawn to the truth, and truth is powerful. The Gospels refer to Jesus as "the truth." When Jesus asks us to speak the truth in love, he has in mind truth made known in him through the Father. We discover in Jesus truths about ourselves and our destiny that we could miss if not for him. His truth often flies in the face of more conventional wisdom. Jesus also gives us a model for truthful living. The eighth commandment enjoins us to speak and live the truth we have in Jesus. In that way we will bear witness to the truth.

For Review...

1. Name one title given to Satan in Scripture.

2. How might you critique the "rags to riches" American myth?

3. What's the difference between racial prejudice and racism?

4. What's the difference between direct and indirect racism?

5. What is the link between women and poverty?

6. According to the text, who suffers from sexism?

Reflection

— How would you describe the dominant image of older people and of growing old that exists in our society?

— What is your image of older people and of growing old?

— Based on both of these images, are there societal attitudes and practices that you would like to see put into place? What are they?

Model of Morality

Blessed Pope John Paul II

In 1996 Pope John Paul II addressed a group of scientists. In his talk he stated that evolution is the most plausible explanation of the development of the universe. He saw no attack on Catholic beliefs in the statement. He said simply, "truth cannot contradict truth." That is, accurate science and true beliefs are not enemies. Rather, they point to the same reality. Scientists who dismiss God in their theories fall short of realizing the truth. Religious believers who don't appreciate scientific contributions to the search for truth are misguided.

John Paul II served as pope for over twenty-five years. He served the Church in many capacities for much of the past century. During that time he stood unwaveringly against many lies. He knew the evils of Nazism, which advocated the superiority of one ethnic group over others to the point of carrying out genocidal killings. He was an outspoken critic of Communism, which proposed that "the state" should control every aspect of people's lives and need bow down to no higher power. He also challenged capitalism. He criticized the excessive materialism and individualism that can accompany capitalism. He saw them result in excessive wealth for a few at the expense of deprivation for the majority of people. Pope John Paul condemned these lies. He was even directly involved in the downfall of Communism in Eastern Europe.

No one questioned the integrity of Pope John Paul II. During his time as pope he traveled to places no pope ever visited, at great hardship to himself. He visited practically every country on earth. He was so firm in his convictions that he became the first pope ever to set foot inside a Jewish synagogue and a Muslim mosque.

"Steadfast," "resolute," and "dedicated entirely to God" described him. An untiring voice for those whose voices are muted by circumstance or oppression, he never held back from upsetting people when he saw falsehood flourishing. He used his time as pope to proclaim without ceasing the beauty and truth of the Catholic story. For Pope John Paul II, that story conveyed the truth that sets us free.

> **"**Ignorance, contempt, and disownment of truth are the cause and the root of all evil, which disturbs individuals and populations.**"**
>
> Pope John Paul II,
> "Vatican Council II: Light for the Church and for the Modern World"

Celebrating Morality

Let us pray . . .

Lord Jesus, may we be counted worthy of
being witnesses to your truth. Help us to
be truthful in speech and honest with
others. Help us to avoid rash judgment
and to learn the art of speaking well of
others. Help us to stand up for ourselves
and others when honesty and reputation
are on the line. May we find a home in
your truth and reflect that truth in all our
dealings with others.

Amen.

Concluding Prayer:
A Reading from Ephesians

"So then, putting away falsehood, let all
of us speak the truth to our neighbors, for
we are members of one another. . . . Let no
evil talk come out of your mouths, but
only what is useful for building up, as
there is need, so that your words may give
grace to those who hear. . . . Put away from
you all bitterness and wrath and anger
and wrangling and slander, together with
all malice, and be kind to one another,
tenderhearted, forgiving one another, as
God in Christ has forgiven you.**"**

Ephesians 4:25, 29, 31–32

Litany based on the Lord's Prayer

— Our Father, who art in heaven . . .

May we witness to your truth.

— hallowed be thy name . . .

May we witness to your truth.

— Thy kingdom come, thy will be done . . .

May we witness to your truth.

— on earth as it is in heaven . . .

May we witness to your truth.

— Give us this day our daily bread . . .

May we witness to your truth.

— and forgive us our trespasses, as we
forgive those who trespass against us . . .

May we witness to your truth.

— And lead us not into temptation . . .

May we witness to your truth.

— but deliver us from evil . . .

May we witness to your truth.

Amen.

14

GENEROSITY AND JUSTICE

Chapter Overview

- The seventh commandment involves the topics of stealing, the use of private property, and the necessity of making amends.
- The tenth commandment helps us appreciate the need to follow the way of Jesus in order to avoid the sins of envy, avarice, and greed.
- Justice applies the seventh commandment to the pursuit of the common good.
- Catholic social teaching offers guidance for achieving social justice.

The seventh and tenth commandments bring us to a discussion of material things. Violation of these two commandments has led to breakdown within families, hostility in communities, widespread deprivation, and warfare between nations. That is, stealing and covetousness are personal matters with immense social consequences, as well as social matters with devastating personal consequences. In this chapter we will explore the many faces of stealing, the necessity of making amends for what we have stolen, our right to private property, the nature of "coveting," the importance of charity, justice as the moral character of society, and the Church's social teaching.

Before we begin . . .

The seventh and ninth commandments are challenged by three practices often associated with American culture: materialism, consumerism, and individualism.

1. Give examples of each of these practices.

2. What practices and activities are the opposite of materialism, consumerism and individualism?

Let us pray . . .

God, our Father, we thank you for your generosity in giving us your Son, Jesus, who in turn gave himself for all. May we reflect the same spirit of generosity in what we do with our own wealth and possessions and in the way we treat the goods of others. Open our eyes to the needs of people who lack basic necessities and guide us in our attempts to distribute your gifts justly. Amen.

The Seventh Commandment

"You shall not steal."

 Exodus 20:15

The most obvious application of the seventh commandment is that we are not to steal. That is, "every manner of taking and using another's property unjustly is contrary to the seventh commandment" *(Catechism, #2454)*.

There are many ways to violate this commandment:

- taking another's property against the will of the property's owner
- holding on to goods that have been lent to us
- keeping lost objects without making an effort to discover who owns them
- business fraud, corporate corruption,
- paying unjust wages
- defrauding our employers by doing shoddy work, being lazy on the job, or stealing from our workplace
- inflating prices that take advantage of the hardship of others
- tax evasion
- forging checks
- wasting goods, such as food and the earth's resources, meant for the common good
- damaging public or private property
- failing to honor legally and morally just contracts such as those that pertain to goods that are purchased, sold, or rented or labor that is contracted
- refusing or failing to pay our debts

We have a right to own property and the seventh commandment forbids others from unjustly taking it from us. However, there is an important principle underlying this commandment. In giving the earth to us, God intends its use for all of mankind. In other words, the goods of this earth are destined for the whole human race. "The right to private property does not abolish the universal destination of goods" *(Catechism, #2452)*. Our things are not just for own use. As stewards of God, we are called also to use them in ways that benefit others. We are called to exercise his gift of charity. **A**

Activity

List five ways you feel the seventh commandment is violated in society today.

Material Things: God's Gifts or Our Possessions?

Man's dominion over inanimate and other living beings granted by the Creator is not absolute; it is limited by concern for the quality of life of his neighbor, including generations to come . . . [CF. CA 37–38]

 **Catechism, #2415**

In the book of Genesis, we learn that God created humans in his own image and commanded them to "be fruitful and multiply, and fill the earth and subdue it" (*Genesis 1:28*). Thus, he asked us to care for the resources of the earth, labor to make good use of them, and enjoy the many things that he gives us through the earth's resources. God intends that the gifts of creation be for everyone. Nonetheless, ownership of private property, provided it is acquired in a just manner, is a right given to us by God.

We normally refer to all those things that "belong" to us as our possessions. The implication is that they are private property, to be used in whatever way we see fit. Scripture begins with a different view of humanity's relationship with material things. We are not owners but stewards. The word "steward" is used to describe us human beings as caretakers of the things of the earth. We are to be caretakers especially of those things designated as our possessions. We don't have an absolute right to use our possessions as we'd like. To the contrary, we need to view them in light of concern for the quality of life of our neighbor—including the quality of life we are bequeathing to future generations.

The right to private property, then, coincides with the responsibility to find ways to make our goods benefit others. In this regard, the following advice is given: *Those who hold goods for use and consumption should use them with moderation, reserving the better part for guests, for the sick and the poor. (Catechism, #2405).* **G**

Group Talk

Discuss the following statements in terms of possible conflicts between private property rights and concern for the quality of life of others.

1. People should not purchase gas-guzzling vehicles that pollute the air.

2. People who can afford them have a right to purchase high-priced items.

3. People who amass a large income should be free to do whatever they want with their money.

4. It's wrong to spend most of one's time on personal pleasures.

5. People have a moral obligation to sign up to donate their organs upon death.

The Seventh Commandment: Special Issues

Slavery

The seventh commandment forbids anything that leads to the enslavement of human beings. Think of it this way: enslavement is stealing the essential dignity of others. Buying, selling, or exchanging human beings as though they were pieces of merchandise is theft in its most brutal form. To reduce people by means of violence to being sources of profit is a grave sin against human dignity.

Slavery is a crime that robs humans of their diginity and often their lives. It belongs in the same category as subhuman living conditions, arbitrary imprisonment, deportation, and disgraceful working conditions. Slavery poisons human society. It harms those who are enslaved as well as those who participate in its evil practice. Most of all, slavery is an example of extreme disrespect to the Creator.

Shoplifting

Beginning about fifty years ago a new phenomenon emerged in America—the shopping mall. Soon malls dotted the modern landscape the way cathedrals dotted the medieval landscape. Resplendent with a vast array of goods for purchase, malls lured people to them. Shoppers were eager to buy or at least possess more things. But what happens if one doesn't have the money, or doesn't want to spend money on particular items? Does the desire to possess them go away? To the contrary, sometimes the desire increases. Is it possible to get some of the wonderful things on display in stores without paying for them? If it were possible, would it be acceptable? Even if it is morally wrong, is it really all that bad to take something without paying for it? After all, stores have plenty of shirts. What's the harm in taking one or two? The fact of the matter is that shoplifting is a form of theft and thus is an offense against the seventh commandment. **G**

Reparation

Commutative justice obliges us to safeguard property rights, pay our debts, and fulfill the obligations to which we have freely committed ourselves. "Without commutative justice, no other form of justice is possible" *(Catechism, #2411)*. Commutative justice requires that we make **reparation** whenever we have stolen property from another or used it in an unjust manner. The seventh commandment requires us to return stolen goods. If the stolen property has disappeared, we are to return the equivalent in kind or in money. If we have participated in stealing from another or have in some way benefited from a theft, we are obliged to make reparation in proportion to our responsibility and to the amount we have gained. **R**

commutative justice— the obligation, required by the seventh commandment, to respect the rights of others

reparation— making amends for harming another; returning stolen property

Group Talk

Form a group of five. Have each person take one of the following roles. Discuss shoplifting. As a group, determine a reasonable punishment for shoplifting.

1. a store manager where shoplifting occurs

2. a teenager found shoplifting

3. parents of the teenager

4. a police officer called to the store

5. a teenager invited to offer an opinion

Reflection

Discuss the moral implications of the six following incidents.
Suggest possible ways of making reparation appropriate for each incident.

—A classmate's family is away. A party begins with a few friends and soon escalates to a large gathering. Before the night is over, the home suffers great damage.

—A group of teens walking through a public park purposely break playground equipment.

—A boy borrows a portable CD player from a friend. His friend doesn't ask for it back, so the boy decides to keep it without asking his friend.

—A girl finds a wallet outside of a store and notices a license with a name and address in it. The wallet contains $50.00. She takes the money and throws the wallet away.

—A boy borrows $6.00 for lunch without intending to pay it back.

—A girl asks a classmate to download a copyrighted CD for her.

For Review...

1. What does the seventh commandment forbid? List some ways that we can violate this commandment.

2. In what sense is private property not an absolute right?

3. Explain the difference between being an owner and a steward.

4. What does the seventh commandment say about slavery and shoplifting?

5. What is reparation? How can we apply the principle of reparation to the seventh commandment?

The Tenth Commandment

"You shall not covet . . . anything that belongs to your neighbor."

Exodus 20:17

"For where your treasure is, there your heart will be also."

Matthew 6:21

envy—
"sadness at the sight of another's goods and the immoderate desire to have them for oneself" *(Catechism, #2553)*

avarice—
"a passion for riches and their attendant power" *(Catechism, #2552)*

greed—
the desire to amass limitless earthly goods

The tenth commandment makes it clear that our attitudes can be as destructive as our actions. Thus, the commandment forbids envy, avarice, and greed.

- **Envy** eats away at the person who is envious as well as at the relationships that the person has. Envy is, first of all, sadness at the thought of another's good fortune. It also means perversely delighting in someone else's misfortune. A serious expression of envy is wishing grave harm to a person or persons whom we envy and knowingly persist in the envy; this is a mortal sin. Envious people can never be satisfied. They are like deprived children who when offered a hot dog want a hamburger or when offered a hamburger want a hot dog. Nothing will satisfy. Envy poisons the Body of Christ.

- **Avarice** is an excessive and unquenchable desire for wealth, power, or other forms of gain. An example of avarice is Ebenezer Scrooge in Charles Dickens, *A Christmas Carol*. Like Scrooge, avaricious people become addicted to the object of desire. Avarice can consume people, making them blind to the demands of the commandments and the needs of others. Instead of worshiping God, they worship money, power, or something they cannot get enough of.

- **Greed** is a desire to amass more and more possessions. It often expresses itself in oppressing and doing violence to others. A greedy person is liable to take advantage of others and trick them out of their belongings. Jesus warned: "Be on your guard against all kinds of greed; for one's life does not consist in the abundance of possessions" *(Luke 12:15).* **A**

Activity

— Read Luke 12:16–21. List three lessons that this parable teaches.

— Give examples of envy, avarice, and greed from recent news stories or from history.

Ways to Observe the Seventh and Tenth Commandments

Would you like to see God glorified by you? Then rejoice in your brother's progress and you will immediately give glory to God. [St. John Chrysostom, Hom. in Rom. 71, 5: PG 60, 448.]

✝ **Catechism, #2540**

Good will. Wishing someone well is a seed out of which God's kingdom grows. Catholics tend to wish one another well during the Christmas season both in word and in action. We even call it "the season of giving." The tenth commandment calls upon us to be well-wishers in all of our dealings with others.

Detachment. Detachment from material goods means cultivating a deep appreciation for things and for the ways they benefit ourselves and others. Detachment flows from preferring Jesus to everything else and thus is necessary for entering into the kingdom of God. Detachment from material goods does not mean dismissing their value. Detachment counteracts theft, envy, avarice, and greed because it reminds us that people are more important than things and that everything must be viewed in light of concern for others.

Trust in God. To truly obtain our deepest needs, we are called to trust in God the Father's loving care, follow the gospel of Jesus the Son of God, and cooperate with the grace of the Holy Spirit which satisfies the desires of our heart. In the Beatitudes, Jesus reveals a path of life that will lead us to happiness, peace, and beauty. To follow this path, he invites us to become poor in spirit *(Matthew 5:3)*. Poverty of spirit invites us to trust in God and to become humble as Jesus was humble, "so that by his poverty you might become rich" *(2 Corinthians 8:9)*.

Charity

Charity is the theological virtue by which we love God above all things for his own sake, and our neighbor as ourselves for the love of God.

✝ **Catechism, #1822**

A story from the Jewish tradition tells of two brothers who shared farmland. One year there was a particularly bountiful crop of grain. The one brother, who was not married, decided to take most of the grain to his brother's barn. "After all," he reasoned, "my brother has a large family and needs the grain more than I do." At the exact same time, the other brother was gathering grain to take to his brother's barn. "My brother has no family to look after him. He needs the grain more than I do."

The two brothers met halfway between their barns. When they realized what each one was doing, they laughed and hugged each other. On that very spot they built an altar to God.

(adapted from John Shea, *An Experience Named Spirit* [Chicago: The Thomas More Press, 1983], pages 7–8)

An altar deserved to be built where these two brothers met. It was truly holy ground. Their spirit of charity made it holy. Charity expresses itself in loving kindness, generosity, friendship, and communion. When we love God and our neighbor as ourselves, we have little inclination towards theft, envy, avarice, or greed. On the contrary, with the gift of charity we have a desire to imitate God's

*"Now the whole group of those who believed were of one heart and soul, and no one claimed private ownership of any possessions, but everything they owned was held in common. . . . There was not a needy person among them, for as many as owned lands or houses sold them and brought the proceeds of what was sold.

They laid it at the apostles' feet, and it was distributed to each as any had need."*

Acts 4:32, 34–35

No doubt Christianity grew at least partially because of its practice of giving and sharing. The Apostles and other members of the early Church obviously believed that generosity with material goods was an important part of Jesus' plan for building up the kingdom of God.

Charity, then, is a hallmark of living the Christian life. It takes us in the exact opposite direction from the stealing and covetousness condemned by the seventh and tenth commandments. **R**

generosity by sharing what we have with one another, especially with those of us who have immediate need.

Indeed, the Acts of the Apostles reports that generosity and charity were distinguishing characteristics of the early Church.

For Review...

1. Define envy, avarice, and greed.

2. Describe some positive ways to observe the seventh and tenth commandments.

3. Why is a spirit of detachment necessary to combat envy?

4. What is the virtue of charity?

5. Describe a characteristic of the early Church.

Reflection

— Studies indicate that generous people tend to live longer. Why do you think that might be the case?

— Is being generous beneficial for oneself as well as for others? For example, do you think that generous people are usually happier?

— Rate yourself in terms of generosity. Think back on an incident when you were either generous or not generous. What was the experience like?

Justice

The Church makes a judgment about economic and social matters when the fundamental rights of the person or the salvation of souls requires it. She is concerned with the temporal common good of men because they are ordered to the sovereign Good, their ultimate end.

Catechism, #2458

Generosity, respect, and joy in the good fortune of others reflect the spirit of the seventh and tenth commandments on a personal level. Justice applies the seventh commandment to the societal level. Morality is not just about personal acts that are right or wrong. Morality also concerns itself with what is right or wrong in our society. For over one hundred years now the Church has frequently addressed this social dimension of morality. The Church therefore gives us principles for reflection, criteria for judgment, and guidelines for action in the social arena.

All dimensions of a particular community or society can help or hinder its members —not just the actions of particular individuals. Justice is the Christian virtue that applies morality to society and aims at creating fairness within that society. Lack of justice is a form of theft: "Not to enable the poor to share in our goods is to steal from them and deprive them of life. The goods we possess are not ours, but theirs [St. John Chrysostom, *Hom. in Lazaro* 2, 5: PG 48, 992.]" *(Catechism, #2446)*.

Although it may seem obvious, it is actually a fact that can be easily overlooked: Deep-seated social problems are problems affecting real people. For instance, if the mother of a friend of yours loses her job, that would put a personal, human face on the social problem of unemployment. Sometimes when we hear about social problems such as factories

shutting down and moving to other countries or people left to live homeless on city streets, we can forget that these news stories and statistics are about real people who are suffering. These people are our brothers and sisters. **A**

Activity

1. Make a list, as complete as possible, of what you consider to be major justice-related problems that exist today.

2. Identify, as best you can, causes of these problems—both underlying, deep-seated causes as well as more immediate causes.

3. Name societal values that might contribute to any of these problems or that might stand in the way of our society overcoming them.

4. Identify ways that society might be changed so as to alleviate or minimize these problems.

Injustice in Our Society

- Homelessness plagues our big cities. Today, many families need the services of shelters. Veterans, especially of the Vietnam War, make up a sizable portion of people living on the streets. Many homeless people are unable to work due to mental illness or other problems.

- Healthcare, income, and housing for the wealthiest people of the world are the best they have ever been. Meanwhile, adequate health care, employment opportunities, and affordable housing are often found lacking among poorer segments of society.

- The United States prides itself on guaranteeing education for all children. Nonetheless, illiteracy and insufficient education remain serious social problems in the country. Many unemployed persons or persons in low-paying, dead-end jobs do not have enough skills or education to help them move out of poverty. Many people in our prisons are either illiterate or poorly educated.

- In North America, hailed as the "breadbasket of the world," an alarming number of people suffer from malnutrition. Surprisingly, people who perform the essential task of harvesting crops are among the poorest paid and often work under the harshest conditions of any workers.

- Recycling and other anti-pollution measures have greatly increased in our communities, but waste and pollution remain serious problems. The problem is intensified by the common practice of constantly accumulating and then discarding things. Neglect of the environment affects everyone, especially people living in poorer areas and, potentially, members of future generations.

Expanding Our Moral Imagination

The list above paints a bleak picture of our society. Certainly, the picture is not complete. Much could be said that would portray a positive image of our society. However, a quick look at any evening news broadcast reminds us that the picture painted in the list is painfully realistic. Unfortunately, our society is not all that it could and should be. The first thing we might notice about the list of statements is that it expresses various ways that groups of people are suffering. As such, it is definitely a list of moral problems.

However, if we view it solely from a personal morality perspective we might conclude that individually we are not responsible for this suffering. We might also feel that these problems are too overwhelming for us to tackle; anything we could do as individuals would make only a small dent toward solving them. To confront issues such as these, we need more than a personal morality approach. Our teaching on justice expands our moral imagination beyond a focus on the behavior of individuals. Justice shifts our focus to identifying underlying causes and seeking long-term solutions to deep-seated social problems.

//Wash yourselves; make yourselves clean; remove the evil of your doings from before my eyes; cease to do evil, learn to do good; seek justice, rescue the oppressed, defend the orphan, plead for the widow.//

 *Isaiah 1:16–17*

Common Good and Personal Good Are One

The concept of the **common good** is an important principle of Catholic social teaching. The common good is "the sum total of social conditions which allow people, either as groups or as individuals, to reach their fulfillment more fully and more easily" *(Catechism #1906)*. In fact, our dignity as human beings depends upon the pursuit of the common good. The principle of common good states that society should be organized so that, as much as possible, the entire community, as well as individuals within that community, benefit from society's actions. Political authority, if it is truly legitimate, must be committed to using morally acceptable means to ensure the common good of its citizens. Thus, the common good and the good of individuals are ultimately one and the same.

Here's an example of the way the common good works. Imagine that you are in an algebra class grouped with a handful of students who are gifted in math and others who are much less mathematically gifted. Your teacher faces a dilemma. Does he aim his teaching at those students who are stronger or those who are weaker in math? If he directs his teaching to the poorer students, the better ones may feel cheated or bored or uninterested. If he directs his teaching toward the better students, the poorer ones will feel lost and left out. As a result, they may become disheartened and bored and also possibly disruptive. In either case the atmosphere of learning will be negatively affected. Even trying to maintain a medium-level pace would likely leave everyone dissatisfied.

In this classroom, unless the good of each student is addressed in some way, all the students will ultimately suffer. The teacher needs to be attentive to the first principle of the common good: The betterment of each community member leads to the betterment of all of its members. The teacher would also do well to put into practice two additional principles of this concept: Those who are more likely to be left out require special attention, and all members of a community should have opportunities to contribute to the betterment of their community. In summary, then, concern for the common good seeks individual and society-wide development through increased equality and active participation of all members.

> **common good—**
> a long-standing concept advocating that society should be organized so that, as much as possible, both individuals and the entire community are equally thriving

Principles of the Common Good

1. The betterment of each community member leads to the betterment of all its members.

2. Those who are more likely to be left out require special attention.

3. All members of a community should have opportunities to contribute to the betterment of their community. **G**

Group Talk

Imagine that you are an algebra teacher who has a class filled with students who have a wide range of math ability. How might you incorporate the three principles of the common good into your teaching of the class?

Common Good Applied to Social Problems

How is the common good played out in society at large? For instance, how can it be applied to poverty and homelessness? Surely, the presence of people who reach the depths of poverty and end up homeless has a negative impact on all members of a community. At the very least, the realization that some fellow community members are sleeping out in the cold should disturb the good sleep of all but the most heartless citizens. A society in which there exists a wide gap between the fortunes of the very rich and the misfortunes of the very poor creates an increasingly unstable social and economic situation. When poor people feel hopeless, even wealthier people can feel their security threatened.

Common good asserts that everyone's life is enriched when each person's life is enriched, even on an international scale. Most especially, common good reminds us that we are all in this together. Wherever we are going as a society, ultimately we are going together. The concept known as the common good offers us an ideal that we can strive for as we ponder how best to help people. The common good calls for a strong sense of social responsibility and of mutual concern among all community members. Justice affirms that when the lot of the poorest members of local and even international society improves and the voiceless gain a voice, then everyone gains. **R**

For Review...

1. What shift in perspective does justice bring to our moral imagination?

2. How is lack of justice a form of theft?

3. Define *common good*.

4. Name the three principles of the concept of the common good.

5. Explain this statement: "Everyone's life is enriched when each person's life is enriched."

Reflection

Look over again the process of moral decision making described in chapter 7. Choose a particular social problem and apply that process to the problem. What insights about the problem are uncovered by submitting it to the process?

• poverty in wealthy countries

• hate groups

• increases in the elderly population

• pressures experienced by single-parent families

• inadequate social and recreational activities for teens

• pressures experienced by disabled persons

• domestic abuse

Catholic Social Teaching

From its beginning, the Church has considered justice to be an integral dimension of Jesus' message. Indeed, down to the present day many examples could be cited that illustrate concern for justice among Christians in word and in action. Words of Jesus recorded in the Gospels ring out with cries on behalf of poor and downtrodden members of society. Even more strikingly, the actions of Jesus demonstrate his concern for people who are suffering or overlooked. Numerous accounts from the first centuries indicate that the early Christians saw the work of justice as a hallmark of what it means to be a follower of Christ.

During the late Middle Ages, taking advantage of cheap labor and increased opportunities for trade, some people saw the possibility of amassing great wealth. In the midst of this fervor for wealth and possessions, Saint Francis of Assisi rejected the rich life into which he had been born and instead chose voluntarily to live like the poorest of the poor. Strangely enough, he gained many followers for his movement—women and men who felt drawn to live a simple life as the appropriate response to the call of the Gospels. The Franciscan movement was a radical living out of the gospel and of the Christian principles of justice.

Still later, industrialization brought with it big city poverty. Many holy women and men founded religious communities and Church organizations to care for homeless beggars, widows, orphans, the unschooled, and the physically and mentally ill. Perhaps your school itself represents part of the legacy of these Christian advocates of justice from the past.

The year 1891 marks an important date for modern Catholic teaching on justice. At the time in Europe, "the poor" meant especially factory workers and their families. To call attention to their needs, Pope Leo XIII issued an encyclical letter called **On the Condition of Workers**. In this encyclical the pope made it clear that the Church intended to speak out on social and economic issues and to serve as an advocate for the poor, as Jesus himself was. This encyclical began a trend that continues today. It stands as the first of many official Church statements addressing issues of justice. Church leaders continue to speak out for justice today. Because of its many pronouncements, the Church counts itself as a strong voice calling for justice in the world. In response, Church members are challenged to think about how justice can be manifest in their living out of the moral life. **R**

On the Condition of Workers— the 1891 encyclical of Pope Leo XIII voicing concern for industrial workers; the first of a series of documents comprising modern Catholic social teaching

Reflection

1. Read portions of a Church document that deals with justice. Select three short passages that you think contain key teachings about the topic. Write down each passage, then write a brief statement of your own about how this message could be applied to specific situations today.

2. Interview someone involved in a Church ministry directed toward helping people in need (for example, a nurse or chaplain in a Catholic hospital, a volunteer at a shelter for the poor, an aide at a convalescent home, or a reading tutor at a school or prison). Ask the person how this work is an expression of his or her Christian faith. Write a report on your interview.

Seven Themes of Modern Catholic Social Teaching

In 1996 the U.S. Catholic bishops identified seven themes underlying Catholic social teaching. These themes run through the many statements on justice made by Catholic leaders during more than a century. Through these statements, Catholic leaders hope that the Church and its members will serve as a beacon of justice in the world.

1. Life and Dignity of the Human Person

In a world warped by materialism and declining respect for human life, the Catholic Church proclaims that human life is sacred and that the dignity of the human person is the foundation of a moral vision for society. . . .We believe that every person is precious, that people are more important than things, and that the measure of every institution is whether it threatens or enhances the life and dignity of the human person.

2. Call to Family, Community, and Participation

In a global culture driven by excessive individualism, our tradition proclaims that the person is not only sacred but also social. How we organize our society—in economics and politics, in law and policy—directly affects human dignity and the capacity of individuals to grow in community. The family is the central social institution that must be supported and strengthened, not undermined. While our society often exalts individualism, the Catholic tradition teaches that human beings grow and achieve fulfillment in community.

3. Rights and Responsibilities

In a world where some speak mostly of "rights" and others mostly of "responsibilities," the Catholic tradition teaches that human dignity can be protected and a healthy community can be achieved only if human rights are protected and responsibilities are met.

4. Option for the Poor and Vulnerable

In a world characterized by growing prosperity for some and pervasive poverty for others, Catholic teaching proclaims that a basic moral test is how our most vulnerable members are faring.

Giving material goods to those in need is a sign of fraternal charity and a work of justice pleasing to God.

5. The Dignity of Work and the Rights of Workers

In a marketplace where too often the quarterly bottom line takes precedence over the rights of workers, we believe that the economy must serve people, not the other way around. Work is more than a way to make a living; it is a form of continuing participation in God's creation. If the dignity of work is to be protected, then the basic rights of workers must be respected—the right to productive work, to decent and fair wages, to organize and join unions, to private property, and to economic initiative.

6. Solidarity

Our culture is tempted to turn inward, becoming indifferent and sometimes isolationist in the face of international responsibilities. Catholic social teaching proclaims that we are our brothers' and sisters' keepers, wherever they live. We are one family, whatever our national, racial, ethnic, economic, and ideological differences. Learning to practice the virtue of solidarity means learning that "loving our neighbor" has global dimensions in an interdependent world.

7. Care for God's Creation

On a planet conflicted over environmental issues, the Catholic tradition insists that we show our respect for the Creator by our stewardship of creation. Care for the earth is not just an Earth Day slogan, it is a requirement of our faith.

Applying the Seven Themes of Catholic Social Teaching

- Jorge spent most of his childhood and youth living on the streets of his small Mexican village. Recently, he has survived by making a small amount of money as a taxi driver. His "taxi" is really a bicycle fitted with a chair in the back that he pedals about town in search of passengers. In his village far too many young men try to make their living this way, and competition is fierce. Now that he is twenty, married, and with a young son, Jorge wants more than to survive. The only hope he sees is to join the thousands who make their way to Mexico City each day seeking some kind of work or to make the dangerous crossing into the United States.

- Since freshman year Sanghee and Kerry have been numbers one and two in their class academically. Now seniors, both have applied to and been accepted at prestigious Ivy League colleges. Sanghee's parents can afford to send him there, and he is looking forward to attending the school of his choice next year. Kerry's mother, however, tells her that even

with the scholarship and loan money promised her, the family cannot possibly afford to send her to the school of her choice. Instead, Kerry will join the large contingent of students from her school who will be attending the local state college next year.

- Darius and Sean, who are African American, have become friends with some classmates who are white. One day the pair wandered into a park in an all-white neighborhood, searching for their friends. Along the way they encountered suspicious looks, and a park guard changed directions to follow them as they passed. When Darius and Sean finally met up with their friends, they were asked, "Have any trouble getting here?" They

just shrugged their shoulders and said, "None at all," knowing how much race continues to be a dividing line in much of our society.

- When Alice's husband died, her sister Marie moved in with her. With the help of a local agency that brings them weekly meals, together they manage to maintain the house. However, both Alice and Marie are growing increasingly fearful of venturing outside of the house alone, even to the senior citizens' bus stop down the street. Neither wants to consider moving to a retirement home. None of the ones they have visited look much like "home" anyway—more like hospitals or warehouses to them. And so the two elderly women live more and more isolated lives and make do with less and less association with the world outside their home. **A**

Activity

Apply one or more of the principles of justice to the above situations.

- Describe another situation in which each principle is violated.
- Describe a concrete way that each principle could be put into practice.

Option for the Poor and Vulnerable

piral of poverty—
spiral of poverty—
poor people being in a
situation that makes
overcoming poverty
almost impossible

urbanization—
growth of cities
worldwide

One problem crying out for justice today is the amount of poverty that exists both here in North America and around the world. According to the United Nations, the richest one-fifth of the world's population receives over eighty percent of the world's income while the poorest one-fifth receives less than one percent. Again, without pointing blame at individuals, it is accurate to say that this statistic describes an injustice.

In large measure, poor people are not just poor; they are trapped in a **spiral of poverty**. That is, they are caught up in a system that makes breaking out of poverty extremely difficult. Jorge's story on the previous page illustrates the spiral of poverty. Since he needed to support himself even as a child, he attended school only sporadically. Thus he lacks marketable skills or even the basics of an education. He works all day driving his taxi, but he makes barely enough to live. He can put aside nothing for the future. His work is not leading up to any better paying job. If he follows the worldwide trend, he will surely make his way to a big city. There he will find far too many people searching for far too few jobs.

The authors of a study on the worldwide phenomenon of **urbanization**, the growth of cities, describe the Jorges of the world in these terms:

Cities draw displaced rural populations with the promise of jobs and by the lifestyles seen on television. But once they reach the city, most find no steady work. Or the work is offered only or mostly to women because they have been taught by their culture to expect less, to be more docile, and because they are more likely to be conveniently short-term workers who will eventually leave their jobs without pensions or benefits for marriage and childcare. Early in the morning women leave for work in factories where there is no job security, no worker safety, no union. Later, the children go to work—sometimes hustling in the streets. Men, finding no work, lose their place in the household economy and often abandon their families. Or people are forced to consider options for survival that are offensive to their culture and their conscience. They steal, deal in drugs, or enter into prostitution. . . . Cities become the graveyards of what once was the functioning structure of traditional family life.

John C. Raines and Donna C. Day-Lower, *Modern Work and Human Meaning* [Philadelphia, PA: The Westminster Press, 1986].

Large numbers of people, especially in poorer countries, are both poor and power-less to make changes. Unfortunately, the call for "economic development" in poorer countries sometimes misses the point that "true development concerns the whole man. It is concerned with increasing each person's ability to respond to his vocation and hence to God's call [cf. CA 29.]" (*Catechism, #2461*). If economic development does not bring benefits such as living wages and job security to those who are poor, then such development does not serve justice. The way to help poor people is not only to alleviate their poverty temporarily but to search for ways that they may increase their ability to work and to live as people of dignity so that poverty is less likely to occur long term.

The Archbishop of Cincinnati explains this principle of justice in these words: *When we say that we owe preferential respect and special attention to the poor, we are not saying that the poor should not be held accountable for their participation in society according to the same standards as everybody else. Rather, we are saying that they require respect and attention so as to be able to take their appropriate part in the social system and thus not only benefit from it but contribute to it. When we think of our obligations to the poor, we must not allow ourselves to think in terms of "them" and "us." To one extent or another, we are all dependent, all disabled, all without power, and all underproductive. Ultimately, we all stand poor before the Lord.*

Archbishop Daniel E. Pilarczk, *Bringing Forth Justice* [Cincinnati: St. Anthony Messenger Press, 1999.] **R**

...Conclusion

As implied in the seventh and tenth commandments, generosity and seeking the good of others are key characteristics of living the moral life. Justice is essential to a full application of the commandments. Jesus wants us to do all that we can to alleviate suffering experienced by those around us—this is a basic component of his moral message. Justice takes this concern of Jesus and applies it to the entire social sphere. It recognizes that caring for those in need means attending to all the causes of their need, both individual and social. Justice adds an important and a necessary dimension to the Christian moral life.

For Review...

1. What two messages did Pope Leo XIII proclaim by issuing On the Condition of Workers?

2. What trend did Pope Leo's encyclical begin?

3. What are the seven themes of Catholic social teaching?

4. What does it mean to say that many people are trapped in a spiral of poverty?

5. Define urbanization. How is urbanization a symptom of worldwide poverty?

Reflection

1. Find someone who has visited or spent time in an economically poor country. Interview the person to find out his or her impression of conditions there. Report your findings to the class.

2. The Catholic Campaign for Human Development is an agency of the Church dedicated to helping poor people help themselves. Send away for literature from this organization and report on a program that it has sponsored.

Model of Morality

John Cushma

The Catholic Campaign for Human Development sets as its goal helping people who are poor to help themselves. One way it alerts young people about its programs is a multi-media youth arts contest. In 2003 the winner of that contest was John Cushma.

At the risk of embarrassing him, it appears that, even at his young age, John Cushma from Seton-LaSalle High School in Mount Lebanon, PA, is not a stranger to winning awards. He lives an active life and involves himself in many activities. However, he consistently links his activities with concern for people in need.

For instance, he didn't simply involve himself in traditional scouting projects. Instead, he used his time as a Boy Scout to collect canned goods for the local food pantry. Later, appalled at the realities of homelessness he made and served meals at a homeless shelter.

John demonstrated even deeper awareness of the plight of people who are poor through his poem that won his award, "Breaking the Cycle of Poverty." In his speech at the awards ceremony John described how he made the connection between generosity and justice.

As a senior. . .I was required to take a course called "Social Justice." For eighteen weeks, my teacher, Mr. Mark Lang, opened the classes' eyes to the cycle of poverty that traps one in eleven American families. . .How can there be children in America who are too poor to receive an education? It doesn't seem fair. Unfortunately, charity, as I've practiced it, was just a bit of temporary assistance. The poor need social justice so that the root causes of poverty can be eradicated:

- *Adults need [to be] trained for jobs that earn a living wage.*
- *Affordable housing must be made available.*
- *Impoverished children must be able to secure a quality education.*
- *We need programs that will help poor people achieve the self-sufficiency that they desire.*

Hopefully, John's journey from collecting cans to concern for justice is mirrored in Catholic high schools across the nation. Through John and others like him, the Catholic Campaign for Human Development will receive needed assistance in creating conditions in which people can care for themselves using their own resources.

Celebrating Morality

Let us pray . . .

Jesus, we praise you and thank you for taking on all the suffering of the world and making it your own. When we look around us—deeply, caringly, through your eyes—we discover people who are hurting in many ways. May we find you in those who are hungry or alone. May we visit you in those who are sick or imprisoned. As part of our moral quest, may we search for ways to use our material possessions creatively and generously. May we exhibit a spirit of good-will and charity in all of our interactions. Help us to transform our world so that it more closely resembles the vision you gave us. Amen.

Meditation

An early Christian writer's description of what it means to be Christian:

We are a community with a common religious feeling, unity of discipline, a common bond of hope. We meet in gathering and congregation to approach God in prayer, massing our forces to surround him. . . . Every man once a month brings some modest coin—or whatever he wishes, and only if he does wish, and if he can; for nobody is compelled; it is a voluntary offering. You might call them the trust funds of piety. For they are not spent upon banquets nor drinking-parties nor thankless eating-houses; but to feed the poor and to bury them, for boys and girls who lack property and parents, and then for slaves grown old and shipwrecked mariners; and any who may be in mines, islands or prisons. . .Such work of love (for so it is) puts a mark upon us, in the eyes of some. "Look," they say, "how they love one another" (for themselves hate one another); "and how they are ready to die for each other." . . .So we, who are united in mind and soul, have no hesitation about sharing property. All is common among us—except our wives.

Tertullian, quoted in John Haughey, ed.,
The Faith That Does Justice
[New York: Paulist Press, 1977]

Let us pray . . .

Christ our brother, you are the just one. You confronted injustice in your own life, even unto death, and gave us the dream of a just world in which we all can share. Empower us with the grace of the Holy Spirit. Guide us as we seek to uproot injustice. Grant us the courage to work with those who are poor and those who are discriminated against. Fill your people with hope. Amen.

Morality and Scripture

The Bible

The Catholic *canon*, or authorized version, of the Bible contains seventy-three books—forty-six in the Old Testament and twenty-seven in the New Testament. Catholic Bibles have seven Old Testament books or parts of books not included in other Christian Bibles. When these books are included in a Protestant Bible, they are usually found in a section called the *Apocrypha* or *Deutero-canonical Books*. The word *apocrypha* comes from a Greek word that means "hidden things."

The apocryphal books are not found in the present Hebrew Scriptures but were included in an early Jewish canon that included Greek writings, the *Septuagint*. Protestant Reformers of later centuries did not accept these books. Catholic translations of the Bible include *The New American Bible* and *The New Jerusalem Bible*. Some translations, such as *The New Revised Standard Version*, which is used in this book and in the Catechism, are accepted by Catholics and Protestants.

Salvation History

The history of salvation begins with creation, reaches its highest point in Christ, and lasts until the end of time. It is the story told in the Bible—the story of God's saving actions for humans. Important events of salvation history in the Old Testament include God's promise to Abraham, the Exodus, the covenant given to Moses, the Israelites' entering the land of Canaan, and the establishment of the kingdom of Israel under David. In the New Testament, salvation history is seen as coming together in the life, death, and Resurrection of Jesus. It continues today in the life of the Church.

The Covenant

The Bible records the events associated with the covenant and God's plan for humans. Here is a brief look at those events.

- After God created everything in the world, humans chose to turn away from him. Instead of abandoning them, he promised to send them a messiah some time in the future. Meanwhile, God promised to be with people, slowly bringing them back to himself. *(See Genesis 3:15.)*

- The story of Noah shows us how God made his covenant of love with humans, even though humans were not always faithful to him. He saved Noah and his family from a great flood. He promised to be with the descendants of Noah forever and gave them a sign of his eternal love. *(See Genesis 9:12–15.)*

- Centuries later, God chose a Middle Eastern nomad named Abram to explain his covenant more fully. He promised to make Abram and his wife Sarah the parents of a great nation, God's own chosen people. *(See Genesis 12:2–3.)*

- God further revealed his intentions to humans by entering into a covenant with Moses and the Israelites at Mount Sinai. He promised to save them if they, in turn, would keep his commandments. *(See Deuteronomy 30:15–20.)*

- The prophets continually reminded the people to be faithful to their covenant with God. They told of his great love that would come to the people in the form of a Messiah who would free them forever from the chains of sin and death. In the fullness of time, he revealed himself in his own Son, Jesus Christ. Through Jesus we know what God is like. *(See John 3:16 and John 14:5–14.)*

- During his lifetime, Jesus chose twelve Apostles and entrusted them with the task of continuing his teaching. They were to form his Church, to preach and write the gospel (the good news about God's saving love) to people in all nations. *(See Matthew 28:16–20.)*

The Moral Law

There are four expressions of moral law:

1. **Divine law** is the plan of God's wisdom to direct all human activity to good.
2. **Natural law** is the law that is written in your heart that helps you know what is good and what is evil.
3. **Revealed law** is law as it is revealed in the Old and New Testaments.
4. **Civil and Church** laws are established by nations and by the Church to promote the common good and to guide the decisions of each person.

The Ten Commandments and What They Mean

1. I am the Lord your God. You shall not have strange gods before me.
   - Place one's faith in God alone.
   - Worship, praise, and thank God the Creator.
   - Believe in, trust, and love God.
2. You shall not take the name of the Lord your God in vain.
   - Speak God's name, and that of Jesus and the saints, with reverence.
   - Don't curse.
   - Don't call on God to witness to a lie.
3. Remember to keep holy the Lord's day.
   - Gather to worship at the Eucharist.
   - Rest and avoid unnecessary work on Sunday.
4. Honor your father and your mother.
   - Respect and obey parents, guardians, and others who have proper authority.
5. You shall not kill.
   - Respect and protect your life and the lives of others.
6. You shall not commit adultery.
   - Be faithful and loyal to spouses, friends, and family.
   - Respect God's gift of sexuality, and practice the virtue of chastity.
7. You shall not steal.
   - Respect the things that belong to others.
   - Share what you have with those in need.
8. You shall not bear false witness against your neighbor.
   - Be honest and truthful.
   - Avoid bragging.
   - Don't say untruthful or negative things about others.
9. You shall not covet your neighbor's wife.
   - Don't lust after another person's spouse.
   - Practice modesty in thoughts, words, dress, and actions.
10. You shall not covet your neighbor's goods.
    - Rejoice in others' good fortune.
    - Don't be jealous of others' possessions.
    - Don't be greedy.

The Great Commandment

"You shall love the Lord your God with all your heart, and with all your soul, and with all your strength, and with all your mind; and your neighbor as yourself."

Luke 10:27

The Beatitudes

Blessed are the poor in spirit,

  for theirs is the kingdom of heaven.

Blessed are they who mourn,

  for they will be comforted.

Blessed are the meek,

  for they will inherit the earth.

Blessed are they who hunger and

  thirst for righteousness, for they will

  be filled.

- You depend on God rather than on things, and you believe that helping others is more important than acquiring things.
- You are aware of the sufferings of others and walk with them in their grief; your grieving is not dominated by selfishness.
- You are humble, patient, and gentle with yourself and with others.
- You stand up for what is right and for the rights of others; you work for a more just world and the fullness of God's kingdom.

Blessed are the merciful,

  for they will receive mercy.

- You readily forgive others from the heart, refusing to hold a grudge, and you forgive yourself as you seek God's forgiveness and the forgiveness of those you have hurt or harmed.

Blessed are the pure in heart,

  for they will see God.

Blessed are the peacemakers,

  for they will be called children of God.

Blessed are they who are persecuted for the

righteousness' sake,

for theirs is the kingdom of heaven.

- You recognize God's image in yourself and in those around you, and you treat others with reverence.
- You live peacefully with others and promote peace between people and groups.
- You make a stand for what you believe in, even when you suffer emotional or physical pain as a result of your decision.

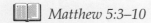 *Matthew 5:3–10*

Spiritual Works of Mercy

Counsel the doubtful.
Instruct the ignorant.
Admonish the sinner.
Comfort the sorrowful.
Forgive injuries.
Bear wrongs patiently.
Pray for the living and the dead.

Corporal Works of Mercy

Feed the hungry.
Give drink to the thirsty.
Clothe the naked.
Shelter the homeless.
Visit the sick.
Visit the imprisoned.
Bury the dead.

Sacraments and Morality

The Seven Sacraments

Sacraments of Initiation

The Sacraments of Initiation celebrate people's relationship with Christ and their full membership in the Church.

- Baptism
- Confirmation
- Eucharist

Sacraments of Healing

In the Sacraments of Healing God's forgiveness of sins and healing are given to those suffering physical and spiritual sickness.

- Reconciliation (Penance)
- Anointing of the Sick

Sacraments at the Service of Communion

These sacraments celebrate people's commitment to serve God and the community.

- Holy Orders
- Matrimony

The Sacrament of Reconciliation

The Sacrament of Reconciliation has four main parts: contrition, confession, penance, and absolution.

- **Contrition**. This involves the examination of conscience and the realization that one has sinned. With true contrition or repentance, there is a sincere sorrow for our sins and a genuine intent to try to do better in the future. When contrition is motivated by love of God, it is called perfect contrition. When it is motivated by something other than this (such as guilt, the repellent nature of the sin, fear of eternal punishment), it is called imperfect contrition.

- **Confession**. To be reconciled with God and the Church, we must first carefully examine our conscience and then tell a priest all the grave sins we have committed since our last confession. Although it is not necessary to confess our venial sins, it is still a practice that the Church strongly recommends.

- **Penance**. The priest may offer some brief spiritual advice before giving us a penance to perform to show the sincerity of our repentance and our willingness to repair the harm caused by sin. The main types of penance are fasting, prayer, and almsgiving. We then pray the Act of Contrition.

- **Absolution**. Our one-to-one confession of grave sins to a priest followed by absolution is the ordinary way we participate in the Sacrament of Reconciliation. The word absolve means "to clean" or "to take away stain." In the Sacrament of Reconciliation, bishops and priests act in Jesus' name to forgive sins.

Indulgences

The doctrine and practice of indulgences are linked to the effects of the Sacrament of Reconciliation. An indulgence is a remission before God of the temporal punishment due to sins whose guilt has already been forgiven (*Catechism, #1471*). Thus, some of the faithful departed are being purified in purgatory. Since these individuals are still members of the communion of saints, a way we can help them is to gain indulgences for them, so that their temporal punishment may be remitted.

The Sacrament of the Eucharist

Jesus said, "I am the living bread that came down from heaven. Whoever eats of this bread will live forever; . . . Those who eat my flesh and drink my blood have eternal life, and . . . abide in me, and I in them" *(John 6:51, 54, 56)*. Jesus, acting through the ministry of Holy Orders offers us his Body and Blood until he comes again. In fact, it is truly Jesus, present through the priest, who is offering the Eucharistic sacrifice.

This Communion increases our union with Jesus, forgives our venial sins, and helps us to resist the temptation to give in to mortal sin. By receiving Jesus in the Eucharist, the bonds of love between Jesus and ourselves are strengthened and thus bonds of unity and love within the Mystical Body of Christ, the Church, are also strengthened.

To respond to Jesus' invitation to receive his Body and Blood in Holy Communion, we must prepare ourselves for the joy and importance of this moment. We must be in a state of grace, and, if we are aware of any mortal sin on our soul, we must refrain from receiving Communion until we have been absolved of our sin in the Sacrament of Reconciliation.

Order of Mass

Mass follows a pattern, with some differences according to the feast or season of the liturgical year. The two great parts of Mass are the Liturgy of the Word and the Liturgy of the Eucharist.

Introductory Rites

- Entrance Chant
- Greeting
- Rite for the Blessing and Sprinkling of Water
- Penitential Act
- *Kyrie*
- Gloria
- Collect

Liturgy of the Word

- The first great part of the Mass; the assembly listens to and responds to God's word in Scripture.
- First Reading (usually from the Old Testament)
- Responsorial Psalm
- Second Reading (from New Testament Letters)
- Gospel Acclamation (Alleluia)
- Gospel Dialogue
- Gospel Reading
- Homily
- Profession of Faith (Creed)
- Prayer of the Faithful (the "Amen" of which ends the Liturgy of the Word)

Liturgy of the Eucharist

- The second great part of the Mass; the Church offers praise and thanksgiving to God.
- Preparation of the Gifts
- Invitation to Prayer
- Prayer Over the Offerings
- Eucharistic Prayer
  - Preface Dialogue
  - Preface
  - Preface Acclamation
  - Consecration
  - Mystery of Faith
  - Concluding Doxology
- Communion Rite
  - The Lord's Prayer
  - Sign of Peace
  - Lamb of God (*Agnus Dei*)
  - Invitation to Communion
  - Communion
  - Prayer After Communion

Concluding Rite

- Greeting
- Blessing
- Dismissal

Fast, Abstinence, and Days of Penance

All Christians, by the nature of their lives, are obliged to live in a spirit of penance whereby their exterior act of prayer, self-denial, and charity bear witness to the inner values of their faith. All the Fridays of the year and the entire Season of Lent are days of penance. Works of penance include voluntary abstinence, fasting, prayer, works of charity, and other acts of self-denial. Proportionately grave circumstances—sickness, dietary needs, social obligations—excuse a person from the obligations to fast and abstain, but not from seeking out other forms of penance.

All Catholics in the United States, from their eighteenth birthday until their fifty-ninth birthday, are required to fast on Ash Wednesday and Good Friday unless a serious reason prevents them from doing so. Fasting is the limitation to one full meal and two lighter means in the course of a day, with no food in between meals.

Abstinence generally refers to refraining from eating meat on certain days. Catholics who are fourteen years of age or older are expected to abstain from eating meat on Ash Wednesday, Good Friday, and, in the United States, on all of the Fridays in Lent. The obligation to abstain from meat binds Catholics from the age of fourteen throughout life.

The Eucharistic Fast

To help prepare spiritually for the Eucharist, Catholics fast for one hour before Communion. They take no food or drink except water and medicine. The fast for those who are elderly or sick is fifteen minutes.

Holy Days of Obligation in the United States

Catholics are required to attend Mass on Sunday unless a serious reason prevents them from doing so. Catholics also must participate in Mass on certain holy days. In the United States the holy days of obligation are the feasts of:

- Mary the Mother of God (January 1)
- Ascension of the Lord (forty days after Easter or the Sunday nearest the end of the forty-day period)
- Assumption of Mary (August 15)
- All Saints' Day (November 1)
- Immaculate Conception of Mary (December 8)
- Christmas (December 25)

Glossary

acedia—not caring, apathy, boredom (p. 149)

acquaintance rape—forcing sex on someone known by the assailant (p. 234)

actual grace—the help God gives us for a particular need to help us conform our lives to his will (p. 9)

ageism—discrimination against people solely on the basis of their age (p. 256)

alienation—an experience of isolation and separateness from God and others (p. 50)

almost-committed sexual intercourse—morally wrong sexual activity that presumes that it is acceptable when the two people have expressed a degree of commitment to each other, such as during engagement (p. 231)

Anointing of the Sick—celebration of healing and care for the sick; a statement about our call to pray for and assist those who are suffering (p. 49)

apathy—an attitude of not getting involved, not caring, not acting when action is called for (p. 94)

avarice—"a passion for riches and their attendant power" *(Catechism, #2552)* (p. 266)

Baptism—birth into new life as God's adopted children; entry into the Church (p. 49)

Beatitude saints—people who take the Beatitudes' message to heart and attempt to live it (p. 28)

Beatitudes—the teachings of Jesus in the Sermon on the Mount on the meaning and way to true happiness (p. 28)

blasphemy—speech or action that shows disrespect or contempt for God or persons or things dedicated to God (p. 154)

calumny—telling lies defaming someone's character (p. 246)

capital punishment—the death penalty; state-sanctioned execution of persons convicted of serious crime (p. 206)

cardinal virtues—prudence, justice, fortitude, and temperance; permanent readiness of our will and intellect that exercise control over our actions, provide discipline for our passions and emotions, and direct our behavior to be disciples of Jesus (p. 110)

Catechism of the Catholic Church—a "synthesis of the essential and fundamental contents of Catholic doctrine, as regards both faith and morals, in the light of Second Vatican Council and the whole of the Church's Tradition" *(Catechism, #11)* (p. 55)

Catholic morality—the way that we live our lives as children of God in response to Jesus under the guidance of the Holy Spirit at work in the Catholic Church (p. 7)

character—the attributes and features that make up our individuality (p. 102)

charity—(sometimes called love) the theological virtue representing the core of the Christian life. Charity is the virtue "by which we love God above all things for his own sake, and our neighbor as ourselves for the love of God" *(Catechism, #1822)*. Charity is the virtue that places concern for God, manifest especially through concern for others, above everything else. *(p. 107)*

chastity—integration of sexuality reflecting our unity as body and spirit; responsible sexual expression (p. 225)

common good—a long-standing concept advocating that society should be organized so that, as much as possible, both individuals and the entire community are equally thriving (p. 271)

communion of saints—this title refers to two realities. First of all, it designates the "holy things" such as charity and the Eucharist, by which the unity of the faithful is brought about. Second, it refers to the unity in Christ of all the redeemed, those on earth and those who have died (p. 43)

community of good character—a community that promotes rather than obstructs the exercise of virtue; a community that is energized by the practice of values (p. 117)

commutative justice—the obligation, required by the seventh commandment, to respect the rights of others (p. 265)

Confirmation—strengthens our bond with Christ and the Church; helps us bear witness by our words and deeds (p. 49)

conscience—"the interior voice of a human being, within whose heart the inner law of God is inscribed" (*Catechism, Glossary*) (p. 2)

conscience—a moral decision-making ability (or action) centering on what a person has already done or ought to do in the future. It involves an awareness that there is right and wrong, a process of discernment, and finally judgment. (p. 63)

conscientious objector—one who for moral or religious reasons is opposed to serving in the military (p. 216)

covenant—a solemn agreement between God and human beings involving mutual obligations and agreements (p. 9)

culpability—the degree to which people are responsible for their actions (p. 91)

date rape—rape that occurs in the context of a date or a dating relationship (p. 234)

Decalogue—literally "ten words," refers to the Ten Commandments (p. 142)

deterrence—punishment or fear of punishment can help prevent crime (p. 208)

detraction—revealing personal, derogatory information without sufficient reason (p. 246)

dignity—the respect owed to all human beings because they are made in God's image (p. 8)

discrimination—a situation in which people suffer disadvantages simply because they are members of a particular group (for example, age, race, gender) (p. 253)

domestic church—the family as a holy community and a microcosm of the universal Church (p. 162)

ecclesia—a Greek word for a duly summoned assembly; also means Church (p. 48)

emotional-relationship sexual intercourse—morally wrong sexual activity presumed as being acceptable when the two people involved feel love for each other (p. 230)

encyclical—an official letter from the pope, usually addressed to all Church members (p. 56)

envy—"sadness at the sight of another's goods and the immoderate desire to have them for oneself" (*Catechism, #2553*) (p. 266)

erroneous conscience—when a person follows a process of conscientious decision making but unwittingly makes a wrong decision (p. 70)

Eucharist—hearing and pondering God's word; receiving and becoming the Body of Christ (p. 49)

euthanasia—"an action or an omission which, of itself or by intention, causes the death of handicapped, sick, or dying persons—sometimes with an attempt to justify the act as a means of eliminating suffering" (*Catechism, Glossary*). (p. 191)

explicit violence—a situation in which someone is physically harmed or killed by direct action (p. 203)

extraordinary means of life support—medical procedures that offer little hope of benefit and which cause undue or excessive burdens to the patient or his or her family (p. 194)

faith—a gift from God and a human act by which we believe in him and all that he has revealed; the theological virtue of seeking to know and to do God's will (p. 104)

fecundity—fruitfulness; bearing children (p. 225)

foot washing—the activity Jesus performed prior to the Last Supper that becomes the model for all Christian service (p. 31)

fortitude—courage; strength when confronted with difficulties and perseverance in pursuing that which is good (p. 111)

genuine—not hiding behind a role or image; seeking honest communication with others (p. 114)

gossip—participating in the spread of injurious information about someone (p. 246)

grace—the gift of the Holy Spirit; participation in God's Trinitarian life; the help God gives us to live out our vocation (p. 9)

greed—the desire to amass limitless earthly goods (p. 266)

"hard sayings" of Jesus—teachings such as the Beatitudes and the Last Judgment that overturn commonly held values and priorities (p. 32)

hell—"The state of definitive self-exclusion from communion with God and the blessed, reserved for those who refuse by their own free choice to believe and be converted from sin, even to the end of their lives" (*Catechism, Glossary*) (p. 91)

hero—someone who follows her or his conscience in the face of difficulties (p. 62)

heterosexuality—sexual attraction toward persons of the other gender. Heterosexual activity is sexual activity engaged in by persons of different genders. (p. 235)

hidden violence—a situation in which someone is harmed or killed indirectly, because of various social factors (p. 203)

Holy Orders—men promise to devote their lives in service of the Church as deacons, priests, and bishops (p. 49)

Holy Trinity—one God in three Persons; the Father, the Son, and the Holy Spirit (p. 9)

homosexuality—sexual attraction toward persons of the same gender. Homosexual activity is sexual activity engaged in by persons of the same gender. (p. 235)

hope—trusting in God, in everything that Christ has promised, and in the help of the Holy Spirit. Hope focuses on obtaining eternal happiness in heaven and the help from God (grace) to achieve it. (p. 106)

Incarnation—"the mystery of the wonderful union of the divine and human natures" (*Catechism, #483*) in Jesus, the Son of God (p. 23)

informed conscience—a conscience that is educated and developed through constant use and examination (p. 69)

integrity—honesty, genuineness, and consistency in behavior patterns (p. 113)

justice—the virtue stating that all people have rights and should have their basic needs met; "the firm and constant will to give God and neighbor their due" (*Catechism, #1836*) (p. 111)

just-war principles—a set of principles outlining conditions when use of violence would be acceptable (p. 213)

kingdom of God—God's reign or rule—proclaimed by and present in Jesus—in which people serve one another, share their goods with one another, and refuse to retaliate with violence against others (p. 30)

lax conscience—when a person does not employ a process of conscientious decision making, thereby not facing or thinking about the morality of actions that he or she performs (p. 68)

legalism—attitude of strict observance of laws, regardless of circumstances and possible harm to people involved (p. 35)

lived values—qualities and concerns that we demonstrate as being important through our actions (p. 114)

lying—"saying what is false with the intention of deceiving one's neighbor" (*Catechism, #2508*) (p. 245)

magisterium—the teaching office of the Church (p. 52)

Marriage—celebration of the family as the foundation for involvement in the moral life of the community (p. 49)

mean-world syndrome—the proposal that increased television viewing leads to a perception of the world as being a more hostile, dangerous place (p. 172)

minimalism—an attitude of doing only the least that is required by law in our moral life (p. 36)

moral muscle—pushing ourselves to do more than the minimum in our moral life (p. 36)

morality—the goodness or sinfulness of human acts (p. 2)

mortal sin—an action so destructive that it mortally wounds our relationship with God; complete rejection of God (p. 91)

motives—the reasons people do what they do (p. 128)

natural law—God's fatherly instruction that is written on the human heart and accessed by human reason (p. 2)

nonviolence—conflict-resolving techniques that do not rely on physical or psychological injury of an opponent (p. 216)

nuclear deterrence—the proposition that when two nations possess the ability to inflict nuclear damage on each other, then neither nation is likely to use its nuclear weapons in the first place (p. 214)

nuclear proliferation—any increase in the number of nations that possess nuclear weapons or that have the capability to build them (p. 214)

On the Condition of Workers—the 1891 encyclical of Pope Leo XIII voicing concern for industrial workers; the first of a series of documents comprising modern Catholic social teaching (p. 273)

ordinary means of life support—medical procedures that offer sufficient or reasonable benefits without excessive or undue burdens to the patient or his or her family (p. 194)

original sin—disobedience against God by the first human beings. This sin marks all human beings as needing the salvation brought about through Christ. (p. 90)

perjury—lying under oath (p. 247)

physician-assisted suicide—a person who is incurably ill killing himself or herself with the help of a physician (p. 196)

prime time—the evening hours when television viewing is heaviest (p. 173)

prudence—the virtue that helps us make a correct judgment about what to do and to choose the right way to do it (p. 111)

rabbi—Hebrew for teaching, a term frequently applied to Jesus (p. 55)

racial prejudice—strong dislike for members of a race other than one's own (p. 254)

racism—subordination of persons who belong to a particular race due to attitudes, actions, or institutional structures at work in a society (p. 254)

rape—forcing sex on an unwilling partner (p. 234)

rash judgment—judging another person unkindly (p. 246)

reconciliation—an experience of reuniting and reconnecting with God and others (p. 50)

recreational sexual intercourse—morally wrong sexual activity as the pursuit of pleasure with no constraints other than mutual consent (p. 230)

rehabilitation—programs aimed at training and reforming wrongdoers so that they no longer commit crime (p. 208)

reparation—making amends for harming another; returning stolen property (p. 265)

retribution—restoring the social order by punishing wrongdoers, thus declaring that certain behaviors are not tolerated in society (p. 209)

sanctifying grace—a share in God's life; a gift from God that enables the soul to live with him and respond to his friendship (p. 9)

scandal—wrongdoing that serves to disillusion or harm more vulnerable people; "an attitude or behavior which leads another to do evil. . .a grave offense if by deed or omission another is deliberately led into a grave offense" (*Catechism*, #2284) (p. 247)

scrutinize—to examine or look over with care various dimensions of a challenging situation so that overlooked aspects can come to light (p. 136)

selective conscientious objector—one who believes that the particular war in which he or she would be called to fight is against his moral or religious principles (p. 217)

Sermon on the Mount—a part of the Gospel according to Matthew in which Jesus preaches important moral teachings, including the Beatitudes (p. 23)

sexism—attitudes, practices, and institutional structures that oppress people solely on the basis of gender (p. 255)

sin—when people act contrary to their conscience and purposely choose to do wrong; "a deliberate thought, word, deed, or omission contrary to the eternal law of God" (*Catechism, Glossary*) (p. 71)

sin of commission—purposely doing an action that is harmful to oneself or another (p. 91)

sin of omission—not doing an action that is called for (p. 91)

sinful social structures—ways societies are structured resulting in unjust distribution of power, benefits, and privileges (p. 96)

skepticism—in general, a doubting and questioning attitude. As defined by Pope John Paul II, a lack of belief that there are fundamental truths, dismissing any sense of right or wrong (p. 204)

social sin—a term comparable to "structures of sin" referring to sinful structures resulting from personal sin and leading to social conditions and institutions that do not embody God's law of love. (p. 96)

"The Splendor of Truth"—an encyclical on morality by Pope John Paul II (p. 76)

spin—giving a self-serving slant on a news story; manipulation of the truth intended to deceive (p. 250)

spiral of poverty—poor people being in a situation that makes overcoming poverty almost impossible (p. 276)

stated values—qualities and concerns that we claim are important to us (p. 114)

superstition—attributing magical power to certain practices (i.e. rubbing a rabbit's foot, carrying a lucky coin) or things (i.e. crystals, tarot cards, statues). "Reliance on such power, rather than trust in God, constitutes an offense against the honor due to God alone, as required by the first commandment" (*Catechism, Glossary*). (p. 151)

temperance—self-control and balanced lifestyle (p. 112)

The Challenge of Peace—1983 pastoral letter of U.S. bishops addressing issues of war and peace (p. 211)

The Gospel of Life—1995 encyclical by Pope John Paul II about the value and sacredness of human life (p. 203)

theological virtues—faith, hope, and charity; good habits, given by God and directed toward him as their object or major focus (p. 104)

urbanization—growth of cities worldwide (p. 276)

venial sin—an action that weakens our relationship with God (p. 91)

vices—bad qualities, habits, or patterns of behavior that incline us to actions that are harmful to ourselves and others (p. 102)

virtues—good qualities, habits, or patterns of behavior that incline us to live justly; character strengths manifested on a consistent basis in decision making (p. 102)

vocation—calling to love and serve God both now and forever (p. 16)

youth culture—the belief that young people have values, interests, and activities distinct from those of other age groups (p. 177)

Index

For permission to reprint copyrighted material, grateful acknowledgment is made to the following sources:

America Press: Quote from "An unlikely martyr" by Thomas Michel, S. J. in *America* Magazine, July 19–26, 1997. Text copyright 1997.

Costello Publishing Company, Inc., Northport, NY: From *Vatican Council II: The Conciliar and Post Conciliar Documents, Volume I, Revised Edition*, edited by Rev. Austin Flannery, O. P. Text copyright © 2003 by Costello Publishing Company, Inc.

The Crossroad Publishing Company, New York: Reflections by Dr. Takashi Nagai and Martin Niemoeller in *All Saints* by Robert Ellsberg. Text copyright © 1997 by Robert Ellsberg.

John C. Haughey, S. J.: From *The Faith That Does Justice*, edited by John C. Haughey, S. J. Published by Paulist Press, 1977.

Libreria Editrice Vaticana: From *Declaration on Procured Abortion* by Sacred Congregation for the Doctrine of the Faith. Text copyright © 1974 by Libreria Editrice Vaticana.

Rev. Jean Mortimer, Leeds, UK: "Glimpses of Glory" by Rev. Jean Mortimer. Originally published in *Exceeding Our Limits*: *Prayer Handbook of the United Reformed Church*, 1991.

Paulist Press, Inc., New York/Mahwah, NJ, www.paulistpress.com: Untitled poem from *Moral Discernment* by Richard M. Gula, S. S. Text copyright © 1997 by Richard Gula.

Religious Task Force on Central America and Mexico, www.rtfcam.org: Quotation by Jean Donovan from *A message too precious to be silenced: The four U.S. church women and the meaning of martyrdom* by Margaret Swedish. Published by the Religious Task Force on Central America (Washington, D. C.), September 1992.

St. Anthony Messenger Press: From *Bringing Forth Justice* by Archbishop Daniel E. Pilarczyk. Text copyright © 1999 by Daniel E. Pilarczyk.

Sojourners, 800-714-7474, www.sojo.net: From "Incarnating Ethics" by Glen Stassen in *Sojourners* Magazine, March–April 1999.

United States Conference of Catholic Bishops, Washington, D. C.: From "Breaking the Cycle of Poverty" speech by John Cushma. Text copyright © 2003 by United States Conference of Catholic Bishops.

Westminster John Knox Press: From *Modern Work and Human Meaning* by John C. Raines and Donna C. Day-Lower. Text copyright © 1986 by John C. Raines and Donna C. Day-Lower.

Photo Credits

iii Masterfile; v Masterfile; vii Sean Locke/the Agency Collection/Getty Images; 0-1 Robert Glusic/Corbis; 2 l Scala/Art Resource, NY; 2 r Masterfile; 3 c Phil Schermeister/Corbis; 3 b Masterfile; 4 Royalty Free/Corbis; 5 Peter Cade/Stone/Getty Images; 7 Erich Lessing/Art Resource, NY; 8 Franco Origlia/Corbis; 10 t Jeffery Allan Salter/CORBIS SABA; 10 b Ocean/Corbis; 12 Ocean/Corbis; 13 Steve Mason/Photodisc/Getty Images; 15 The Art Archive/Galleria Nazionale dell'Umbria Perugia/Gianni Dagli Orti; 16 Bob Donnan/Sports Illustrated/Getty Images; 17 David Grossman/The Image Works; 18 Masterfile; 20-21 John August Swanson; 22 Peter Turnley/CORBIS; 23 Nicolo Orsi Battaglini/Art Resource, NY; 24 The Art Archive/Queretaro Museum Mexico/Gianni Dagli Orti; 25 Cameraphoto Arte, Venice/Art Resource, NY; 26 Rob Lewine/Tetra Images/Corbis; 29 Britt Erlanson/Cultura/Getty Images; 31 c John August Swanson; 31 r John August Swanson; 32 Réunion des Musées Nationaux/Art Resource, NY; 34 Ariel Skelley/CORBIS; 36 Kathy McLaughlin/The Image Works; 37 Danny Lehman/CORBIS; 40-41 Masterfile; 42 Erich Lessing/Art Resource, NY; 43 Jim Cornfield/CORBIS; 44 Bettman/Corbis; 45 The Art Archive/Piccolomini Library Siena/Gianni Dagli Orti; 46 The Art Archive/Museo del Prado Madrid/Gianni Dagli Orti; 47 The Art Archive/Museo del Prado Madrid/Gianni Dagli Orti; 48 Chuck Savage/CORBIS; 50 Alberto Pizzoli/Sygma/Corbis; 51 Design Pics/Con Tanasiuk/Getty Images; 53 Reuters/CORBIS; 54 SUCHETA DAS/Reuters/Corbis; 56 Andy Caulfield/Riser/Getty Images; 57 John August Swanson; 58 Andrea Jemolo/CORBIS; 60-61 Chase Jarvis/Photodisc/Getty Images; 62 Time & Life Pictures/Getty Images; 63 Masterfile; 64 Rhoda Sidney/The Image Works; 65 Masterfile; 67 Tom & Dee Ann McCarthy/CORBIS; 68 Chase Jarvis/Photodisc/Getty Images; 71 Werner Forman/Art Resource, NY; 72 bg Gerrit Greve/Corbis; 72 fg Gerrit Greve/Corbis; 73 t Gerrit Greve/Corbis; 73 b Alinari/Art Resource, NY; 74 Bettman/Corbis; 76 Brand X Pictures/Punchstock; 80-81 Eastcott Momatiuk/The Image Bank/Getty Images; 82 Peter Hvizdak/The Image Works; 83 Manu Sassoonian/Art Resource, NY; 84 Tracy Frankel/The Image Bank/Getty Images; 85 Eric Pearle/Photodisc/Getty Images; 86 Manu Sassoonian/Art Resource, NY; 87 SW Productions/Photodisc/Getty Images; 88 Jon Riley/Riser/Getty Images; 89 david sanger photography/Alamy; 90-91 Eastcott Momatiuk/The Image Bank/Getty Images; 92 Masterfile; 93 Bob Daemmrich/The Image Works; 95 Ghislain & Marie David de Lossy/Getty Images; 96 Mark Ludak/The Image Works; 98 Antoine Serra/Sygma/Corbis; 100-101 Mike Powell/Allsport Concepts/Getty Images; 103 Jim Zuckerman/CORBIS; 104 l Masterfile; 104 r Masterfile; 105 Lori Adamski Peek/Stone/Getty Images; 106 Randy Faris/CORBIS; 108 Erich Lessing/Art Resource, NY; 110 Kelly-Mooney Photography/Corbis; 112 Richard Lord/The Image Works; 113 Brand X Pictures/Fotosearch; 114 Gary Buss/Getty Images; 115 Mike Powell/Allsport Concepts/Getty Images; 117 Jose Luis Pelaez, Inc./CORBIS; 118 Masterfile; 120-121 Raimund Linke/Masterfile; 122 Paul A. Souders/CORBIS; 124 Bob Daemmrich/The Image Works; 125 Masterfile; 126 t Reed Kaestner/Corbis; 126 b Reed Kaestner/Corbis; 127 Corbis; 129 Lisa Peardon/Taxi/Getty Images; 131 bg Burstein Collection/CORBIS; 131 fg Burstein Collection/CORBIS; 132 Royalty Free/Corbis; 133 Paul Barton/CORBIS; 135 SW Productions/Photodisc/Getty Images; 137 iStockphoto.com/AVTG; 138 AFP/Getty Images; 140-141 Archive Timothy McCarthy/Art Resource, NY; 142 Mark Karrass/Corbis; 143 Tate, London/Art Resource, NY; 144 SW Productions/Photodisc/Getty Images; 146 Réunion des Musées Nationaux/Art Resource, NY; 147 Erich Lessing/Art Resource, NY; 148 National Trust Photo Library/Art Resource, NY; 149 Sonda Dawes/The Image Works; 151 John and Lisa Merrill/Corbis; 152 Masterfile; 153 Moses breaking the Tablets of the Law and the Adoration of the Golden Calf, illustration from a catechism 'L'Histoire Sainte', published by Charles Delagrave, Paris, late 19th century (colour litho), French School, (19th century)/Bibliotheque des Arts Decoratifs, Paris, France/The Bridgeman Art Library International; 155 Michael S. Yamashita/CORBIS; 156 Kathy McLaughlin/The Image Works; 158 Danita Delimont/Alamy; 160-161 Jack Hollingsworth/Corbis; 162 Rob Lewine/Tetra Images/Corbis; 164 Bob Daemmrich/The Image Works; 165 Brand X Pictures/Punchstock; 166 Image Source/CORBIS; 168 Ed Bock/CORBIS; 169 bg Images.com/Corbis; 169 fg Images.com/Corbis; 170 Robert Daly/Stone/Getty Images; 172 ER Productions/CORBIS; 175 Francis Dean/Dean Pictures/The Image Works; 176 Darama/CORBIS; 178 Ed Boettcher/Corbis; 180-181 Valueline/Punchstock; 182 Smithsonian American Art Museum, Washington, DC/Art Resource, NY; 183 Lawrence Manning/Corbis; 184 Valueline/Punchstock; 187 Christopher Fitzgerald/The Image Works; 188 t Sunset on Coast, Minozzi, Professor Filiberto (1877-1936)/Private Collection/Photo © Whitford & Hughes, London, UK/The Bridgeman Art Library International; 188 b Sunset on Coast, Minozzi, Professor Filiberto (1877-1936)/Private Collection/Photo © Whitford & Hughes, London, UK/The Bridgeman Art Library International; 191 Jonathan Morgan/Stone/Getty Images; 192 Joel Stettenheim/CORBIS; 193 Royalty Free/Corbis; 194 Science Photo Librar/Alamy; 195 Jim West/The Image Works; 197 Tom Stewart/CORBIS; 198 Hulton Archive/Getty Images; 200-201 Cameraphoto Arte, Venice/Art Resource, NY; 202 Philip Condit II/Stone/Getty Images; 205 iStockphoto.com/Berc; 207 Jim West/PhotoEdit; 209 iStockphoto.com/LOU OATES; 210 Doug Menuez/Photodisc/Getty Images; 211 Peter Turnley/CORBIS; 212 SW Productions/Photodisc/Getty Images; 214 Corbis; 215 Corbis; 216 Hulton Archive/Getty Images; 217 Ernst Haas/Getty Images; 218 Bettmann/CORBIS; 220-221 Masterfile; 222 t Skjold/The Image Works; 222 b Brand X Pictures/Getty Images; 223 Erich Lessing/Art Resource, NY; 224 bg The Art Archive/Biblioteca Comunale Trento/Gianni Dagli Orti; 224 fg The Art Archive/Biblioteca Comunale Trento/Gianni Dagli Orti; 226 Flying Colours Ltd/Digital Vision/Getty Images; 228 t Spike Mafford/Photodisc/Getty Images; 228 b Spike Mafford/Photodisc/Getty Images; 229 t Spike Mafford/Photodisc/Getty Images; 229 c Spike Mafford/Photodisc/Getty Images; 229 b Spike Mafford/Photodisc/Getty Images; 230 Esbin-Anderson/The Image Works; 231 Jutta Klee/CORBIS; 233 Cheryl Maeder/CORBIS; 234 Bill Varie/CORBIS; 235 Digital Vision/Getty Images; 236 Brand X Pictures/Getty Images; 237 Bill Lai/The Image Works; 240-241 Scala/Art Resource, NY; 242 Réunion des Musées Nationaux/Art Resource, NY; 243 Steve Skjold/The Image Works; 247 Brand X Pictures/Punchstock; 249 bg John August Swanson; 249 fg John August Swanson; 251 Steven Rubin/The Image Works; 252 The Art Archive/Gianni Dagli Orti; 254 Ryan McVay/Photodisc/Getty Images; 256 Michael J. Doolittle/The Image Works; 257 Ken Fisher/Stone/Getty Images; 258 Sherab/Alamy; 260-261 Arcaid/Masterfile; 262 Bart Geerligs/Taxi/Getty Images; 263 David Fraizer/The Image Works; 264 The Art Archive/Maritime Museum Kronborg Castle Denmark/Gianni Dagli Orti; 266 Ed Pritchard/Stone/Getty Images; 268 Royalty Free/Corbis; 269 Bruce Ayres/Stone/Getty Images; 272 Sean Sprague/The Image Works; 275 John Maier, Jr./The Image Works; 276 Joel Stettenheim/CORBIS; 278 iStockphoto.com/Juanmonino